PATIENT-CENTERED HOSPITAL CARE

AMERICAN COLLEGE OF HEALTHCARE EXECUTIVES MANAGEMENT SERIES

Anthony R. Kovner, Series Editor

Kathryn J. McDonagh
Editor

PATIENT-CENTERED HOSPITAL CARE

REFORM FROM WITHIN

MANAGEMENT SERIES
American College of Healthcare Executives

97   96   95   94   93   5   4   3   2   1

Library of Congress Cataloging-in-Publication Data

Patient-centered hospital care : reform from within / Kathryn J. McDonagh, editor.
     p.   cm. — (Management series / American College of Healthcare
Executives)
     Includes bibliographical references and index.
     ISBN 1-56793-002-6 (hardbound : alk. paper)
     1. Hospitals—Personnel management.   2. Organizational change.   3. Work
design.   4. Hospital care—Quality control.   I. McDonagh, Kathryn J.   II. Series:
Management series (Ann Arbor, Mich.)
     [DNLM: 1. Hospital Administration—organization & administration.
2. Patient Satisfaction.   3. Quality Assurance, Health Care—organization &
administration.   4. Leadership.   WX 150 P2975 1993]
RA971.35.P38   1993   362.1′1′068—dc20
DNLM/DLC for Library of Congress   93-14569 CIP

Health Administration Press
A division of the Foundation of the
   American College of Healthcare Executives
1021 East Huron Street
Ann Arbor, Michigan 48104-9990
(313) 764-1380

CONTENTS

129327

FOREWORD

The time is right for this book. The American health care system as we have known it for many decades is breaking up. Health care providers are fighting for survival in a competitive marketplace. Health insurers sit on the brink of disaster. The public is up in arms over problems of access and quality. Industry is going to war with doctors and hospitals because of the high costs of providing health care to their employees. Federal and state legislators meet and generate an array of bills to "fix" the system. We all suffer. Nothing is working very well. The stage is set for a change.

The change comes in this decade—the last ten years of a millennium. It is a change of epoch, a change of paradigm, a change of mind. The 1990s are an era of destructuring and restructuring. It is a time for health care providers to face the challenges of access, cost, and quality with bold new initiatives. This book is an important part of the changes I foresee. It suggests a new strategy for optimal utilization of human resources—work redesign.

Work redesign is a bright light on the horizon. It is a strategy of empowerment that puts the center of action inside the health care organization. Work redesign asks the important questions: Who should be doing what? How can we maximize the human potential of our organization and improve the health of the community we serve?

I often dream of the perfect health care organization. I don't know just what that means. I do know it means liberating the talent and creativity of everyone in the organization. I dream of an organization that says, If you want to do it and you can do it, you may do it. Imagine an organization with no artificial constraints of licensure—an organization that says, We do not look for the degree after your name; we look at what you can do. Imagine an organization that is licensed but is free to deploy its human resources as it sees fit. Work redesign could generate such an organization.

Imagine an organization that escapes the boxes on its organizational chart. Imagine a circular organization where health care is provided by teams and the patient is the director of care—an organization that is patient, family, and community centered. Such an imagined organization will stretch the limits of your credibility. Yet, that is what this book is about—it pushes the edges of the envelope. You are the designer. You can change the work of your organization. You can make it happen!

Antitrust legislation, licensure, tort law, onerous third party requirements, inefficient utilization of health care professionals—all of these are wasting hundreds of millions of dollars annually in the United States. I believe we waste more than we need. A 30–40 percent waste factor is more than we can afford. It is time to take design seriously. Until we change the social, political, and economic context of health care, we will be powerless to change what is happening in health care. Yet, the first step is to change ourselves.

The first step is to change the way we do business. That is work redesign. The second step is to change what is happening in our communities— community health care redesign. The two changes are related. The goal is a designed health care system that prevents and treats disease in the most efficient and effective way imaginable.

The goal of a medical care system should be to create healthier communities. We do not yet meet this outcome criterion. We will never meet it until we take our role seriously as health care designers of the future.

I recommend this book. It is a step in the right direction. It asks the tough questions. Even more importantly, it provides you with some answers. Each contributor has something important to say. Listen well! You are the designer. You are the architect of the future of health care.

Leland Kaiser, Ph.D.
Health Care Futurist

PREFACE

There are a multitude of components and concepts related to work redesign or operational restructuring in hospitals. This book is designed to address those various components in detail and yet integrate the common themes that run through all aspects of work redesign. Each of the chapters was prepared by different contributing authors; therefore, there are a variety of perspectives and experiences relayed in each of the chapters. Although the experience and approaches to work redesign vary among organizations, there are several common threads that permeate this book. One of these threads is the theory behind work redesign and why it is so essential that American hospitals redesign their structures to better meet the needs of the emerging health care system. Additionally, the concept of hospital redesigning as a continuous quality improvement process and a continually evolving journey is one that pervades this book as well.

The first chapter, "The Art of Redesigning Hospitals," introduces the concept of work redesign within the total array of programs currently being developed in hospitals today. A theoretical approach explains where the concept of redesigning hospitals fits into the total picture of health care reform.

The second chapter, "Work Redesign: Theory, Approaches, and Lessons," provides a more in-depth and systematic review of what work redesign is, with a very practical, experiential case study of the ProACT® model from Robert Wood Johnson University Hospital.

Chapter 3, "Assessing and Preparing the Organization for Work Redesign," includes information on conducting an internal assessment of individual hospitals to determine what model would best fit the organization, theories of stakeholder management, and how to avoid "jumping on the bandwagon." Various redesign models are described in detail, including perspectives on how these models evolved. Many relevant examples and references from work redesign programs from across the country are included as well.

Chapter 4, "Case Management: Work Redesign with Patient Outcomes in Mind," discusses a very key component of the work redesign model since case management is one of the most important and innovative programs addressing organizational inefficiencies along the continuum of care today. This chapter describes in detail the concept of case management, which is necessary to process patients effectively and efficiently through the complex health care system.

Chapter 5, "A Model for Measuring Outcomes of Work Redesign," reviews the importance of measuring the effect of work redesign on quality outcomes. The authors describe the questionnaires, which include qualitative and quantitative indicators, used to evaluate the success and outcomes of work redesign at Saint Joseph's Hospital of Atlanta. This chapter includes research components related to work redesign and should be helpful for readers about to embark on redesign processes.

Chapter 6, "Financial Impacts of Work Redesign," includes the development of a business plan or approach to work redesign in order to effectively negotiate the initiation of such a program. This chapter also includes information on a cost-benefit analysis for work redesign, a framework for evaluating financial issues such as up-front investment and long-term return on investment.

Chapter 7, "Work Redesign: Getting Ready for and Dealing with the Change," deals with the many issues of implementation related to work redesign. This chapter also describes the importance of team building and the issues related to boundaries that are created by licensure, regulation, and historical hospital organizational structures. Implementation issues such as professional territorialism and corporate culture change are discussed in depth. Work redesign models at Saint Joseph's Hospital of Atlanta and Vanderbilt University are described throughout the chapter.

Chapter 8, "Breaking Molds: Hospital Education, Work Redesign, and the American Work Force," deals with the impact of redesign on roles and job descriptions in the hospital. These authors describe the experience of Saint Joseph's Hospital of Atlanta and World Education as the issue of education and training evolved in this program. The emerging multicultural American work force requires organizations to face the issues of functional illiteracy and the lack of training and service concepts in businesses. These are critical issues facing the American business world at large and, specifically, hospitals in the United States.

Chapter 9, "Work Redesign: A Journey, Not a Destination," discusses the concept of redesigning and changing the organization as a journey, not as a destination. Concepts of organizations as learning entities and other futuristic perspectives puts work redesign into a total context of continuous quality improvement and evolution. This final chapter pulls together the concepts introduced throughout the book and looks toward the future vision for a changing health care world.

ACKNOWLEDGMENTS

This book is dedicated to my many colleagues who have dreamed of doing things differently and creating new visions in hospitals. The challenges facing our health care system have opened up new opportunities to make this possible. With courage and fortitude these dreams can at last become reality.

Kathryn J. McDonagh
Editor

1

THE ART OF REDESIGNING HOSPITALS

Kathryn J. McDonagh

The final two decades of this millennium have been marked by changes so drastic and unexpected—the fall of the Berlin Wall, the destruction of communism as it was known for many decades, global economic shifts, the rapid rise in new technologies, the loss of industrial and manufacturing jobs, the changing characteristics of the work force, and political upheavals in the United States and abroad—that it is sometimes difficult to see through the chaos to what the vision for the future may be.

It is important to pause and examine the common threads that permeate these events and use those as guiding principles for planned change in the unsettling world of health care. Some of the themes of these social upheavals include a relentless struggle for human freedom, a movement for ecological protection, power shifts away from formerly omnipotent corporations and individuals, a move from domination to partnerships, and a shift toward collaboration instead of fierce competition (Toffler 1990).

These global trends are clearly manifesting themselves in the health care arena. Some examples from the health care world are shown in Table 1.1.

These trends are promoting change at an unprecedented rate, which when combined with new laws and the restrictive rules that characterize the highly regulated health care field, make the challenges for the health care executive great. "Yet many hospitals have not found the answers to the dilemmas in the environment. They grapple with the old way of doing things because they can't think creatively enough to see the new visions. Many hospitals, like other organizations, resist the changes that are necessary for their survival. Overcoming the difficulties facing hospitals will require creative, resourceful leadership" (McDonagh 1990, 270).

Table 1.1   The Effect of Global Trends on Health Care

Global Trend	*Impact on Health Care*
Struggle for human freedom and self-determination	Educated patients wanting adequate health care information and autonomy to make health care decisions that affect their lives.
Ecological preservation	Impact on health care, health promotion, and disease prevention efforts rising in order to reduce waste of resources and technology on lifestyle-related health problems.
Power shifts	Once omnipotent physicians now having practice regulated by federal government and insurers interested in managing care and reducing costs.
Competition to collaboration	Costly duplication of services in communities and promotion of medical arms race being replaced by mergers, acquisitions, and collaborative ventures.
Changing work force	Predominantly female work force in health care no longer willing to settle for poor working conditions and lack of authority. Shared governance models and feminization of leadership revolution under way.
Rapid rise in technology	Technology provides new cures, but alternative health modalities put an emphasis on caring, stress reduction, and lifestyle modifications.

Barbara Donaho, program director for the innovative and nationally recognized Strengthening Hospital Nursing: A Program to Improve Patient Care, which was developed by the Robert Wood Johnson Foundation and the Pew Charitable Trusts, thinks that hospitals can learn much from the American business sector. "Unlike industry, healthcare has been a lumbering giant that doesn't move fast and doesn't respond to societal changes as they occur. We can no longer afford this time lag. Healthcare must be a part of the larger changes that are going on—the renewed focus on quality, cost effectiveness and employee and consumer satisfaction. We can't go on behaving like a totally different kind of animal. We need to learn from industry" (Donaho 1992, 9).

Times of adversity often bring about creative new opportunities. The concept of work redesign is one of the most creative answers on the health care horizon. Work redesign involves changing the work and job parameters of many staff throughout hospitals. The stage of evolution that the health care system is in currently is a combination of recognition that the "old ways" are not working anymore and a flurry of new and creative ideas of how to adapt to the rapidly changing environment. This can be a puzzling time for health care executives as they attempt to determine which new ideas to implement in their own hospitals. Setting priorities in organizations as complex as hospitals can be difficult. Application of the best solutions can be even more challenging. There is often a "jumping on the bandwagon" phenomenon—a manager, eager to experiment with new ideas or to gain a reputation as an innovator, selects a model of change that may not fit well with the corporate culture of the organization. This can prove fatal for the new plans since people will strongly resist a plan that does not fit well or that they have not had a hand in designing or selecting.

There is almost no phase of hospital operations that has not been altered in the last several years in response to the changing environment. Models of hospital innovations include the development of product line management, matrix organizations, shared governance, new care delivery models, case management, managed care, and work redesign. Each of these changes addresses different aspects of the organization. Some have been more successful than others in various settings. The complexity of hospitals often demands that more than one of these operational changes needs to occur simultaneously. Care must be given to selecting compatible models and involving staff at all levels. Resources to accomplish these massive changes must also be provided and be realistic.

It is a common misperception that instituting one model of change, such as shared governance, work redesign or a new care delivery model, alone will suffice. These concepts are not interchangeable. They represent inextricably linked parts of the entire hospital system. Therefore, attention needs to be paid to the entire system and its component parts.

The essential components of a hospital's care system include the following:

- mission and philosophy
- structural design of the system
- care delivery model
- incentive programs
- ongoing system evaluation and improvement

Examples of planned changes that can occur within any of these components are shown in Table 1.2.

What is important to realize is that no one of these programs meets the needs of the entire system. For the organization to work in harmony, multiple changes need to occur at various levels simultaneously with congruent philosophies or outcomes planned. Such expected outcomes should be improved quality of care, better service levels, cost savings, and improved patient, physician and staff satisfaction.

Within that context, this book will focus on structural changes or work redesign models that make the work of health care providers more patient centered. What needs to be done for the patient is studied in such a way that it results in the most effective outcomes in the most efficient manner. A fresh look at how things are done in hospitals is necessary after many years of traditional bureaucratic organizational structures that did not focus on the patient, but rather the providers' convenience and the perpetuation of administrative structures. In other words, to be patient driven means to build

Table 1.2   Essential Components of a Hospital's Care System and Associated Planned Changes

Components of the Hospital System	Planned Changes
Mission and philosophy	Reexamination of hospital mission
	Development of community outreach programs to enhance mission
	Values integration programs to strengthen mission internally
	Development of shared governance program
Structural design of system	Work redesign programs
Care delivery model	Primary nursing
	Team nursing
	Total patient care
Incentive programs	Gain-sharing and bonus programs
	Professional salary programs
	Career advancement programs
Evaluation and improvement	Continuous quality improvement programs
	Total quality management

a dynamic system of care delivery that fosters empowerment of all staff to respond to the needs of the patients, rather than the routine of the system (Hagland 1991).

New, more collaborative and egalitarian professional models of care delivery are vastly improving patient satisfaction as well as the satisfaction of the health care work force. This retooling of hospitals and how they function is an integral part of the health care reform movement today. Patients, insurers, the public tax payer, and even health care providers recognize that the system needs a comprehensive overhaul or reform process. It has become a major agenda item in national and local politics. The public is no longer willing to financially support an expensive system whose outcomes do not correlate with the vast amount of dollars being spent. The disease-oriented or medical model design of our current health care system emphasizes costly new technology at the expense of public health and primary care efforts that yield much more positive patient outcomes. Our American fascination with high technology, combined with declining individual responsibility for health, has created an imbalance between the utilization of technology and common sense approaches such as prenatal care and access to primary care for many. Consumers are now assuming a role as partners in the health care structure, not the passive patients of the past (Ferguson 1992). These factors are all creating the impetus for major health care reform measures.

Work redesign represents a major shift in organizations, disrupting long-held beliefs and shaking up existing power structures. Thomas Hanrahan (1991) and others feel strongly that the traditional hospital structure needs a major overhaul as opposed to a tune-up or repair. Many managers wonder if smaller incremental changes would be preferable to an upheaval in the status quo. After all, there are already so many changes occurring in hospitals. The answer to that dilemma depends on your interest in survival in the increasingly competitive health care marketplace. Hospitals that do not systematically assess their organizations and begin a series of concurrent changes in operations may not survive or at least thrive in this environment.

It also depends on what your hospital is doing currently to be patient focused. If there are good solid foundations and structures in place that emphasize the patient and provide good service, it would be wise to keep and strengthen those parts and build equally strong systems to support that ideology. For instance, if the professional nursing care provided in your hospital is one of the key strengths and attributes of the organization, don't risk weakening that role, but rather work to enhance it even more by redesigning the roles that support that essential function. With increased outpatient testing, surgery, and the use of new technologies outside the hospital, the primary reason for patients to come to today's hospital is for nursing care (Gilmore 1991). Not losing sight of such core, fundamental concepts will be important as hospitals redesign for the future. Some hospitals in their haste to throw out all the old ways and start all over again have dismantled the nursing organization and thus thrown the baby out with the bath water. This is not what work redesign is all about.

It is vital to approach work redesign in a systematic way. Working within the framework of a strategic vision for the whole organization is essential. Understanding the mission of the hospital is the first step that the board, management, physicians, and staff need to collectively concur on. Then, an internal and external assessment should be conducted to under-stand where the organization stands as far as the competition and in the eyes of those who work there. The strengths, weaknesses, opportunities, and threats need to be assessed so that priorities can be established as a comprehensive strategic plan is developed. Work redesign should be a vital part of that overall plan. The approach and type of work redesign plan should be congruent with the mission of the hospital, the philosophy of the workers, and, most of all, the needs of the patients.

The various approaches and models of work redesign described in this book can be modified and individualized to meet the needs of each organization. It is imperative, though, to understand that this planned change process will represent a radical change throughout the hospital. It will disrupt the organization, but if managed appropriately, can unleash the creative concepts of many staff members eager to improve the way they care for the patient. This book describes the experiences of many people, including the critical issues related to implementation, that should help make this journey to the "hospital of the future" more enjoyable and successful.

All of these organizational changes are not possible without successful relationships with people. Organizations may be often represented by orga-nizational charts, mission statements, job descriptions, and other symbols, but the reality is that organizations are people, drawn together for a common purpose. At times, the structures that support the organizational endeavors need revision such as work redesign, but these necessary changes will not succeed without the involvement and support of the people that make up that organization. "Beneath the strategic challenges that health care organizations are experiencing are critical working relationships" (Gilmore 1991, 228). To be successful, the health care leader needs to recognize this by building and maintaining effective working relationships as the foundation for work redesign. Leland Kaiser (1991) envisions hospitals of the future as places for healing; healing does not necessarily connote curing, but rather physical and spiritual healing. The architecture, environment, policies, and people should all promote a positive healing experience for the patient. Somehow over the last several decades this concept has been lost in hospitals. It is essential for hospitals to regain some of the essence of why they were developed years ago. Creating patient-focused environments, unencumbered by restrictive bureaucratic structures and the old way of doing things, is the first step toward bringing healing back to our hospitals.

References

Donaho, B. 1992. "Strengthening Hospital Nursing: A Program to Improve Patient Care." *Gaining Momentum: A Progress Report.*

Ferguson, T. 1992. "Patient, Heal Thyself." *The Futurist* 26 (January/February): 9–13.

Gilmore, T. N. 1991. "Building and Maintaining Effective Working Alliances." In *Managing Hospitals*, edited by S. Rovin and L. Ginsberg. San Francisco: Jossey-Bass Publishers.

Hagland, M. 1991. "Restructuring Care: Patient Focus is Key to Innovation." *Hospitals* (5 August): 26–29.

Hanrahan, T. F. 1991. "New Approaches to Care Giving." *Healthcare Forum Journal* 34 (4): 33–38.

Kaiser, L. 1991. "Hospitals of the Future." Presentation at Saint Joseph's Hospital of Atlanta, Atlanta, GA, 22 March.

McDonagh, K. J. 1990. "The Future of Shared Governance in Nursing." In *Nursing Shared Governance: Restructuring for the Future*, edited by K. J. McDonagh, 263–77. Atlanta, GA: K. J. McDonagh and Associates.

Toffler, A. 1990. *Power Shift: Knowledge, Wealth and Violence at the Edge of the 21st Century.* New York: Bantam Books.

2

WORK REDESIGN:
THEORY, APPROACHES, AND LESSONS

Mary Crabtree Tonges

Much has been written recently about work redesign in nursing (Eubanks 1990; Sovie 1989; Moritz, Hinshaw, and Heirich 1989; Lawrenz 1989), and this movement has the potential to become one of the most significant trends of the early 1990s. But what exactly is work redesign? And precisely what does it mean to "redesign" someone's work and "restructure" roles and systems? This chapter presents an overview of the theoretical framework for work redesign, describes potential pitfalls to avoid in implementing an alternative care delivery system, and discusses the human resources implications for health care workers.

Theoretical Framework

Work redesign is defined as "changing the actual structure of the jobs people perform" (Hackman and Oldham 1980, 44). Traditionally, this has been accomplished by either taking a management engineering approach—measuring the work load and fitting people into jobs developed from studies of the work—or by using an organizational development approach—focusing on creating a strong organization in which people work well together (Lawrenz 1989). Hackman and Oldham suggest that the differences

This chapter is adapted, with permission, from "Work Redesigns: Sociotechnical Systems for Patient Care Delivery," *Nursing Management* 23, no. 1 (January 1992): 27–32.

in these approaches can be conceptualized by envisioning employees in jobs as pegs in a pegboard. Management engineering emphasizes reshaping the holes (jobs) while organizational development looks at making changes in the pegs (people) (Hackman and Oldham 1980). A more useful approach may lie in striking a balance between adapting jobs to people and adapting people to jobs. The Sociotechnical Systems (STS) approach to work redesign is such a method and is recommended by experts in this field (Hackman and Oldham 1980, 44; Mohr et al. 1989).

The STS approach is a framework or perspective that looks at work as a system and considers both the technical aspects—the work done and how it is accomplished—and the social aspects—the relationships among the people doing the work (Mohr et al. 1989). The goal of STS is to develop alternatives that "neither compromise the integrity of people to achieve work efficiency nor compromise productivity to make people happy," that is, to "jointly optimize" both the social and technical systems in organizations (Hackman and Oldham 1980, 63, 68).

There are two particularly important benefits to using the STS approach. First, this approach recognizes that the incremental productivity gains that can be achieved by doing more of what is already being done and doing it better are limited. Instead, changes have to be made in both how the work is designed and how the people are organized. Second, the STS approach encourages a holistic or purpose-oriented perspective rather than focusing on problems. This is important because it facilitates the development of creative solutions (Nadler 1981).

The following example illustrates how a group that focuses on fixing problems within a system can become limited in their quest for solutions by the existing system itself. In many hospitals, nursing staff are involved in running errands to other departments for "stat" specimens and supplies and equipment. Since this system is frequently fraught with problems, interdepartmental task forces are created, and they try to resolve the issues by developing new procedures and forms, such as special requisitions and sign-in logs, to make the system work better. These efforts are rarely successful because attempts to fix bad systems generally do not result in long-term improvement. Rather than focusing on what is *not* wanted, it is more useful to take a clean-slate approach and identify the purpose of the system and what *is* wanted. This exercise could lead to the realization that alternative methods of transporting items to and from the patient care unit that do not involve the nursing staff do exist, ultimately resulting in a successful change in the way this work is done.

The STS approach can be described as a seven-step process, shown in Figure 2.1 (Hackman and Oldham 1980; Mohr et al. 1989). Initial planning begins with an assessment of whether work redesign is an appropriate potential solution for the situation, and the feasibility of the project in terms of institutional and employee support and readiness for change (Hackman and Oldham 1980). The work is frequently accomplished through the organization of a steering committee and a design team task force. The process continues through the steps of conducting technical and social analyses, generating and evaluating alternatives (redesigning), planning for implementation, implementing, and evaluating the results. As Figure 2.1 illustrates, this is a spiral-like process in which feedback from evaluation serves as a basis for continuing redesign and ongoing changes.

Systems theory tells us that when one part of a system changes, other components are affected, and the need for new patterns of interaction provides opportunities for further restructuring in other parts of the organization that interface with the redesigned area (Hackman and Oldham 1980). Thus, initial restructuring creates a ripple effect, and numerous small waves of innovation begin to spread through the organization. It is not surprising that widespread support and participation at all levels of the organization are critical to successful work redesign.

Figure 2.1   Steps for Work Redesign in the STS Process

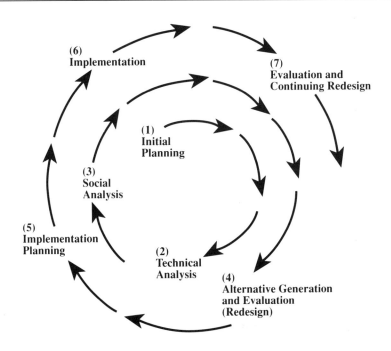

Application of Work Redesign to Nursing

Although nurses do not generally think of their practice as a process producing a product, Zander (1985, 229) points out that

> "nursing" entails a provider, a consumer, an outcome (product), and a production process. The production process occurs within the context of the larger milieu (environment), which includes multiple resources and their access routes.

Thus, nursing can be conceptualized as a production process to which work redesign methods can be appropriately applied.

Recognition of the importance of nursing's links to its environment is imperative. Nursing care must be viewed as an integral part of a total patient care delivery system designed by all involved departments (Lawrenz 1989). An interdisciplinary approach to work redesign acknowledges the essential interdependence of personnel and departments as components within the hospital as a system delivering patient care. This system is a configuration of coordinated services, not the sum of separate unrelated parts; that is, the best nursing division, medical staff, pharmacy department, and so on, do not make the best hospital if they do not work together effectively as a system of patient care (Ackoff 1989).

Collaborative interdepartmental redesign not only facilitates improvements in quality but can also create new opportunities for increased productivity. Most efforts toward improving productivity to date have focused on activities within departments. Opportunities for continued gains now lie in the interactions between departments.

The chance to totally design a new system is rare; however, when "stable" organizations temporarily become unstable during periods of turbulence, the defenses of the organization against change are down (Hackman and Oldham 1980, 44). This creates an opportunity to redesign work and fit these innovations with the surrounding organizational systems before a new state of stability is established and those who are ready with an engaging vision and a plan for making that vision a reality can achieve real change (Hackman and Oldham 1980, 255, 271). For nursing, the severe shortage of professional registered nurses was clearly such an opportunity. In most settings, the availability of RNs has become less of a problem, but the affordability of nurses' time is an increasingly compelling issue.

Reduced to its simplest terms, work redesign is really just thinking about how it is and inventing how you would like it to be. Nursing's challenge is to take apart our production process and recombine the involved components in new ways to create alternative practice and care delivery systems that can meet the needs of today and successfully take the profession into the future.

It is important to remember that nursing care delivery has been restructured before. The changes from case method of assignment to team nursing to primary nursing represented fundamental alterations in the organization of nursing care that were deemed appropriate to the needs of the time. Thus, restructuring nursing care delivery is not a totally new idea nor a cause for concern. Rather, it represents an exciting opportunity for positive change.

Putting Theory into Practice

Flannery and Williams (1990) predict that the successful "new look" hospital of the 1990s will be organized around patient care delivery as an outcome rather than by functional areas, such as nursing, pharmacy, or housekeeping. The need to restructure patient care delivery systems is supported by Schetter (1990), who indicates that the most promising new models combine operations redesign with clinical and economic case management. These models contain the elements of case management within a restructured care delivery system and display the following key features:

- restructured operations in which selected aspects of nursing care and other clinical and nonclinical tasks are delegated to the lowest appropriate level,
- decentralization of services to the patient care unit level, and
- integrated case management in which nurses, physicians, and other health professionals utilize critical paths as tools to manage the delivery of high-quality, cost-effective care.

Robert Wood Johnson University Hospital (RWJUH) has been engaged in an extensive work redesign project since early 1987. This work resulted in the creation of the Professionally Advanced Care Team (ProACT®) model (described in detail in Tonges 1989).

During 1986 RWJUH faced the simultaneous imperatives of increased demand for patient care services and reduced availability of professional nurses and other workers. The shortfall in availability of nurses was due to the national shortage, and the supply of other types of workers was also very limited because of an extremely low unemployment rate locally. The hospital was experiencing an accelerating demand for beds and had to continue to provide care despite increasing labor shortages. Faced with these problems, there was definitely an institutional readiness to commit all of the resources of the organization to work redesign.

Successful work redesign on this scale requires an institutional commitment and systematic institutionwide change. The commitment of the board and CEO is essential for the support needed to marshal the resources of the organization for the project; "top down" support is invaluable.

Success in reconfiguring the delivery of patient care also requires an institutional approach to change. The development of ProACT at RWJUH has involved numerous disciplines and departments. It is essential that the model be woven into the fabric of the institution. It cannot be a separate nursing initiative because nursing shortages may come and go, but this work must have sustained support rather than being linked to a crisis in nursing.

Nurse executives and managers who want to sell their programs effectively and obtain institutional commitment must interpret these programs in terms of organizational objectives, as opposed to the narrower view of just what is good for nursing. The senior nursing management sponsors and champions of this project were successful in linking it to the hospital's needs and goals and did receive widespread institutional support.

The groundwork for the project began even earlier with an analysis of the work on a busy medical-surgical unit and consideration of all the factors affecting the work of the unit. The work analysis looked at four issues:

1. What work is being done?
2. Is each task/action necessary? Should it be done?
3. If so, who is doing it?
4. Who should or could be doing it?

The findings indicated that a disturbingly high percentage of nurses' time was being spent in indirect nonnursing activities. A review of the literature revealed that these findings were supported by other similar studies (American Hospital Association 1988; Swenson, Wolfe, and Schroeder 1984). The situation was definitely not unique to RWJUH. Model development was then begun on the basis of this objective data.

Simultaneously within the institution, the Support Services Division had independently begun to look at a new model for themselves in which they collapsed the departments of housekeeping, dietary, and materials management, to create multipurpose decentralized roles. Thus, the redesign project was an institutional effort that nursing took the lead in bringing together.

Through the process of choosing the initial pilot or demonstration unit, four criteria for unit selection were identified. As the model has been expanded, these criteria have been applied in subsequent choices and have been found to be valid:

1. *The right nurse manager*: Because nurse managers are instrumental in planning and implementing new care delivery systems on their units, consideration of the nurse manager is of paramount importance in unit selection. The right nurse manager is competent,

seasoned, enthusiastic about the model, respected by staff and physicians, and knowledgeable about hospital systems.

2. *Key physician support*: Physicians are very important and legitimate stakeholders in the delivery of patient care and must be involved in its redesign. It is essential to identify the formal and informal physician leaders on the unit and ensure their cooperation and support.

3. *Sufficient RN vacancies*: Some vacancies are necessary to allow for the conversion of salary dollars to pay for new services.

4. *Clinical care manager candidates (unit based)*: If a model includes new positions such as the clinical care managers (CCMs) who assume case management responsibilities within the ProACT model, it is important that there are qualified candidates among the current unit staff who can be promoted.

The work at RWJUH is evolutionary, and there are many opportunities to learn as it progresses. The lessons gleaned from this experience thus far that may be helpful to others interested in embarking on a work redesign project can be summarized as follows (adapted from a list originally developed by Maryann F. Fralic, senior vice president of nursing, Robert Wood Johnson University Hospital):

Restructuring the Environment versus Reshaping Behavior

It is much easier to restructure the environment than to reshape behavior. Staff need help and support to internalize new and redesigned roles, and managers have to allocate and spend time working with staff learning unfamiliar behaviors such as delegation.

Clinical Care Manager and Primary Nurse Role Confusion

The clinical care manager position is new, and there is potential for role blurring and diffusion with the primary nurse. Implementation of different roles requires a great deal of attention, clarification, and reclarification.

Matrix Manageability

Staff providing clinical and nonclinical support services at the unit level in the ProACT model receive direction from the nurse manager through a matrix reporting relationship. Managing the matrix relationships requires frequent interdepartmental negotiation and a high level of trust. It is imperative to have good relationships with the other departments and to work at these alliances.

The Trials and Tribulations of Evaluation

Creating and implementing a good evaluation plan is extremely important but very challenging. Sufficient resources must be allocated to accommodate the exponential growth of the evaluation effort as the model is expanded to additional units while data are still repeatedly collected from current units.

No Missing Pieces Allowed

It is better to wait than to implement if all key positions are not filled. If the new system does not meet staff expectations, it will be viewed negatively and rejected.

Budgetary Pitfalls to Avoid

There are many budgetary complexities involved in creating and managing a budget-neutral model. The system that has evolved and seems to work best in this setting entails the transfer of salaries from departments providing new services to nursing cost centers each pay period during the start-up year. Appropriate positions and salary dollars are then reallocated to the involved departments in a more permanent manner for the next year's budget.

Nurse Manager Job Redesign

When the care delivery system is restructured and staff's work is redesigned, the role of the nurse manager must also change. This is a highly significant second-generation redesign issue that has only recently begun to be recognized and addressed (American Organization of Nurse Executives 1990, 1). With improved support on the unit, nurse managers will have the opportunity to function at a higher administrative level in a broader role. They will have increased responsibility for strategic planning for their units, contribute to the progress of the entire service and division, cultivate specific areas of managerial expertise, and interact with other areas as fully functioning department heads.

Variance Analysis and Peer-Review Systems

Variance analysis and case manager effectiveness evaluation systems are two additional important next-generation redesign activities. Data about the factors causing either positive or negative variances from expected length of stay must be collected and analyzed—preferably using an automated system—to identify systemic problems and opportunities to improve resource utilization and patient throughput. This information can be organized and reported in various formats including, very importantly, length of stay by DRG for each nurse case manager. Objective data about the effect of individual nurse case managers on length of stay are an essential element for inclusion in a peer-review system to evaluate performance in this important new position.

Acceptable Modification versus Integrity of Basic Concepts

Finally, anyone involved in the ongoing development and implementation of an alternative practice and care delivery model will face and struggle with this question: How can the model be safely modified as roles evolve and implementation is expanded to new units without damaging the integrity of the original concepts upon which it is based? The answers can be found through a clear vision of the model and an examination of proposed changes on a case-by-case basis.

Human Resources Implications

Labor shortages have been a driving force in the movement to redesign hospital nursing practice and patient care delivery, and these shortages may continue and intensify ("RN Population Seen Declining" 1990). Friedman (1990) states, "In the 1980's, hospitals closed for lack of payment or lack of patients; in the 1990's, hospitals will close for lack of staff." Given these projections, it is extremely important to examine the human resources implications of work redesign.

Redesigned jobs and systems offer many advantages to both employees and organizations, but working and managing in restructured environments also present new challenges and demands for managers and staff.

Attractive New Roles

The creation of new positions provides attractive alternatives for health care workers that were not previously available. For example, the CCM position offers qualified RNs an opportunity to advance to a distinctly different, exciting role with a highly desirable salary and schedule. The chance to do challenging, new, and different work for a higher salary has obvious recruitment and retention implications.

Supportive and Satisfying Work Environment

Models that provide increased clinical and nonclinical support and assistance to primary nurses, enabling them to stay at the bedside and reinvest saved time in direct patient care, definitely facilitate professional nursing practice. When support systems are decentralized and moved to the unit level, ancillary personnel can be incorporated in the unit staff as coworkers. This change makes it possible for support staff to feel part of a team providing high-quality patient care, to see the need for and importance of their work, and to feel accountable and appreciated.

For job enrichment specifically for nurses, competitive and comparable salaries are very important but will not suffice as a total strategy. Nor are clinical ladders the answer if they merely compartmentalize levels of performance within the traditional staff nurse role. It appears that what nurses really need and want is a practice environment and role that allows them to actualize their professional potential and practice to their very best and fullest ability. Thus, salary, scheduling, and other external issues are important because they will dissatisfy if they are not right, but in and of themselves they cannot satisfy because that has to come from within, and through the work itself (Herzberg, Mausner, and Snyderman 1959; Herzberg 1966).

Increased Opportunities for Advancement

Improving opportunities for advancement is critical to retention. Dismantling jobs to create fewer roles with broader scope can accomplish this objective by establishing new career paths. For example, the support service host/hostess position in the ProACT model combines elements of previous housekeeper, dietary aide, supply clerk, and nurse aide positions and, at a higher salary, represents a step up and out of what previously were limited opportunity support services jobs.

Restructured Reporting and Interdepartmental Relationships

Lastly, there are the issues of (1) the increased complexity of matrix reporting relationships; (2) the need to redesign the roles of nurse managers and give them the new skills required to manage today's "new breed" nurse and other staff who have different values, priorities, and expectations; and (3) the challenge of managing these multidisciplinary teams of new and traditional workers in a restructured environment. Nurse managers and other department heads will need a great deal of management training and development to function effectively in restructured environments, and the position of nurse manager will be among the most important in the hospital.

Other Issues

As models evolve and begin to move more deeply into the redesign process, a few other very significant issues emerge:

1. When the number of functions assigned to a position increases, the training process has to lengthen. Increased education and orientation costs are a concern, and it takes longer for replacements to become fully competent.

2. Again, in multipurpose roles, there may be conflicting demands for service from the same person at the same time. For example, a clinical services technician who normally provides unit-based pharmacy technician, EKG, and phlebotomy services in the ProACT model may not be able to meet the simultaneous demands of a code situation without assistance from the central departments.

3. The functions of the central departments may become those of hiring, scheduling and training, and the question of who in the matrix actually supervises the multifunctional employee has to be carefully examined and addressed.

Clearly, there are many important issues to consider.

The health care industry continues to operate in a relentlessly turbulent environment, and the key to surviving and thriving is to be exquisitely well informed, prepared for and responsive to the changes. Today's reduced availability and affordability of professional registered nurses drives the need to adapt nurses' responsibilities and create new systems in which fewer, higher-paid nurses can provide quality patient care. Work redesign is an appropriate and feasible solution to this problem, but there is a strong need for care in implementation and for sensitivity to the human resources implications for all staff members affected by the changes.

References

Ackoff, R. 1989. "The Interactive Planning Model." Presented at Strengthening Hospital Nursing: A Program to Improve Patient Care Conference, Orlando, FL, 7 September.

American Hospital Association. 1988. "Issues and Strategies." *Proceedings, Invitational Conference on the Nursing Shortage*. Chicago: AHA, Center for Nursing, 7 October.

American Organization of Nurse Executives. 1990. "AONE to Conduct National Study of Nurse Manager Role." *The Nurse Executive* 2 (9): 1.

Eubanks, P. 1990. "Nursing Restructuring Renews Focus on Patient-Centered Care." *Hospitals* (20 April): 60, 62.

Flannery, T. P., and J. B. Williams. 1990. "The Shape of Things to Come." *Healthcare Forum Journal* 33 (3): 14–20.

Friedman, E. 1990. "Farewell to the 80's: What have we learned and where are we heading?" Presentation at the American Hospital Association Annual Convention, Washington, DC, 30 July.

Hackman, J., and G. Oldham. 1980. *Work Redesign.* Menlo Park, CA: Addison-Wesley Publishing.

Herzberg, F. 1966. *Work and the Nature of Man.* Cleveland: World.

Herzberg, F., B. Mausner, and B. B. Snyderman. 1959. *The Motivation to Work.* New York: Wiley.

Lawrenz, E. 1989. "Work Redesign." *Perspectives on Staffing and Scheduling* 8 (6): 4.

Mohr, B., G. Thomas, J. Ranney, and S. R. Lamb. 1989. *A Socio-technical Approach to Designing High Performance Organizations.* Participants' Reference Binder, Bethel, ME, 17–26 July.

Moritz, P., A. S. Hinshaw, and J. Heirich. 1989. "Nursing Resources and the Delivery of Patient Care: The National Center for Nursing Research Perspective." *Journal of Nursing Administration* 19 (5): 12–17.

Nadler, G. 1981. *The Planning and Design Approach.* New York: John Wiley and Sons.

"RN Population Seen Declining after the Year 2000: HHS Predicts Shortage Could Top 800,000 by 2020." 1990. *American Journal of Nursing* 90 (9): 97, 110.

Schetter, C. O. 1990. "Can Today's Care Delivery System Deliver Tomorrow?" Presentation at the American Hospital Association Annual Convention, Washington, DC, 1 August.

Sovie, M. 1989. "Clinical Nursing Practices and Patient Outcomes: Evaluation, Evolution, and Revolution (Legitimizing Radical Change to Maximize Nurses' Time for Quality Care)." *Nursing Economics* 7 (2): 79–85.

Swenson, B., H. Wolfe, and R. Shroeder. 1984. "Effectively Employing Support Services: The Key for Increasing Nursing Productivity." *Modern Healthcare* 14 (16): 101–102.

Tonges, M. C. 1989. "Redesigning Hospital Nursing Practice. The Professionally Advanced Care Team (ProACT™) Model, Part 1." *Journal of Nursing Administration* 19 (7): 31–38.

Zander, K. 1985. "Analyzing Your Workplace." In *Political Action Handbook for Nurses*, edited by D. Mason and S. Talbott, 227–39. Menlo Park, CA: Addison-Wesley Publishing.

3

Assessing and Preparing the Organization for Work Redesign

Vickie Mullins Moore, M. Gibby Kinsey, and Marilyn Dubree

Work redesign is not a concept that a hospital administrator casually drops on the table at a management meeting one day. It is a comprehensive and systematic change process that requires a detailed assessment of the organization and a well-thought-out plan for implementation. If done in a collaborative fashion with hospital staff, the process of assessing the organization and determining the most appropriate work redesign model can be the start of a new way of thinking creatively for the future.

Organizational Assessment

Prior to undertaking an operational restructuring effort, there are several key areas that require assessment and clear definition. An environmental assessment of the organization should be conducted to assist the leadership of the organization in determining the best approach to improve the chances of the success of the project.

The environmental assessment will give a picture of the readiness of the organization to embark upon a change project of this magnitude. The strengths, weaknesses, opportunities, and threats that are known to the organization should be discussed in terms of how they will affect the organization's ability to restructure (Allawi, Bellaire, and David 1991). Following are factors that should be considered in the environmental assessment.

Philosophy and Mission

The philosophy and mission of the organization should be reviewed and will provide a basis for determining the strategic objectives for the restructuring effort. What are the values inherent in the organizational philosophy, and are they well understood and demonstrated in daily operations? This may provide a basis for trust between the staff and administration as questions about the project unfold and anxiety about job security occurs.

Strategic Plan

The strategic plan of the organization as it relates to market share, specialty services, and plans for growth and expansion should be considered. Is the hospital community based, rural, tertiary, academic? Who does it serve? What competitive advantages already exist that could be capitalized upon? What is the average occupancy of the hospital and is that expected to change for any reason?

The strategic objectives of the project related to cost, quality, customer satisfaction, and service must be consistent with the hospital's strategic plan to be accepted.

Magnitude of Return Required

The magnitude of return required on the investment of resources is important to understand before initiating the project. How quick does that return need to occur? What is the financial position of the hospital? What is the capital available to support the project implementation?

Restructuring hospital operations will not improve last quarter's operating margin. If the return must be quick and substantial, it is better to apply other strategies that better meet that financial goal. An organization would be wise not to take on a project of this scope until those initiatives had been implemented and achieved to some degree. A restructuring effort takes time before the financial rewards are realized.

Current Operating and Management Capabilities

Current operating and management capabilities should be identified, such as integrated information systems, usefulness of statistical data as a management tool, systems that have already been implemented to increase efficiencies in central departments and on patient units, and the skill, sophistication and creativity of the management staff. Have opportunities to improve operations and quality been addressed through the process of continuous quality improvement? What do the managers need to be better able to do their jobs? What hinders them from being effective? Is the organization run as a business or at the whims of those who have the loudest voices?

Organizational Leadership

The type of organizational leadership that is practiced in the institution needs to be identified and assessed as to how it will facilitate or encumber the restructuring effort. Is the environment bureaucratic or participative? Are those at the top of the organization committed to the successful implementation of the project, or are there some who will need encouragement, coaching, educating, or counseling to support the efforts?

Internal Resources and Consultation Needs

Internal resources and the need for consultation are important to assess before the project begins. Identify the talent within the organization that may provide leadership for the restructuring effort. Although most organizations will require consultative assistance, at least in the initial phases of the project, some may find that there are enough internal resources that consultative assistance will be minimal. Others may require assistance and support for a longer period and at several levels. This need should be identified so that decisions can be made to ensure that the appropriate level of expertise is available.

Human Resource Issues

Human resource issues, such as recruitment and retention statistics for health care professionals and support staff, should be addressed. A data base is necessary for tracking this information before and after implementation. What are the current statistics on FTEs per occupied bed? What are the staffing ratios on the patient care units?

Organizational Culture and Readiness to Change

The culture of the organization and the speed with which change can occur must be assessed. Does the environment foster innovation and creativity? Peter Senge (1990), author of *The Fifth Discipline*, asserts that the only sustainable competitive advantage an organization has is its ability to learn. Does the organization possess the five disciplines of a learning organization or the learning disabilities that cause it merely to be able to react to the past? How successfully can resources be identified and dedicated to the project?

How successful has the organization been in the change process in the past? How has change been managed historically? Does the culture require a great deal of planning time with opportunity to have input and reaction from a variety of sources, or is the decision-making process more centralized? How cohesive is the staff to establish a team to assure the success of the project?

One of the most important components of any organizational assessment is the organization's "readiness to learn." According to Senge (1990), in most companies that fail, there is abundant evidence *in advance* that the firm is in trouble. This evidence goes unheeded, however, even when individual managers are aware of it. The organization as a whole cannot recognize impending threats, understand the implications of those threats, or come up with alternatives.

Let's presume that even the most successful companies are "poor" learners—they survive but never live up to their potential. What if, in light of what organizations could be, "excellence is actually mediocrity"? Senge (1990) further asserts that it is no accident that most organizations learn poorly. The way they are designed and managed, the way people's jobs are defined, and, most importantly, the way we have all been taught to think and interact create fundamental "learning disabilities." These disabilities operate despite the best efforts of bright, committed people. Often, the harder they try to solve problems, the worse the results. What learning does occur takes place despite these learning disabilities—they pervade all organizations, including hospitals, to some degree.

So, what does all of this have to do with operational restructuring or providing patient-focused care? Undeniably, this "readiness to learn" concept is a very new and different phenomenon. But it is one whose time has come for the health care industry and warrants careful attention. In order to survive the upcoming decade, a metamorphosis of the hospital as we know it today will become imperative. The charge for hospital administrators in the 1990s will be multifold but will include at the least the following:

- To change the focus for decision making from "hospital" or "provider-focused" care to "patient-focused" care
- To decompartmentalize and therefore simplify procedures and processes by which services are provided to patients
- To increase the continuity of care provided to patients
- To decentralize as many services as possible to the patient care unit
- To design roles that will ensure the effective and efficient utilization of *all* the staff
- To incorporate a customer service, patient-focused, and continuous quality improvement philosophy throughout the organization

In order to effect this transformation, administrators must do the following:

- Identify the learning disabilities prevalent in their organizations
- Evaluate the effect the disabilities will have on meeting the objectives to provide patient-focused care
- Develop a plan for managing and/or eliminating the disabilities

There are several prevalent learning disabilities in hospitals that are likely to affect decision making in the development and implementation of a patient-focused model. The most problematic disability in hospitals is "I am my position." We are trained to be loyal to our jobs—so much so that we confuse them with our own identities. When asked what one does for a living, most people describe the tasks they perform every day, not the purpose of the greater enterprise in which they take part. Most individuals see themselves within a system over which they have little or no influence. They do their job, put in their time, and try to cope with the forces outside of their control. Consequently, they tend to see their responsibilities as limited to the boundaries of their position. When people in hospitals focus only on their position, they have little sense of responsibility for the results produced when all positions interact (Senge 1990). Employees, particularly the various professionals throughout the hospital (RNs, respiratory therapists, physical therapists, radiology technologists, laboratory technologists, etc.), get caught up with "doing their thing" to or for the patient—and, typically, never at the convenience of the patient. Competition among these caregivers results, and the patient either feels pulled in every direction or gets lost in the shuffle. This disability must be overcome by developing and implementing multidisciplinary teams of caregivers that are empowered to do whatever it takes to provide service in a more patient-focused manner. Only then will the territorialism between and among departments begin to diminish!

Maladaptation to gradually building threats to survival is so pervasive in systems studies of corporate failure that it has given rise to the "parable of the boiled frog"—the second disability prevalent in hospitals. If you place a frog in a pot of boiling water, it will immediately try to scramble out. If you place the frog in room temperature water and do not scare it, it will stay put. Now, if the pot sits on a heat source and if you gradually turn up the temperature, something very interesting happens. As the temperature rises from 70°F to 80°F, the frog will do nothing. In fact, it will show every sign of enjoying itself. As the temperature gradually increases, the frog will become groggier and groggier until it is unable to climb out of the pot. Though there is nothing restraining it, the frog will sit there and boil. Why? Because the frog's internal apparatus for sensing threats to survival is geared to sudden changes in its environment, not to slow, gradual changes (Senge 1990).

This is absolutely no different from a hospital! Hospitals definitely respond to changes in legislation that affect third party reimbursement—and therefore the bottom line—because these changes are, more often than not, sudden. Most hospitals are focused on the short term and the dramatic. They respond to crises well. However, hospitals have been unable to see the slow, insidious processes that have occurred over the past decade or so—the increased specialization, the compartmentalization and fragmentation of services, the lack of continuity of care to our patients, the ever-increasing paperwork that takes caregivers from the patient, and the barriers or obstacles that prevent our caregivers from doing their job. As a result, the American health care industry has become one of the most inefficient industries in the world. Even more importantly, we have failed to realize that our patients are our customers. The care that we have provided for years and years has been provider focused rather than patient focused. In this day and age of managed care, direct contracting, and HMOs, we have to place the patient at the very center of our efforts and our decision making. How does your hospital compare to the "boiled frog" phenomenon?

The next disability is called the "myth of the management team." Standing forward to do battle with these various disabilities is the "management team"—the collection of savvy, experienced managers who represent the hospital's different functions and areas of expertise. Together, they are supposed to sort out the complex cross-functional issues that are critical to the organization. What confidence do we have, really, that typical management teams can surmount these disabilities? All too often, management teams tend to spend their time fighting for turf, avoiding anything that will make them look bad personally, and pretending that everyone is behind the team's collective strategy—maintaining the appearance of a cohesive team. To keep up the image, they seek to squelch disagreement; people with serious reservations avoid stating them publicly, and joint decisions are watered-down compromises reflecting what everyone can live with, or else reflecting one person's view foisted on the group. If there is disagreement, it is usually expressed in a manner that lays blame, polarizes opinion, and fails to reveal the underlying differences in assumptions and experience in a way that would enable the team as a whole to learn (Senge 1990).

Senge asserts that most management teams break down under pressure. Although the team may function quite well with routine issues, when forced to confront complex issues that may be embarrassing or threatening, the "teamness goes to pot." Most managers find collective inquiry inherently threatening. School trains us never to admit that we do not know the answer, and in most organizations we reinforce that lesson by rewarding the people that excel in advocating their own views and do not inquire into complex issues. For example, when was the last time someone was rewarded in your hospital for raising difficult questions about current policies rather than solving urgent problems? Even if we feel uncertain or ignorant, we learn to protect ourselves from the pain of appearing uncertain or ignorant. That very process blocks out any new understandings that might threaten us. The consequence is what is called "skilled incompetence"—teams full of people who are incredibly proficient at protecting themselves from learning or changing (Senge 1990)! Since change—massive and mandatory change—is the operative word for the future, this particular disability must be evaluated and objectively and aggressively managed.

Stakeholder Management

Crucial to the success of any significant change in an organization is a comprehensive analysis of the "stakeholders." Stakeholders include all those individuals or groups who have a vested interest in the problem and its solutions. Stakeholders depend upon an organization for the realization of some of their goals and, in turn, the organization depends on them in some way for the full realization of its goals. Stakeholders can be individuals or departments within an organization, they can be formal or informal leaders, and they can be internal or external to the organization. Stakeholders may strengthen or weaken an organization's efforts to achieve objectives related to change. In fact, when united, stakeholders can prevent change from occurring. Because of this, it is imperative that stakeholder management become a priority in the overall management of any notable change (Center for Applied Research 1993).

Organizations are typically aware of only the most obvious stakeholders and become aware of others only when trouble, or even a crisis, occurs. "Stakeholder mapping" is a method of thorough and detailed assessment of the potential repercussions for *all* stakeholders included in the planned change. It enlightens the organization and positions the organization to deal more proactively and more effectively with inevitable resistance. The unfortunate but rather common practice of "putting out fires" as they develop from dissatisfied stakeholders will become unnecessary if this process is executed appropriately (Center for Applied Research 1993).

The Center for Applied Research outlines the following steps designed to conduct a systematic analysis of stakeholders and their potential impact on the organization (abstracted with permission from the Center for Applied Research's *Stakeholder Mapping*, © 1993, Philadelphia, PA):

1. State the organizational objectives.
2. Brainstorm stakeholders.
3. Characterize stakeholders' attitude toward organizational objectives or planned change.
4. Identify their power with respect to the adoption and/or implementation of the plan.
5. Who influences whom?
6. Rethink solutions to increase successful implementation.
7. Develop strategies.

State the Organizational Objectives

Stakeholder mapping may be used as a general assessment of the potential impact of stakeholders on the organization as a whole or, more specifically, to assess potential support or opposition to a specific objective or planned change. For the general assessment, the group performing stakeholder mapping should be in agreement regarding the mission, goal, and objectives of the organization. For the more specific assessment, they should agree on a set of statements to describe the nature of a specific objective or planned change since stakeholders' possible reactions are what is at issue in this work. An excellent way to ensure this agreement is to list these objectives or descriptions on a flip chart. Discussion will help to clarify ambiguous issues and to surface group values and individual objectives. Nominal group technique is an excellent process for doing this in a more formal way.

Brainstorm Stakeholders

The next step is to brainstorm all the possible stakeholders. They should be identified as specifically as possible—by name, title, group, or department. It is also important to delineate separately any mixed groups that contain both supporters and opponents.

Characterize Stakeholders Attitude toward
Organizational Objectives or Planned Change

At this stage, it is important to examine the issues through the eyes of the stakeholders. How do objectives for the project affect the objectives of the stakeholders? It would probably be helpful to characterize the stakeholders' situation at present, contrast it with their situation after the planned change, and then consider the impact. In general, personal values, such as security, power, survival, status, and achievement, will dominate organizational values, such as efficiency and effectiveness, in influencing the attitudes of stakeholders.

Identify Their Power with Respect to the Adoption and/or Implementation of the Plan

Power should be subdivided into two categories—adoption and implementation. Board members, administrative staff, department managers, and others may be extremely powerful with respect to adoption of the change, but have little influence over the actual implementation. Groups of employees, on the other hand, may be extremely powerful in regard to implementation.

Who Influences Whom?

Stakeholders increase their influence by forming coalitions, opportunistic relationships, or both. These coalitions should be examined by delineating who influences the stakeholder and who they, in turn, influence.

Rethink Solutions to Increase Successful Implementation

The next step, rethinking solutions to increase successful implementation, is somewhat twofold. First of all, one should look at the individuals or groups who are vehemently opposed and powerful and determine whether any strategies exist that could decrease the opposition without alienating support. The second group to examine are those who favor the change, but who are not particularly powerful. Here the thrust is on ways to enhance their power by such means as organizing or information sharing.

Develop Strategies

After conducting the above steps, the group will have a good picture of key opponents and supporters and will have considered a number of options and their possible effect on stakeholders. This information can then be assembled to construct strategies that enhance organizational objectives. The best strategies are those that induce the most cooperative behavior from the most powerful stakeholder groups. Opposition from powerful groups may be reduced by modifying objectives or planned change if this does not compromise important organizational values. If conflict seems inevitable, the stakeholder list supplies important information regarding potential supporters, opponents, and coalitions. Exhibit 3.1 is a worksheet that could be used for stakeholder mapping.

Exhibit 3.1   Stakeholder Mapping

Identify Stakeholders	Attitude toward Restructuring		Stakeholder Power		Coalition	
	Attitude	Stakeholder Objectives and Values That Motivate Their Attitude	Adoption	Implementation	Who Influences Whom	Whom Do They Influence

Source: Abstracted, with permission, from the Center for Applied Research, *Stakeholder Mapping,* © 1993, Philadelphia, PA.

Desired Outcomes

Since every organization has opportunities to implement change, the real key is determining the desired outcome to be achieved as a result of the change process and exactly what type of change the organization can accommodate. The "continuum of operational and organizational development" is a framework for decision making that helps hospitals identify risks, time frames, and organizational requirements necessary for managing change (Figure 3.1). The organization's current position and options for the future can be assessed using this framework (Allawi, Bellaire, and David 1991). As organizations progress along the developmental continuum, they exhibit an increase in skill, abilities, and effectiveness as measured by reduced operating costs, improved service delivery, and improved outcomes.

The authors describe the desired outcomes of operational restructuring for hospitals in each stage along the continuum. For a hospital in Stage 1, the desired outcome is clearly to alter basic operations in order to turn around the financial viability of the organization. The organization may be lacking the basic systems to coordinate care to achieve minimal efficiencies. The resources to produce the changes may not be available within the organization, and strong leadership and consultative assistance may be required for restructuring efforts to be initiated and effectively implemented.

The hospital in Stage 2 may not identify a real need to make changes because currently it is functioning well, but must do so in order to defend its position in the marketplace (Allawi, Bellaire, and David 1991). The hospital in this stage usually does not have a strong market leader and may typify the community hospital offering a full range of services. Basic operational systems are usually in place, and there are adequate resources to initiate organizational change. In order to defend its market share, the strengths in providing care must be identified and enhanced to make an impact on the overall organization, highlighting this aspect of care to customers and establishing a reputation as a result. The most obvious example of a service with the potential to affect the total organization is nursing care. By strengthening and enhancing nursing service, providing support services necessary to improve efficiencies, quality care will be improved. The hospital may well be able to improve its market share and be in a position to begin to take advantage of opportunities to differentiate itself in the market in the future.

The hospital in Stage 3 is in a position to differentiate itself from others in the market (Allawi, Bellaire, and David 1991). This hospital may have one or more service lines that provide opportunity for achieving excellence in quality, cost, efficiency, and customer satisfaction. The desired outcomes

Figure 3.1   Continuum of Operational and Organizational Development

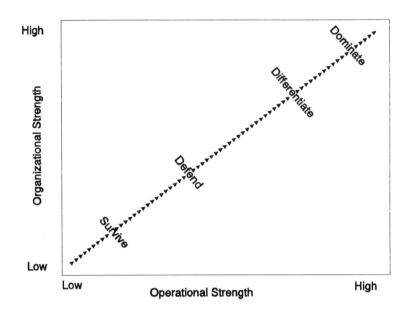

<table>
<tr><td>**Stage 1**
SURVIVAL</td><td>Organizations with an absence of operational processes or the management skills to make critical changes. Change requires new controls and management tools.</td></tr>
<tr><td>**Stage 2**
DEFENSE</td><td>Organizations undifferentiated in their markets and inwardly focused on managing resource use and cost efficiency. Change is based on long-term skill development and functional area improvement.</td></tr>
<tr><td>**Stage 3**
DIFFERENTIATION</td><td>Organizations that strive to be responsive to customer requirements along the dimensions of cost, service, and clinical outcomes. Change is focused on achieving excellence within clinical areas.</td></tr>
<tr><td>**Stage 4**
DOMINATION</td><td>Organizations that are prepared to set "world class" performance standards in achieving the best possible outcomes at the lowest cost, across multiple product lines.</td></tr>
</table>

Source: Reprinted, with the permission of Healthcare Forum, from S. Allawi, D. Bellaire, and L. David, "Are You Ready for Structural Change?" *Healthcare Forum Journal* 34 (July/August 1991): 40.

for this organization are to improve service standards and operational efficiencies, reduce the cost of providing services, and improve quality in these clinical areas. The leadership of the organization is usually visionary and has the luxury of internal resources to both lead and support operational restructuring efforts to achieve the goals.

The hospital in Stage 4 is a role model for other hospitals. This hospital has several market leaders established as centers of excellence, resources are abundant, and services are provided efficiently, at the lowest cost and with the best possible outcome (Allawi, Bellaire, and David 1991). This nirvana exists only in the dreams of the CEOs of hospitals in the first three stages; however, there are a few centers across the country that come close in one or more of the dimensions of cost, quality, service, and customer satisfaction. Change is focused on the ability to respond to market changes, reimbursement, and customer demands quickly and effortlessly. Leadership for quality and service improvements comes from front line employees empowered to set performance standards.

Continuous Quality Improvement

Are restructuring efforts, regardless of the magnitude, simply a component of continuous quality improvement? Absolutely! Continuous quality improvement (CQI) is a customer-focused, quality-driven philosophy and process that relies on each member of an organization to build quality into every step of service development and delivery. The core of CQI, and perhaps its most basic principle, is that systems can always be improved. Organizations that use CQI make the continuous search for improvement in the processes used to create products and services a way of life (Orlikoff and Totten 1991). Gurus of operational restructuring throughout the country insist that restructuring is a journey—not a destination! Certainly this is analogous to the philosophy of CQI.

Dennis O'Leary, president of the Joint Commission on Accreditation of Healthcare Organizations (JCAHO), differentiates between quality assurance and continuous quality improvement: "Quality assurance has been traditionally viewed as a blame-finding, compartmentalized activity focused on generating specific requirements for individual departments of the hospital, often with the goal of meeting external regulations or standards. CQI, on the other hand, is based on a different philosophy and set of assumptions" (Orlikoff and Totten 1991, 14). What W. Edwards Deming, Joseph M. Juran, and other experts discovered while researching the sources of quality problems was that the problems, and therefore the opportunities to solve them, were part of the systems and processes used to create products or provide services. Rarely were they attributable to the lack of will, skill, or intention of individual workers. Even when people were causing defects, the root of the problem could most often be traced to poor job design, leadership failure, or unclear purpose.

Now, let's examine the reasons hospitals are restructuring operations. The most significant reason for changing the way hospitals function is simply that hospitals are inefficient. According to Bain Farris (1991), the CEO of Saint Vincent's Hospital in Indianapolis, Indiana, "The hospital of today was designed for the 1920's." In fact, hospitals have changed very little in the past several decades, and their traditional, bureaucratic structures designed for the industrial age are creating a multitude of problems in this highly complex age of information. Due to the explosion of new technology in the 1980s, hospitals today are extremely compartmentalized and specialized. As a consequence of all of this, the care that we provide is hospital focused rather than patient focused. True, it appears that patients receive high-quality clinical care, but they pay a terrible price in terms of confusion, lack of continuity, impersonal care, and cost (Urmy 1991).

For example, did you know that the typical patient comes in contact with as many as 55 different people in a typical four-day hospital stay? And did you know that obtaining a simple chest x-ray in a hospital takes one to two hours, involves 40 steps (80 percent of which have nothing at all to do with the actual procedure), and necessitates the involvement of at least 50 employees? Of even greater concern is that nurses spend as little as 16 percent of their time at the bedside providing direct patient care, compared to 44 percent of their time spent scheduling and coordinating activities and documenting what they have done (Lathrop 1991). The purposes, therefore, of restructuring operations in hospitals are

- first and foremost, to change the focus for decision making from hospital- or provider-focused care to patient-focused care;
- to decompartmentalize and therefore simplify procedures;
- to evaluate and streamline processes and systems by which services are rendered;
- to decentralize as many services as possible to the patient care unit;
- to design roles that will ensure the effective and efficient utilization of all the staff—particularly the professional staff; and
- to increase the continuity of care provided to patients.

Without a doubt, these objectives are congruent with and complimentary to the objectives for continuous quality improvement.

Model Descriptions

There are several types of work redesign models that have been developed for hospitals.

Nurse Extender Model

Providing less skilled employees to assist nurses to provide care is probably the most frequently used strategy to restructure patient care delivery and relieve the burden of shortages of health care professionals. The nurse extender may perform clinical tasks under the direction of the nurse as well as support functions traditionally associated with central departments, such as transportation, housekeeping, dietary, materials management, and clerical tasks. Training is usually provided at the institution to include the job responsibilities to meet the needs of the hospital or through area vocational programs. Titles vary for the nurse extender but include patient care technicians, nursing assistants, and medical technicians, for example. The nurse may delegate tasks appropriately to the nurse extender, thereby relieving her to perform the duties associated with professional practice.

The cost to train and employ nurse extenders is minimal. Because the staffing mix of professionals to support staff can be changed when using nurse extenders, this model can result in reduced salary costs. The model addresses the need expressed by nurses to provide support to relieve them of nonnursing tasks. Depending upon how this model is implemented, it may also provide opportunity for an increase in the amount of time the professional has to provide direct patient care.

The major shortcoming of this model is that it does not address the structural inefficiencies, such as scheduling, coordinating, documenting, and employee downtime, that cause an increase in the cost of providing care. Simply adding nurse extenders to the staffing mix does not address the fragmentation caused by specialization and by central departments providing care for the convenience, efficiency, and productivity of the department, rather than the patients' needs. Quality improvements are not addressed with a pure nurse extender model, and the types of tasks that may be delegated to nonskilled support staff in some models may be questionable from a quality perspective.

Patient-Focused Approach

Booz-Allen & Hamilton Healthcare Consultants (1990) developed a care delivery model with a patient-focused approach that has been implemented in several hospitals nationwide with varying degrees of modification. The main premise of this model is to restructure operations so that services are provided around the needs and convenience of the patient. In order to accomplish this, caregivers from a variety of backgrounds are cross-trained to provide almost all of the services their patients need. Continuity is provided across shifts and days of hospitalization, allowing the patient to interact with fewer caregivers. Since services are provided on the patient unit to the extent possible, there is less time required for scheduling of tests in central departments and transporting patients off the unit. Patients with similar diagnoses, care requirements, ancillary resource consumption, and length of stay are clustered, allowing care to become more predictable and protocol driven. Documentation can become exception based as a result (Lathrop 1991).

This model provides a basis for dealing with the structural inefficiencies such as fragmentation of services, compartmentalization of duties and overspecialization of health care personnel, and unacceptable service levels. Because employees are cross-trained, the model helps relieve the staffing difficulties caused by the shortage of health care professionals. The cost of providing care can be reduced as a result of the long-term efficiencies that can be achieved with a patient-focused approach. All constituents—staff, physicians, and patients—are better satisfied with this method of delivering care in the hospitals surveyed.

However, if this model is not implemented carefully and with a great deal of input from health care professionals, there is a hazard of cross-training personnel to the point that the lines become blurred between professional and support roles. Hospitals must be careful to avoid the trap of making "mini-nurses" out of everyone for the sake of breaking down barriers among the professional disciplines. Critics contend that excessive cross-training and overdelegation results in lowered quality of care and dissatisfied health care workers who entered certain professions based on their skills and affinities for those roles. Patient aggregation is difficult to achieve in all cases, particularly in hospitals with high occupancy rates or with significant census fluctuations overall or from unit to unit. Extensive operational restructuring has a cultural and behavioral component that can be expected to cause human resource concerns. Finally, the cost of implementation is high—so high, in fact, that some hospitals may believe it prohibitive if resources are scarce and operating margins narrow.

Expanded/Alternate Roles

Expanding, enhancing, and altering the professional practice of nursing is another method of restructuring patient care delivery. One such model has been developed at Robert Wood Johnson University Hospital. The Professionally Advanced Care Team (ProACT®) model combines the expansion of the nursing role with deployment of ancillary support services to the patient unit. Primary nurses manage and provide nursing care during the patient's hospitalization; clinical care managers coordinate the entire hospital stay with nursing staff, physicians, and other health care professionals. The clinical care managers coordinate the care for a number of patients based on diagnosis and work load. Professional and ancillary support services, including pharmacy, housekeeping, dietary, and materials management, are deployed to the patient unit to provide maximum support to the staff and patient and to improve the quality of service provided (Tonges 1991). Mary Crabtree Tonges stresses that cross-training is not a component of this model; rather, the goal is to define the work of the professional nurse and then provide the support needed to accomplish those components of care that can be delegated.

The ProACT model has resulted in increased satisfaction from patients, staff, and physicians. This model has demonstrated a reduction in the length of stay for targeted DRGs, and quality indexes have shown positive trends. The model was designed to be budget neutral for salaries as it was implemented on the pilot units. However, there is an expectation that the impact the clinical care managers have in controlling hospital resource utilization and maximizing reimbursement will result in cost savings (Tonges 1991).

The role of the clinical care manager encompasses broad evaluation and comprehensive planning for the patient, managing the patient unit in the absence of the nurse manager, providing direct care to patients at times, as well as seeing new admissions (Tonges 1991). Thus, there is potential for role confusion with not only the nurse manager, but also with the primary nurses at the bedside. This role can also lead to frustration in trying to assume all responsibilities adequately. The lack of cross-training may lead to additional personnel needs for the patient unit to fulfill all of the decentralized support functions. Additionally, fragmentation of services, even though they are provided on the patient unit, may occur due to the lack of cross-training of team members.

Work Step Analysis

As the development of a chosen model unfolds, the need to assess the work to be done and who is best suited to do it must be considered. This is referred to as *work step analysis*, a crucial and potentially volatile point in the change process. Therefore, much thought should be given to the approach that will be taken to leading this effort. It is important that the operational restructuring effort not be associated only with tasks—a very sensitive point with staff that cannot be taken lightly. However, staff must be assisted to understand their professional disciplines are not based on tasks, but on process and outcomes. Tasks are a means by which the processes are carried out to achieve the desired outcome, but by no means should be considered the sum total of the role of a health care professional. Staff who get caught up in "I am my position because of the tasks I perform" will provide a great deal of challenge to the process of assessing and redefining who is best suited to perform or share tasks in order to get the job accomplished.

A work group or project team should be designated to begin this process. All members of the team must learn what each discipline incorporates into the basic education for that area of practice and the amount of education and training that the support personnel undergo to prepare them for their roles. This can prove to be very enlightening for the staff and can also provide for a greater appreciation for each other.

In order to proceed with model development, work step analysis should be undertaken. As with each step of this process, the training needs of the project team must be assessed. Work redesign, although not a science, can be supported and facilitated by several skills and techniques that provide adequate conceptual background and skill development, expediting the work of the project team.

Redesigning jobs entails a seven-step process used at Vanderbilt University Hospital (Booz-Allen & Hamilton Healthcare Consultants 1990):

1. Unbundle current jobs into a discrete list of tasks.
2. Target and eliminate redundant, unnecessary, and highly complex tasks.
3. Define the minimal skill level required to perform each task.
4. Identify deferrable and time-dependent tasks.
5. Rebundle work into jobs that meet the organization's goals.
6. Define organizational models to support newly defined jobs.
7. Develop supporting operational practices for new jobs.

Each of these steps can help the project team see the opportunities for restructuring the work to be done. These steps were used at Vanderbilt for both analysis prior to job restructuring and later as a framework for work redesign training for hospital staff and leadership. Noted below are examples of the activities and outcomes of each step.

Step 1

Unbundle current work into tasks. This step is critical to developing a new paradigm for patient care. Until the current work is identified, no real analysis can occur. There is often a perception of much greater understanding of the work of others in the organization than is really true. Depending upon the scope of integration desired, the review of task lists will be an education for all involved. Most disciplines and departments minimally know the work of other areas. Moreover, this review will reveal opportunities to create efficiencies and eliminate redundancies.

Step 2

Target and eliminate redundant, unnecessary, and highly complex tasks. The review of task lists produces a new awareness of efforts expended by multiple individuals and departments, of processes that have achieved a high level of complexity, and of tasks that are unnecessary but that have not been eliminated. Changes resulting from this step are usually less threatening and are a welcome relief from excess and time-consuming work steps. At Vanderbilt, this step produced process simplification on the pilot unit, which helped to regain time for clinical and service work. Streamlining the clinical documentation system was another outcome of this effort.

Step 3

Define the minimal skill level required to perform each task. The completion of this step will produce a review indicating skill, regulatory, and training requirements. Each previously listed task should reflect who currently completes the task and who could do the task. This summary will not be the answer to who should do the tasks, as that cannot be determined until other aspects of the work are considered. However, examination of the minimal skill level required will help to shift thinking from "we have always done it this way" to "perhaps there is an alternative approach." The product of this review will be a summary of requirements. The process of review may be uncomfortable for project team members as they revisit why tasks are done the way they are currently and by which person. At Vanderbilt, professional territory became evident at this step. Also, questions of quality arise around who *could* do a task versus who *should* do a task.

Step 4

Identify deferrable and time-dependent tasks. Identifying the time-dependent tasks can assist in rebundling tasks in a way that balances work load (Table 3.1).

Step 5

Rebundle work into jobs that meet the organization's goals. This step is the most challenging of all the steps of work redesign. The opportunity to

Table 3.1 Identification of Types of Tasks

	Deferrable	*Event Dependent on Demand*	*Time Dependent*
Definition	Able to perform when time permits	Requires immediate or timely response	Requires immediate or timely response
Nature of demand	Work load predictable	Work load somewhat predictable; varies by patient	Work load predictable day to day and time of day
Implications for work redesign	Used to balance work load	Used to determine required staffing levels	Used to determine staffing levels

rebuild work into newly defined jobs requires synthesis of organizational goals, stakeholders' input, holistic job criteria, and the feasibility of implementation. First, the time-dependent and regulatory-constrained tasks should be rebundled by job class. Work load should then be balanced by assigning deferrable tasks to appropriate job classes. At the completion of this step, each newly defined job class must be reviewed for appropriateness of work and to determine if an enriched job has been defined. This step at Vanderbilt afforded the project team the opportunity to revisit project goals and to reaffirm them as new roles were created.

Step 6

Define organizational models to support the newly defined jobs. Through this process, questions will surface regarding the relationships of new jobs and who will be the manager of newly integrated work. It is important to resist the urge to answer these questions prematurely. The answers to these structure queries should be driven by the work, as newly defined. The adage of "form follows function" applies in this situation.

New relationships will evolve when work is redesigned, and responses to the following questions must be developed:

- Who is on the patient care team?
- Who supports the patient care team?
- How does each role relate to the patient?

- How do they relate to one another?

The new paradigm of work requires a new set of rules for these guidelines.

Step 7

Develop supporting operational practices for new jobs. The initial aspects of work redesign are defined to allow as much creativity and innovation as possible. Step 7 acknowledges the reality of operational planning and implementation. All of the work, heretofore somewhat academic, must be supported by a plan that includes systems to address the following:

- Training programs
- Quality improvement
- Process descriptions
- Job descriptions
- Performance appraisals

The integration of these work steps into actual work redesign also requires that the model design be placed against the previously established criteria for success. Prior to implementation, testing of the models will identify where problems exist and appropriate preventions may be applied.

These steps for work redesign have been used as a template for reviewing work and redefining roles. A replicable set of steps is essential to expanding this type of change throughout the organization.

Organizational Enablers

Every hospital has its own unique set of strengths and weaknesses. A number of organizational strengths have been identified as enablers for the process of work redesign. These enabling factors consist of programs or innovations already implemented that will act as anchors or critical components of the work redesign process and expedite the change process as well. While assessing the organizational feasibility of the models designed, an assessment of existing enablers is also in order. If such enablers exist and are effective, the work redesign model should be developed to incorporate and enhance these strategies.

Case Management

Case management is defined as a clinical system with goals of achieving patient outcomes within effective and appropriate time frames and resources.

Case management focuses on accountability of an identified individual or group for coordinating a patient's care across the continuum (Center for Case Management 1992).

Case management is an excellent central theme or component of work redesign for several reasons. First, the system promotes a high level of multidisciplinary planning and practice on behalf of the patient. Also, case management models the integration of services in a patient-focused, cost-efficient manner. Case management is a very effective clinical system for controlling and potentially reducing length of stay and cost while maintaining or improving patient outcomes. This system enables staff to detect problems early and intervene to minimize or reverse them. It supports and facilitates continuous quality improvement activities at the bedside. Case management also involves clinicians in the financial aspects of care (Center for Case Management 1992).

Shared Governance

Shared governance is a philosophy that embraces collaborative decision making among professionals who are accountable for patient care (McDonagh 1990). Hospitals that have already implemented shared governance models will find that many of the attitudinal and behavioral changes necessary for work redesign have been made. In particular, unit-based shared governance supports both staff development and involvement and decision making at the point closest to service delivery. At Vanderbilt University Hospital, the pilot unit for restructuring found their unit board, a multidisciplinary group, to be critical for expedient problem identification and solution definition. This collegial model supports staff leadership in continuous quality improvement as well. The skills needed for effective shared governance are even more critical for a newly integrated patient care delivery model, which may include a multiplicity of disciplines.

Documentation by Exception

The use of a streamlined clinical documentation model supports the premise of eliminating redundancy or unnecessary steps. The implementation of a computerized charting-by-exception system was both time saving and satisfaction enhancing for the clinical staff at Vanderbilt. The system was supported by critical paths or protocols (a component of the Vanderbilt University Hospital collaborative care program) and a computerized daily flow sheet system. This system embraced the principles of charting by exception developed by Judy Murphy at Aurora Healthcare Systems, Milwaukee,

Wisconsin. This approach reduced nurse documentation time by approximately 40 percent and increased the available time for clinical practice.

Critical Path System

Critical paths are abbreviated versions of processes or activities that must occur in a timely fashion to achieve anticipated, outlined goals within an appropriate length of stay and resource utilization. Processes outlined in a critical path are multidisciplinary and used by all members of the health care team (Center for Case Management 1992). The use of critical paths document the anticipated care needs of aggregate groups of patients and allow interventions to be organized and sequenced. Patients and their families are better able to anticipate and participate in the plan of care.

At Vanderbilt University, these critical paths also proved to be invaluable as a teaching approach for cross-training. Since the critical paths are multidisciplinary, they mirrored the teamwork and collaboration that restructuring hoped to achieve. Variances from the anticipated course for individual patients are immediately identified and addressed. Aggregate variances identify opportunities to review, alter, and enhance internal systems to improve service delivery and patient outcomes (Center for Case Management 1992). At Vanderbilt University Hospital, the planned approach for collaboration care includes a computerized system of variance analysis that will allow review of variance data for patient and system indicators. This system will ultimately allow real-time review of length of stay and outcome variances and the reasons for those occurrences.

Supply Management Systems

A number of supply management systems exist for patient care areas. Often an area of concern following task review is the inordinate amount of time spent by clinical staff ordering, tracking, and obtaining patient supplies and equipment. Systems in place to expedite the availability of supplies and equipment will enhance efforts focused on time-saving steps for clinical and support staff. A number of hospitals have restructured patient units to allow decentralized supply and equipment storage, which has had a demonstrated decrease in work steps required to obtain these items.

Effective Communication Links

The presence of effective communication links throughout the hospital will facilitate not only communication but information access. As hospitals are restructured to be more patient focused and integrated, the necessity for quick information access will be paramount. These links will be supported by effective computer systems, beeper systems, and electronic mail systems.

Comprehensive Scheduling System

A patient-focused restructuring effort requires a new paradigm for patient scheduling. The redundancy of steps involved in typical patient scheduling holds much opportunity for streamlining. Hospitals with integrated systems for comprehensive scheduling will be able to support a user-friendly effort much better than organizations with freestanding manual systems or non-communicating computerized systems.

Determining the Right Approach for the Organization

Once the environmental assessment has been completed and a vision agreed upon as to the type of restructuring effort that will result in the desired outcomes required by the organization, the internal resources that may be available to direct and support the project should be identified. Although many organizations have internal talent that can be tapped for this project throughout all phases, the internal resources will vary in strength, creativity, vision, leadership, follow-through, and in sheer numbers of resources that can feasibly be dedicated to the effort. It is important to identify the internal resources in the organization early on and also to identify the needs the organization may have for outside assistance throughout the project. A trend in hospitals is to employ internal consultants to reduce the outside consulting services required for operational assessments, project development and implementation, and the development of management systems to support the institution. If the organization has internal resources of this type, they may or may not have experience in operational restructuring at the level required to lead the project, but they can certainly boost the internal leadership capabilities available. Both Vanderbilt University Hospital and Saint Joseph's Hospital of Atlanta used internal consultants during their restructuring planning and implementation. The placement of this position in the organization should sufficiently empower the role to accomplish the work involved in organizational change. Access to executive management is important for both strategies and informational purposes.

The approach to outside consultation will be influenced by several factors in addition to the internal resources available. The desired outcome, the speed with which results must be achieved, organizational culture, leadership style, and the approach the organization chooses to take in development of a model are all important considerations in selecting a consultant.

Many consultants have jumped on the bandwagon of work redesign, so it is important to assess the actual years of experience and successful outcomes that they have demonstrated. Professional references from clients can help in this determination. Work redesign consultants tend to emphasize one of three approaches: a management engineering approach, operational restructuring, or behavioral change. These can all be successful but need to be well suited to the individual organization.

The work redesign project team should reach consensus on the model design and the approach for implementation. This shared vision will serve as a guiding light throughout the challenging change process of redesigning work in the hospital.

References

Allawi, S., D. Bellaire, and L. David. 1991. "Are You Ready for Structural Change?" *Healthcare Forum Journal* 34 (July/August): 39–42.

Booz-Allen & Hamilton Healthcare Consultants Study. 1990. Vanderbilt Hospital, Nashville, TN.

Center for Applied Research. 1993. *Stakeholder Mapping*, distributing by American Executive Conference on Strategic Operational Restructuring: Patient-Focused Healthcare Delivery, The Healthcare Forum, Marina Del Rey, CA.

Center for Case Management. 1992. "Case Management and Managed Care: Clinical Systems for Cost/Quality Outcomes." South Natick, MA.

Farris, B. 1991. "Care 2001." *An Executive Conference on Strategic Operational Restructuring: Patient-Focused Healthcare Delivery*. Presentation at The Healthcare Forum, Marina Del Rey, CA, 13 March.

Lathrop, P. J. 1991. "The Patient-Focused Hospital." *Healthcare Forum Journal* 34 (4): 17–22.

McDonagh, K. J. (Ed.). 1990. *Nursing Shared Governance: Restructuring for the Future*. Atlanta, GA: K. J. McDonagh and Associates.

Orlikoff, J., and M. Totten. 1991. "New Approaches in Quality: CQI." *Trustee* (May): 14–15.

Senge, P. M. 1990. *The Fifth Discipline: The Art and Practice of the Learning Organization*. New York: Doubleday/Currency.

Tonges, M. C. 1991. "ProACT™: The Professional Advanced Care Team Model." *Patient Care Delivery Models*. Rockville, MD: Aspen Publishing.

Urmy, N. 1991. "Shaping the Future of Healthcare: The Vanderbilt Experience." Presentation at The Olympic Challenge: Creating Models of Excellence Through Organizational Redesign, Atlanta, GA, 1 November.

4

CASE MANAGEMENT: WORK REDESIGN WITH PATIENT OUTCOMES IN MIND

Kathleen A. Bower

Introduction

Organizations and departments are embarking on major restructuring and redesign efforts in response to drastic and rapid changes in the health care environment. For many, these efforts are critical to short- and long-term survival. Various approaches have been incorporated in restructuring programs. Case management is one such approach. It focuses on the coordination of patient care across a care continuum of time and settings with the goal of achieving desired clinical and financial outcomes. It is not a strategy that can be introduced in isolation; rather, it must be understood in the context of other organizational issues and changes. This chapter will describe the impetus for moving toward case management, outline central concepts and basic principles, describe case management and its design, and profile issues to anticipate in implementing case management.

Why Health Care Has Entered the Era
of Restructuring and Redesign

The era of redesign has been stimulated by multiple changes in the health care arena. Those changes include the nature and characteristics of patients, the environment in which hospitals and other facilities operate, and the evolving roles of various disciplines, including nursing.

Patient care is increasingly complex as issues of aging and chronic illness multiply. In addition, the social environment for many patients is desperately difficult and demanding because of the diminishing availability of support from family and friends and because of the changes in the economic environment. Patients are being discharged from acute care settings at earlier stages in their recovery, yet there are fewer informal resources available to them at home. Access to care has remained an issue for many, and payment for health care is a problem faced by millions.

Hospitals and other health care facilities awaken each day to new situations and pressures. They must anticipate and respond to constantly changing payer requirements. The payers themselves are changing as employers enter the arena in new and different ways. In some areas, employers are dealing directly with hospitals and other providers to negotiate care for their employees. "Packaged" payment modalities are creating new partnerships as payers (including employers) are designing programs that promote a single payment structure for inpatient and outpatient care as well as the physician component. This approach is likely to continue and to expand.

As the length of inpatient stay decreases, there has been a rapid shift in care settings from inpatient to outpatient. As a consequence, the inpatient portion of the trajectory assumes an ever smaller percentage of total care. The emerging dichotomy is that, as patients have an ever greater need for continuity and coordination in their care, the system is becoming increasingly fragmented.

Hospitals are creating new and different partnerships with physicians, who are responding to dramatic changes in their practice environment. Physicians are caring for an increasing proportion of patients within capitated payment plans and within aggressive cost-containment strategies, leading to an enhanced focus on financial aspects of care. Like other providers and institutions, physicians are being challenged to demonstrate quality and cost-effectiveness.

Within the health care community, nursing is responding to constant changes. Nursing has made stops at various points along the staffing availability continuum. In times of acute shortage, creative approaches to staffing have been developed, and some of those approaches, while addressing immediate problems, have contributed to care fragmentation. Changes in patient population have also affected practice by decreasing the amount of time available to interact with patients and by enhancing the fragmentation created by multiple settings for care. Simultaneously, these changes have created new opportunities for nurses to truly expand their roles in important directions such as case management.

These and other forces have created a mandate for care by design and not by chance. Most of the current care systems ensure at least minimal quality standards. However, as the focus on cost and length of stay continues, the time frame for care is greatly reduced. Clinicians and others no longer have the luxury of time; they must effectively manage patient care in addition to actually providing that care.

Key Principles

The patient must be the focal point of any redesign or restructuring efforts. The related goal becomes identifying and understanding the characteristics and needs of the patient populations served by the organization and restructuring the organization to meet those needs. Inherent in understanding the needs of the patient populations served is the notion of "continuum." Establishing a focus on continuum means understanding patients' needs in all settings in which they receive or need care, and understanding how all of the pieces fit together. Fragmentation of care negatively affects both quality and cost.

All of these priorities focus redesign efforts on quality issues that will also positively influence cost. These priorities ultimately reflect the core values, beliefs, and philosophy of the organization and also influence the management approach and principles within the organization. Although case management is an important emerging concept, implementation will be most successful if the central principles and assumptions are understood and addressed.

Within nursing, a core consideration is that the most important relationship is that between the staff nurse and the patient. It is at the staff nurse level that most interaction takes place with the patient, the patient's family and significant others, and other disciplines. A basic goal, then, is to ensure that this relationship is supported and is maximally effective. In this context an effective nurse–patient relationship means that patient care is coordinated to ensure smooth progression toward desired physiological, psychosocial, emotional, spiritual, and financial outcomes in a manner that is satisfying to patients and their families. Organizational redesign must incorporate means of supporting that staff nurse–patient relationship at the unit and institutional levels.

Case management takes place within the entire organizational environment. It does not cure all problems within the setting. In fact, it may highlight long-standing issues and problems. For example, case management is not a substitute for inadequate basic patient care. Quality begins at this point, and if good basic patient care is not provided, case management will not be a cure. Case management augments a strong clinical system and provides some support in weaker settings, but it is not a quick fix. It is also not a substitute for lack of accountability and responsibility systems. It is a management function to define expectations, monitor the extent to which they are met, and provide feedback and counseling when practice does not meet standards and expectations. Managers manage the system to enable staff to manage the patients.

Coordination as the Central Component of Case Management and Related Structures

Coordination is the primary goal and central function of case management. In this context, "coordination" means the smooth and effective progression toward desired clinical and financial outcomes through the timely and synchronized intervention of various disciplines and departments across time and across settings. When care is effectively coordinated, patients have a supportive, "seamless" experience, which they perceive to be managed along a well-defined plan.

There are three major elements of coordination: unit- or department-based care coordination, continuum-based care coordination, and tools and systems for care coordination.

Continuum-based care coordination is provided through case management. Within nursing, unit-based care coordination is a function of the nursing care delivery system. Emerging tools and systems for care coordination include critical paths and their second-generation counterparts, CareMaps™ and variance management. Each of the major elements of coordination is essential in the overall management of patient care. Experience demonstrates that when unit- or area-based care coordination is effective and when supportive tools and systems are in use, case management (or continuum-based care coordination) can be targeted first at high-cost and high-risk patients.

The Nursing Care Delivery System as the Methodology for Unit-Based Care Coordination

Nursing care delivery systems structure the organization of patient care within a geographic area. They define the span of time over which nursing staff are involved with patients, specify accountability and responsibility, and identify who will do which aspects of care. They answer the question, How will the work get done? Unit-based care coordination is an essential component of any redesign strategy.

Selection of a nursing care delivery system is a very important undertaking. Most nursing organizations have a written philosophy that outlines values and beliefs about patients and patient care. The nursing care delivery system operationalizes the philosophy of nursing; it is the way in which patients experience the philosophy. One of the first steps in redesign within a nursing organization is to examine whether there is congruence between the written philosophy and the nursing care delivery system. Another step is to list the desired characteristics of a nursing care delivery system from three viewpoints: the patient/family, the nurse, and the organization; again, the current care delivery system can be examined in light of those desired characteristics. Using this assessment data, it is then possible to determine the ideal nursing care delivery system, based on philosophy and desired characteristics.

There are basically four nursing care delivery systems: (1) functional, (2) team, (3) total patient care, and (4) primary nursing. Functional, team, and total patient care promote responsibility for tasks and shifts. Coordination within these three systems is at the shift level, and there is no formal structure for day-to-day coordination or coordination across time. Informal or ad hoc coordination may occur, but it is not a standard.

Primary nursing is a system for care delivery in which a nurse is identified to be accountable for the outcomes of the patient's nursing care while the patient is on the unit. Primary nursing is the only system that structures accountability, if accountability is understood to be for outcomes of care. If the goals of nursing care are continuity and accountability but primary nursing is not an acceptable care delivery system, another structure must be implemented to ensure that those goals are met. For example, a separate position of care coordinator can be created. A nurse in this role assumes accountability for coordinating and managing the care of a large group of patients (for example, half of the patient unit) throughout the unit-based length of stay.

In addition to clearly defining the unit-based system for care coordination, it is important to establish effective roles and systems for unit management. The role and effectiveness of the nurse manager are critical in supporting quality patient care and in creating the magnitude of change involved in moving toward case management. The manager is accountable for translating departmental and organizational values, beliefs, and priorities to the direct patient care interface. As noted earlier, managers manage the unit systems so that staff can manage the patients.

It is important to note that case management is not a nursing care delivery system. Rather, case management is a clinical system that spans care areas across the continuum of patient care and is multidisciplinary in nature. The case manager role can be fulfilled by disciplines other than nursing. Accountability in case management is for continuum-based clinical and financial outcomes.

Tools and Systems for Care Coordination

Tools and systems support care coordination at both the unit and continuum levels. Critical paths (and their second-generation counterparts, CareMaps) and variance management represent emerging tools and systems that provide such support.

Critical paths are case-type-specific grids that outline interventions on one axis (usually the vertical) and define a time line on the other axis. CareMaps, the second-generation critical path, incorporate the usual patient problems and desired intermediate goals and discharge outcomes. A sample CareMap is provided in the Appendix to this chapter. CareMaps demonstrate the relationship between quality (via the discharge clinical outcomes) and cost (via the interventions and time line). CareMaps represent patient care from the perspective of all the disciplines usually involved in the care of the identified case type; they must be developed by an interdisciplinary team. In developing CareMaps, the interdisciplinary team outlines the usual and desired care for the patient population. CareMaps can be developed for diagnoses (such as myocardial infarction or pneumonia), procedures (such as coronary artery bypass graft or percutaneous transluminal coronary angioplasty), and conditions (such as failure to wean from the ventilator and boarder babies). The CareMap provides a very visual picture of the usual patient care and assists in identifying overlaps, gaps, and inappropriate sequencing in care activities.

CareMaps can be developed for patient care in all settings. The major adjustment required as the settings change is in the time line. The time frame is defined by the needs of the area. For example, the time frame in the emergency department is best outlined in hours or less, while in the community or ambulatory setting, the time frame may be in months. In CareMaps developed for elective inpatient admissions, the first column should outline the prehospital components of care. This is one step toward viewing the case along the continuum. Additionally, post-acute-care requirements can be outlined on the CareMap.

Because they include patient problems and outcome statements, Care-Maps can serve as the foundation for the nursing care plan. To be most successful, CareMaps should be integrated into the documentation system and eliminate redundancy.

Clinicians use CareMaps as a template or blueprint for the plan of care as they provide care to patients. The CareMap is adjusted based on the information gathered during the initial assessment to meet the unique needs of individual patients. This individualization may involve deleting, modifying, or adding goals, outcomes, or interventions. As care is provided, the status of the patient is compared to that anticipated on the CareMap and variances are identified. Clinical staff record the variances observed, a hypothesis about the cause(s), and what was done about the variance.

Variance identification and management are an important component of using CareMaps. Concurrent variance identification facilitates initiating interventions to mediate or prevent variance. When an individual patient is discharged, the variance data are pooled with those collected regarding other patients within the case type. Periodically, these pooled data are aggregated to determine the number of variances and their associated causes within the case type. The aggregate variances for each case type are then analyzed for patterns and trends by the clinical staff that developed the CareMap, by the department managers, and by an institutionwide group. The department managers and the institutionwide group are also looking for trends and patterns between case types. The issues are prioritized and action plans are developed for high-priority issues. In some instances, the analysis will suggest that the CareMap needs to be revised. The analysis process may also suggest that systems within the organization need to be changed, that additional information is needed, that staff need to be educated, or that new policies and procedures need to be developed. Trends in variances related to patients (such as variances caused by age or living situation) can be used to create a profile for high-risk screening of patients on admission to the system. The process of using CareMaps and managing identified variance is a clinical application of the continuous quality improvement process.

CareMaps function best when communication systems are revised to incorporate them. These communication systems include intershift nursing reports, physician rounds, and interdisciplinary patient-focused meetings. In each of these situations, the CareMap should provide the framework for presenting patients and their current status.

CareMaps and variance management support coordination at both the unit and continuum level. At the unit level, CareMaps provide a framework for continuity of plan, supporting shift-to-shift communication as well as the communication about patients (and their plans of care) on transfer from one unit or setting to another. Likewise, there is continuum-based continuity of plan when CareMaps include care from each setting. CareMaps cannot function in isolation; they must be used within the context of systems for unit-based and continuum-based care coordination and within systems that manage accountability.

When patient populations in particular need of care coordination are identified, three strategies are available. Patient populations can be managed (1) along a CareMap, (2) through the use of a case manager, or (3) with both a CareMap and a case manager.

Case Management as a Methodology for
Continuum-Based Care Coordination

Case management is an approach to coordinating patient care across the continuum or trajectory of care needs, usually crossing multiple settings. In case management, an individual or team has accountability for coordinating the care of identified patient populations. Case managers work with other care providers to ensure the achievement of satisfactory clinical and financial outcomes with patients and their families. The Center for Case Management (1992) defines "case management" as

> a clinical system that focuses on the accountability of an identified individual or group for coordinating a patient's care (or group of patients) across a continuum of care; insuring and facilitating the achievement of quality, clinical, and cost outcomes; negotiating, procuring and coordinating services and resources needed by the patient/family; intervening at key points (and/or at significant variances) for individual patients; addressing and resolving patterns in aggregate variances that have a negative quality-cost impact; and creating opportunities and systems to enhance outcomes. (p. 1)

Case management creates a system continuity of provider, ideally across many or all settings in which patients receive care.

Who Should Be Case Managed?

In the presence of strong unit- or area-based care coordination and effective tools for care coordination, patients selected for admission into a case management program generally represent 20 percent or less of the total patient population. Employing Pareto's Law or the 20/80 Rule, the 20 percent of the patients selected for case management generally fall within high-cost and high-risk categories. In addition to the high-cost/high-risk categories, organizations may choose to case manage other patient populations, such as patients in high-profile product lines or centers of excellence established by the facility.

The high-cost and high-risk categories often represent patients who

1. are chronically ill and experience frequent readmissions, such as those with emphysema or congestive heart failure;
2. fit high-risk socioeconomic profiles, such as the frail elderly, the homeless, or those with inadequate social support;
3. experience significant complications or variances;
4. have multiple conditions or problems requiring treatment; and
5. represent other high-cost treatment modalities, such as transplantation.

Case-managed patients can be within several categories. Case management programs can be organized by the following:

- Diagnosis, procedure, or condition
- Major systems issues or major diagnostic categories
- Age
- Product line
- Program or division
- Physician
- Payer
- Geographic area

These categories are not mutually exclusive, and several will probably be used simultaneously when designing a case management program. Patient volume and institution size will also influence design. For example, in a very small rural hospital, one case manager will suffice for the entire institution and will case manage a wide variety of conditions.

When feasible, program design should facilitate case managers' expertise within a manageable clinical area and should maximize consistent contact and collaboration with other care providers. For example, if a caseload is defined by diagnoses and/or physician, the case manager becomes very knowledgeable and skilled about that patient population. This enhances case managers' effectiveness because they are more skilled at anticipating specific needs and issues for the patients and have the opportunity to develop an effective relationship with the physicians and other team members involved in the cases. Following this strategy, an institution could appoint a case manager for orthopedic or cardiology patients, for example.

The Case Management Process

Case managers function along two primary tracts: (1) using the clinical reasoning (or nursing) process and (2) establishing a network of services for patients. The first step in the process is to identify what patients will be included in the caseload, specify the characteristics for admission, and determine at what point in the trajectory the case manager should become involved. With the first step completed, case managers can then turn to establishing a system that reliably admits patients into the case management system at the appropriate time. This step is influenced by the nature of the patient population, especially the manner in which they enter the health care system. Specifically, case managers can be much more anticipatory when patients are electively admitted. For example, case managers can arrange with the operating room booking staff or admitting office staff to be notified when patients within the identified categories are scheduled for admission. When patients enter the system emergently, other strategies must be developed.

As patients are admitted into the case manager's practice, the clinical reasoning process is initiated, beginning with an initial assessment and collection of baseline data. The data collected usually supplement the data provided by other clinicians, such as physicians, nurses, and social workers—especially when case managers enter a case at a midpoint along the trajectory. Case managers identify specific information essential to the effective management of their patients and incorporate it into their assessment questions.

After the initial data are collected, case managers negotiate desired outcomes with patients, their families, and other clinicians. In addition, they may negotiate anticipated outcomes with the patient's payer. These outcomes must be realistic, measurable, and patient focused. Based on the desired outcomes and assessment of the patient's status, intermediate goals and a plan are outlined. Again, the case manager interacts, negotiates, and communicates with the patients, their families, other clinicians, payers, and other departments within the health care setting or system. The plan explicates responsibility for each activity.

Effective case managers and case management programs establish a network of services that are usually required by patients and their families. This network may include such services as home care, hospice, equipment supply companies, social agencies, and specialists. The network may be within or external to the physical environment in which case managers function. Case managers negotiate or broker services within this network, adding to it as the need arises.

The most significant steps of the case management process are monitoring, evaluating, and revising the plan and desired outcomes based on changing patient status. Case managers are often involved across the various settings in which the patients receive care. The resulting continuity greatly facilitates evaluating for and identifying subtle changes in patient or family status that require modification of the plan.

As the case reaches the desired outcomes or completes the defined case-managed part of the trajectory, the case manager either discharges the patient from the caseload or maintains the patient in an inactive status. A discharge or transfer note summarizes the case. The case manager includes a copy of the note in the patient's record and retains a second copy for future reference.

Periodically, case managers do a retrospective review of their patients to identify consistent impediments in the smooth coordination of patient care. As patterns or trends emerge, case managers substantiate them with data and develop an action plan. The action plan involves members of other departments and may require administrative involvement. The aggregate review of cases reflects a quality improvement component of the case management process.

Case Management Design Factors and Options

Case management design is a reflection of three major factors:

1. The needs and characteristics of the patient populations to be case managed
2. The actual and potential resources within the organization
3. The goals of the organization's case management program

Based on the information outlined within these factors, a case management program can be flexibly designed to meet patient and institutional needs. These factors include whom to case manage and for how long, where case management activities should primarily be located, and who should be case manager.

Target populations for case management were discussed earlier. Patient selection is a critical step because the needs and characteristics of the population will greatly influence case management program design. That influence is felt in all aspects, especially in deciding where case management activities should be focused and for how long, and who should be case manager.

Length and location of case management services

To identify where case management services should be based and for how long they should continue, it is useful to flowchart the trajectory that the case-managed patient populations follow throughout the continuum. The trajectory needs to include the entire care experience, including initial entry into the health care system through termination of services for the identified problem. Each area in which care is received must be included on the flowchart. The trajectory will vary according to the nature and characteristics of the patient population. For example, the trajectory for orthopedic patients begins with identification of the need for a total joint replacement in a physician's office and will be completed 6–12 months later. The trajectory for patients with chronic pulmonary disease will be very different, especially in length.

Case management activities can be provided within the organization (for example, acute care or rehabilitation), within an ambulatory setting, within the community, or in combination. For example, many of the chronically ill included in case management programs, such as chronic pulmonary patients, need care coordination concentrated primarily in the community setting. In this situation, case managers focus on supporting patients in the community to minimize the necessity for readmissions. The nurse case management program at Carondelet St. Mary's in Tucson, Arizona, is an example of this type of process (Ethridge 1991; Ethridge and Lamb 1989). An important design consideration is to place case managers in the settings where they can most effectively meet the needs of their patient populations. Although a case manager may be based in one setting (the acute care setting, for example), it is important that the case management process cross settings to ensure coordination of care. For example, orthopedic case managers may be based primarily in the acute setting but ideally visit elective patients in their homes before admission and extend services into the community after discharge.

The nature of the patient population also influences how long case management services are provided. In the examples discussed above, the chronic pulmonary patients may be case managed for years, while the orthopedic patient may be case managed for weeks or months. The decision regarding length of case management services is influenced by the organization's goals for the program. Initially, the organization may decide to case manage identified patients only when they are actively receiving care within the hospital. As experience is gained with the case management program and as data provide additional support, this decision may be modified to include a prehospital and a posthospital telephone call to the patients. At yet another point, the case management services may be extended into the community.

Caseload size is a matrix function of acuity or complexity of the patients, volume within the identified patient population, and identified scope and nature of the case manager's role. Caseload size will be restricted when the scope of a case manager's practice includes providing direct patient care. It will also be delineated by the number of locations in which the case managers provide services. For example, when home visits are included in the case manager's role, caseloads will, of necessity, be smaller than in those situations where the case managers function within one defined setting. In addition, in case management design, complexity may have less to do with physical acuity and more to do with complex social situations.

Who should be case manager?

Decisions regarding identifying staff to be case manager are included in the overall design of the case management program. One of the first questions that arises is, Which discipline should be case manager? The primary disciplines that are providing case management services are nurses and social service. Returning to one of the fundamental issues—what are the needs and characteristics of the patient population to be case managed—an effective case management program will incorporate both of these disciplines. A case manager who best meets the needs of the patient population can then be identified. Another option is to partner a social worker and a nurse in a case management practice.

Qualifications of the individuals selected to practice as case managers should again reflect the needs and characteristics of the patient population to be case managed but also include some generic criteria. Qualifications related to the patient population include knowledge of the clinical aspects of the patients within all settings in which they will receive care. More generic criteria include good clinical reasoning, problem solving, effective communication (verbal and written), negotiation skills, conflict management, project management, priority setting, knowledge of the principle payers, and collaboration. To be effective in negotiating system and clinician changes, case managers also need to collect, analyze, and discuss data effectively.

In some settings, educational preparation of the case manager candidates will be very important. Some organizations may decide to select only master's-prepared clinical specialists for case management positions. This is where the issue of actual and potential resources within the organization comes into play. Not all settings have access to master's level clinicians and must, alternatively, elect to hire from within alternative educational backgrounds. Within nursing, it is recommended that those selected for case management positions be registered nurses because of the elements of assessment and evaluation and because of the broader education received in programs leading to licensure as an RN.

Identifying to whom case managers report is often a controversial decision within an organization. If there is agreement with the concept that case management is a quality-focused clinical program with financial implications, the decision generally moves toward positioning the program within a clinical department. The nursing department is the most common location for program management. Other models involve program management by utilization management, quality management, product line managers, and finance departments. Ideally, the administration of the program is built and evaluated on a matrix of needs, including negotiated quality and financial outcomes.

The interdisciplinary nature of case management as an essential design consideration

To be effective, case management programs must seek to actively represent all those disciplines and departments that either provide care and services to the patients being case managed or who have a vested interest in the success of the program. There are a variety of strategies to ensure inclusion. One strategy is to include a multidisciplinary steering committee as part of program management and to schedule regular meetings where all parties can discuss program evolution. Another strategy is to elicit needs and goals for the case management program from all departments and disciplines and to regularly evaluate the program vis-a-vis those multi-interest goals. Maintaining clear and open communication regarding the case management program within the organization is an additional approach. The philosophy that emerges in successful programs focuses on case management practice rather than case managers per se.

In case-type-focused case management programs, one formal approach to creating an interdisciplinary case management practice is to develop case management group practices. Membership in a case management group practice is composed of all disciplines and settings within the patients' trajectory. For example, core members in a cardiac group practice would include nurses, physicians, social service, nutrition services, discharge planning, cardiac rehabilitation, and cardiac catheterization. The nurses represent all settings in which cardiac patients are seen: emergency department, intensive care, operating room and post-anesthesia care unit, telemetry, general unit, and home health. Staff from physician offices can be included in this group as well. Consultants and liaisons to the group practice include respiratory therapy, laboratories, radiology, finance, contracting departments, and administration.

A group practice functions by outlining the desired plan of care for each of the diagnoses included in the caseload. This desired plan may be outlined on a critical path or CareMap. In addition, the group establishes communication and other systems for managing the patients across the various settings and departments, often including an initial review and clarification of each member's role in the care of the patient population. Core members of the group meet on a regular basis (often weekly) to review current cases and to resolve immediate system issues. The group collects data regarding the flow of patients through the practice and periodically meets with consulting members of the group to negotiate system changes that will enhance patient care outcomes. When possible, the nurse members of the group practice provide direct care while group practice patients are in their geographic areas.

Although a specifically identified case manager is not always included in a group practice, case managers and group practices can have a potentiating effect on one another. Within this concept, a case manager can function as staff to the group. Likewise, the group practice creates an automatic network of services, clinicians, and colleagues for the case manager.

Whether or not a group practice format is included in the program, case management must be designed within a multidisciplinary framework.

The program will meet with limited success if it is designed or viewed as a "nursing" program, or a "finance" program, or a "utilization management" program. The focus of a case management program must consistently be on the needs and characteristics of the patient population, incorporating the work of all related departments and disciplines. Case management and case manager success are directly related to effective negotiation with all disciplines and departments.

Anticipating Issues and Needs in Implementing a Case Management Program

The transition to a case management program is exciting but must be carefully managed. Part of the effective management of the implementation and ongoing development of a case management program involves anticipating issues and needs. Seven issues or needs will be discussed briefly in relation to effective case management programs:

1. Turf issues and the need for role clarification and integration
2. Educational needs associated with case management
3. Response of the organization to problems identified by the case management program
4. Refocusing the organization toward patient needs
5. Monitoring and evaluating the system
6. Data needs
7. Ongoing development of the case management system

Turf Issues and the Need for Role Clarification and Integration

Turf issues arise simultaneously with the initial discussions about case management. It seems that the development of a case management program can be universally threatening. Competition for "ownership" of case management is sometimes fierce. Anticipate turf issues between case managers and staff nurses, nurse managers, social service, discharge planning, utilization management, and quality management, to name a few. This issue requires clear administrative direction and support to focus the program on patient needs and to match the organization's response to those needs. This is accomplished through negotiating clear goals for the case management program and by formally planning for inclusion rather than exclusion. As noted earlier, this may involve creating a multidisciplinary steering committee.

As the program evolves, clarification of roles becomes essential, especially among those roles that directly interface with the case management program. One useful approach is to facilitate the completion of a role clarification grid. A role clarification grid outlines roles along the horizontal axis and functions or activities along the vertical axis. Roles that should be included in the grid include staff nurse, case manager, nurse manager, social worker, discharge planner, quality management, utilization management, and clinical specialist. It is easier to initially identify current role functions and then use the information to determine what changes are generated by case management and what overlaps and gaps need to be addressed. The discussion process is often vitally useful in establishing collaborative relationships among the various players in a case management program. The grid is a foundation for writing role descriptions.

Along with discussing role clarification and completing a grid, ongoing formal discussions are needed to reflect changes as the program evolves. These discussions can be held by the steering committee but must also be available to the staff directly involved in case management. It is a program administration function to create regular forums in which interested parties can meet to discuss issues and to clarify and reclarify roles.

Educational Needs Associated with Case Management

Meeting educational needs is an ongoing component of program management. Initially, staff need to be introduced to the concept of case management, to gain an understanding of why the program is being implemented within the organization, and to understand the plan for implementation. Case managers need to be educated about role and process as they move into the role. A formally designed orientation program can be established for the transition group as well as case managers appointed after the program is under way. They need education in

- the health care environment, including finance issues, competition, and regulations;
- the requirements of third party payers usually involved in the case-managed patients;
- accessing and analyzing demographic, financial, quality, and other data;
- enhancing clinical skills, especially in settings in which the new case manager has minimal experience;
- management skills, including communication, negotiation, problem solving, program evaluation, the consultation process, and project management; and

• the case management process and system, both generically and as designed for the organization.

In addition to the initial educational needs, attention is needed toward ongoing development of case managers. Again, ongoing development is best accomplished in a formal program that regularly (for example, every six months) assesses the learning needs of the case managers, both individually and as a group, and designs a curriculum to meet those needs.

One effective approach to the ongoing development of case managers is the process of case consultation. *Case consultation* is a process by which case managers present cases to their peers and manager for review and consultation. The cases are discussed, problems clarified, and approaches suggested. There are multiple benefits to this approach:

1. The group setting enhances each case manager's learning.
2. The manager gains insight into the skills and developmental needs of the case managers as individuals and as a group.
3. Patterns of systems issues are identified and can be approached by the group.
4. The sense of isolation that many case managers encounter is reduced through interaction with other case managers and identification of common problems and issues.

Response of the Organization to Problems Identified by the Case Management Program

Implicit in the implementation of a case management program is a commitment to resolving identified issues. In many situations, case management programs highlight unresolved institutional problems. For example, one long-standing issue may be inappropriate timing or content of discharge teaching by staff nurses. A case management program will rapidly reveal this issue and will necessitate that the problem be resolved. Again, a resolution of the problem requires maintaining a patient-centered focus and a problem-solving approach. However, case management is a clinical application of continuous quality improvement processes and, as in any continuous quality improvement environment, administrative commitment to problem solving is critical.

Refocusing the Organization toward Patient Needs

Many of the approaches to the issues discussed previously have been associated with refocusing the organization toward patient needs—an administrative commitment that must be formally stated and structured. Focusing on patients is a wide-reaching process and involves all facets of the organization. This approach may require that each process and role be reexamined in light of the new understanding of patient characteristics and needs as well as the changing health care environment. Basic issues such as staffing patterns and schedules may need to be redesigned for continuity and coordination rather than for staff convenience.

Monitoring and Evaluating the System

Identifying methods for monitoring and evaluating the case management system is an essential issue in program design. The monitors need to be both process and outcome oriented. Evaluation strategies, with data needs identified, must be included in the initial planning phase with baseline data collected where available. The outcome evaluation includes areas such as changes in length of stay, cost per case, readmission rates, patient satisfaction, and clinical outcome attainment. Process monitoring along the established case management standards are also incorporated into program management. Process monitoring includes, for example, verifying that all patients eligible for inclusion in the case management program were actually admitted into it.

Data Needs

Data needs emerge initially and throughout the span of the program. The philosophy and approach to sharing data are vital to the functioning of the case management program and its evaluation. The most effective approach incorporates openness with data and a willingness to share the data with the clinicians involved in the case types. For some institutions where data are guarded and withheld, this will be a radical change in data management strategies. In addition to providing data, it must be formatted to be useful. In other words, data must be converted into information.

Ongoing Development of the Case Management System

Ongoing development of the case management system is an essential component of program management. In a very real sense, program design and development is never complete; it is constantly evolving. Approached in this way, participants in the program have much more freedom to experiment, to create, to explore, and to fail. Care coordination should be included in annual institutional and departmental goals. Case management program managers should be directed to develop specific goals on an annual basis with all the program participants and to report progress formally and informally on a regular basis. In this way, program success can be celebrated and advertised, and development can be maintained.

Summary

Care coordination through case management, nursing care delivery systems, CareMaps, and variance management are important approaches in organizational restructuring. They strengthen the quality-cost link by focusing on the patient and by including direct care providers in all aspects of patient care management. These systems, roles, and tools are consistently demonstrating their effectiveness in managing costs and length of stay (Bower 1992; Koska 1991; McKenzie, Torkelson, and Holt 1989; Cohen 1991). The transition to case management is a major organizational change, incorporating the need to fundamentally modify the mindsets of clinical and administrative staff. It requires vision to properly place case management and the related changes within the context of the organization's environment. It requires commitment at all levels, but especially top administration, to initiate the process and to maintain momentum through difficult times. It means transforming the organization to focus maximum effort on meeting patient needs, but the results positively effect patients, staff, the organization, and the community at large.

References

Bower, K. 1992. *Case Management by Nurses*. Washington, DC: The American Nurses' Association.

Center for Case Management. 1992. "Case Management and Managed Care: Clinical Systems for Cost/Quality Outcomes." South Natick, MA: Center for Case Management.

Cohen, E. 1991. "Nursing Case Management: Does It Pay?" *Journal of Nursing Administration* 21: 20–25.

Ethridge, P. 1991. "A Nursing HMO: Carondelet St. Mary's Experience." *Nursing Management* 22 (7): 22–27.

Ethridge, P., and G. Lamb. 1989. "Professional Nursing Case Management Improves Quality, Access, and Cost." *Nursing Management* 20: 30–35.

Koska, M. 1991. "Clinical Guidelines." *Hospitals* 65: 38–41.

McKenzie, C., N. Torkelson, and M. Holt. 1989. "Care and Cost: Nursing Case Management Improves Both." *Nursing Management* 20: 30–34.

Appendix 4.1 Congestive Heart Failure (CHF) CareMap®

Problem	1 Feb ER 1–6 Hours	1 Feb Floor Telemetry or CCU: Day 1	2 Feb Floor Day 2	3 Feb Floor Day 3	4 Feb Floor Day 4	5 Feb Floor Day 5	6 Feb Floor Day 6
Alteration in gas exchange/perfusion and fluid balance due to decreased cardiac output. Exceed fluid volume.	Reduced pain from admission or pain free. Uses pain scale O² sat. improved over admission baseline on O² therapy.	Respirations equal to or less than on admission.	O² sat = 80. Resp. 20–22. Vital signs stable. Crackles at lung bases. Mild shortness of breath with activity.	Does not require O². Vital signs stable. Crackles at base. Respirations 20–22. Mild shortness of breath with activity.	Does not require O² (O² sat. on room air 90%). Vital signs stable. Crackles at base. Respirations 20–22. Complete activities with no increase respirations. No edema.	Can lie in bed at baseline position. Chest x-ray clear or at baseline.	No dyspnea.
Potential for shock.	No signs/symptoms of shock.	No signs/symptoms of shock. No signs/symptoms of MI.	No signs/symptoms of shock.	No signs/symptoms of shock. Normal lab values.	No signs/symptoms of shock.	No signs/symptoms of shock.	No signs/symptoms of shock.
Potential for consequences of immobility & decreased activity. Skin breakdown. DVT.	No redness at pressure points. No falls.	No redness at pressure points. No falls.	Tolerates chair. Washing, eating and toileting.	Has bowel movement. Up in room & bathroom with assist.	Up ad lib for short periods.	Activity increased to level used at home without shortness of breath.	Activity increased to level used at home without shortness of breath.
Alteration in nutritional intake due to nausea & vomiting. Labored.		No c/o nausea. No vomiting. Taking liquids as offered.	Eating solids. Takes 50% each meal.	Takes 50% each meal.	Taking 50% each meal. Weight 2 lbs. from patient's normal baseline.	Taking 75% each meal.	Taking 75% each meal.

	ER	6–24 Hours	Day 2	Day 3	Day 4	Day 5	Day 6
Potential for arrhythmias due to decreased cardiac output; decreased irritable foci. Valve problems decreased; gas exchanged.	No evidence of life-threatening dysrhythmias.	Normal sinus rhythm with benign ecotopy.	K(WNL). Benign or no arrhythmias.	Digoxin level WNL. Benign or no arrhythmias.	Digoxin level WNL. Benign or no arrhythmias.	Digoxin level WNL. Benign or no arrhythmias.	Digoxin level WNL. Benign or no arrhythmias.
Patient/family response to future treatment & hospitalization.	Patient/family expressing concerns. Following directions of staff.	Patient/family expressing concerns. Following directions of staff.	Patient/family discuss degree of CHF and its causes.	States reasons for and cooperates with rest periods. Patient begins to assess own knowledge & ability to care for CHF at home.	Patient decides whether he/she wants discussion with physician about advance directives.	States plans for 1–2 days post discharge as to meds, diet, activity, follow-up appts. Expresses reaction to having CHF.	Repeats plans. States signs and symptoms to notify physician/ER. Signs discharge consent.
Staff Tasks	*ER*	*6–24 Hours*	*Day 2*	*Day 3*	*Day 4*	*Day 5*	*Day 6*
Assessments/ consults	Vital signs q15min. Nursing assessments focus: lung sounds, edema, color, skin integrity, jugular vein distention. Cardiac monitor. Arterial line if needed. Swan Ganz. Intake & Output.	Vital signs q15min–1hr. Repeat nursing assessments. Cardiac monitor. Arterial line. Swan Ganz. Daily weight. Intake & Output.	Vital signs q4hr. Repeat nursing assessments. Input & Output. Daily weight.	Vital signs q8hr. Repeat nursing assessments. Intake & Output. Daily weight.	Vital signs q8hr. Repeat nursing assessments. Intake & Output. Daily weight. Nutrition consult.	Vital signs q8hr. Repeat nursing assessments. Intake & Output. Daily weight.	Vital signs q8hr. Repeat nursing assessments. Intake & Output. Daily weight.

Continued

Appendix 4.1   Continued

Staff Tasks	1 Feb / ER	1 Feb / 6–24 Hours	2 Feb / Day 2	3 Feb / Day 3	4 Feb / Day 4	5 Feb / Day 5	6 Feb / Day 6
Specimens/tests	Consider TSH studies. Chest x-ray. EKG. CPK q8hr×3. ABG if pulse ox: (range) Lytes, Na, K, Cl, CO₂, Glucose, BUN, Creatinine, Digoxin: (range)	BKG	Evaluate for ECHO. Lytes, BUN, Creatinine			Chest x-ray. Lytes, BUN, Creatinine	
Treatments	O² or intubate IV or Heparin Lock	O². IV or Heparin Lock	IV or Heparin lock.	DC pulse Ox if stable. D/C IV or Heparin Lock			
Medications	Evaluate for Digoxin. Nitrodrip or paste. Diuretics IV. Evaluate for antiemetic and arrhythmias.	Evaluate for Digoxin, Nitrodrip or paste. Diuretics IV. Evaluate for preload/afterload reducers. K supplements. Stool softeners.	D/C Nitrodrip or paste. Diuretics IV or PO. K supplements. Stool softeners. Evaluate for nicotine patch.	Change to PO Digoxin. PO diuretics. K supplements. Stool softeners. Nicotine patch if consent.	PO diuretics. K supplement. Stool softeners. Nicotine patch if consent.	PO diuretics. K supplement. Stool softeners. Nicotine patch if consent.	PO diuretics. K supplement. Stool softeners. Nicotine patch if consent.
Nutrition	None	Clear liquids	Cardiac, low salt diet	Cardiac, low salt diet	Cardiac, low salt diet	Cardiac, low salt diet	Cardiac, low salt diet
Safety/activity	Commode, bedrest with head elevated. Reposition patient q2hr. Bedrails up. Call light available.	Commode, bedrest with head elevated. Dangle. Reposition q2hr. Enforce rest periods. Bedrails up. Call light available.	Commode, enforce rest periods. Chair with assist 1/2 hr. with feet elevated. Bedrails up. Call light available.	Bathroom privileges. Chair ×3, bedrails up, call light available.	Ambulate in hall ×2, up ad lib between rest periods, bedrails up, call light available.	Encourage ADLS which approximate activities at home, bedrails up, call light available.	Encourage ADLS which approximate activities at home, bedrails up with call light available.

Teaching	Explain procedure, teach chest pain scale & importance of reporting.	Explain costs, need for energy conservation. Orient to unit & routine.	Clarity CHF, Dx and future teaching needs. Orient to unit & routine. Schedule rest periods. Begin medication teaching.	Importance of weighing self every day. Provide smoking cessation information. Review energy conservation schedule.	Cardiac rehab level as indicated by consult. Provide smoking cessation support. Dietary teaching.	Review CHF education material with patient.	Reinforce CHF teaching.
Transfer/ discharge coordination	Assess home situation; notify significant other if no arrhythmias or chest pain. Transfer to floor, otherwise transfer to ICU.	Screen for discharge needs. Transfer to floor.	Consider home health care referral.		Evaluate needs for diet and anti-smoking classes. Physician offers discussion opportunities for advance directives.	Appointment and arrangement for follow-up care with home health care nurse. Contact VNA.	Reinforce follow-up appointments.

Copyright 1992, The Center for Case Management, Inc. Reprinted with permission. CareMap® is a registered trademark of the Center for Case Management, South Natick, MA 01760.

5

A MODEL FOR MEASURING OUTCOMES OF WORK REDESIGN

Richard J. Stephen and M. Gibby Kinsey

Although work redesign has become one of the most significant trends of the 1990s, the concept remains in the infancy stage in terms of analyzing the impact of such an effort. Because operational restructuring represents dramatic changes in the way hospitals provide services to patients, hospitals must develop and implement a framework for comprehensively evaluating the outcomes. This chapter provides a detailed review of the process by which this challenge can be met and presents components of the model developed and implemented at Saint Joseph's Hospital of Atlanta (SJHA).

Requirements for Successful Model Development

The process for developing a model to measure and evaluate the outcomes of work redesign is based upon data collection and analysis. As our health care delivery system grows larger and more complex, managers turn more and more frequently to the collection and interpretation of statistical data for help in decision making (Cortis 1972, 5). In work redesign, careful collection and analysis of statistical data will enable health care managers to assess their success in meeting hospital objectives and to make decisions regarding future refinements, enhancements and applications. The development of appropriate statistics requires data collection, analysis, and interpretation of both quantitative and qualitative information sources. The success of these efforts depends on three major requirements: (1) availability, reliability, and validity of data; (2) development of a framework for data collection and analysis; and (3) commitment of resources.

Availability, Reliability, and Validity of Data

Data availability

Data availability involves the recognition of multiple data sources from historical information, existing hospital reports, outside sources, expert opinion, and observations of current operations. Successful data collection begins with an understanding and assessment of various data sources. This requires an understanding of departmental and hospitalwide reporting systems, a review of current literature, discussions with hospital managers regarding their familiarity with information (such as cost, service, quality, satisfaction).

Data reliability

Whenever data are obtained through a sample, such as a sample of time periods, a sample of people interviewed, or a sample of measurements, there is always a chance for error. For example, there is always a chance that different results may be obtained from a sample of different time periods, a sample of different people, or a sample of different measurements. Successful data collection incorporates methods for specifying, selecting, and measuring samples that will ensure reliable data.

Data validity

Data errors can also result from bias or misunderstanding on either the part of the data collector, the data provider, or the data interpreter. Successful data collection and analysis incorporates approaches that will help to ensure the validity of data, such as using a combination of several data collection methods or incorporating a combination of multiple resources (such as internal staff, committees, external consultants) (Costis 1972).

Development of a Framework for Data Collection and Analysis

Operational objectives

A framework for data collection and analysis cannot be developed until objectives for restructuring are formulated. At Saint Joseph's Hospital of Atlanta, our goal has been to develop a health care delivery model in which the patient serves as the catalyst for decision making. The objectives are (1) greater operational efficiency with a focus on controlling costs; (2) increased continuity of care resulting in greater patient satisfaction; (3) greater

Exhibit 5.1 Examples of SJHA Clinical Imperatives

- **Quality of Care**
  1. We will preserve and maintain excellence in patient care.
  2. Every patient will have a primary nurse.
  3. Each team member will be considered unique and of vital importance to the team, and every effort will be made to convey this message to each member of the team.

- **Service**
  1. Every effort will be made to achieve maximum efficiency.
  2. The focus for the service provided to patients and physicians will be to continually improve the process by which the service is provided.

- **Satisfaction**
  Saint Joseph's Hospital of Atlanta will continue to measure, to the greatest extent possible, satisfaction of staff, physicians and patients, and will respond appropriately to findings.

- **Cost**
  The goal will be to control costs.

autonomy and increased empowerment for health care professionals and other employees; and (4) increased physician satisfaction.

Operational imperatives

After objectives for restructuring are clearly articulated, clinical or operational imperatives—the guiding principles or "rules" upon which the model must be developed and implemented—should be formulated and placed in writing. The imperatives must incorporate the values of the organization; they must correspond with the overall objectives for the development and implementation of such a model; and they should address issues related to at least four key areas: (1) quality; (2) service; (3) patient, staff, and physician satisfaction; and (4) cost. Examples of the clinical imperatives established at Saint Joseph's Hospital of Atlanta are shown in Exhibit 5.1.

Components of the model

Using the objectives and the operational imperatives as the foundation, the framework for data collection and analysis can be developed and should include the following components:

Table 5.1   SJHA Performance and Evaluation Measures for Work
Redesign

Measures of Success	*Dimension*	*Component*	*Quantitative Measures*	*Qualitative Measures*
Ecomonic measures	Value-added composition	Process purity and complexity	Number of steps and time associated with the performance of specific activities	
Service measures	Patient convenience	Patient transfers	Number of patient transfers out of the unit	
Quality measures	Continuity of care	Dedicated staff	Number of different staff members in contact with patients	Feeling of patient and physician that they know who to look to for information and assistance
Satisfaction measures	Job enrichment	Overall employee satisfaction	Turnover of staff in all affected departments	Employee's perception of quality of care delivered, desirability of work environment and desirability of "content" of job

Definition of variables. Both quantitative variables (such as number of steps,
percentage of time spent, average procedure time) and qualitative variables
(such as level of satisfaction, description of services, perception of quality)

Methodology	Responsible Department	Timing/Frequency	Expected Outcome
Work flow diagrams of sample ancillary and support services.	Management Services	Pre: Current process. Post: Following integration of new roles.	Reduction in the number of steps and time
Measure number based upon chart review samples of patients during their first 72 hours of stay.	Quality Management and Nursing	Pre: 30 current charts each from CCU and 7 West. Post: Following integration of new roles.	Fewer patient transfers
Prepare description based upon chart review samples during their first 72 hours of stay. For qualitative measures, use patient satisfaction and physician satisfaction surveys for 1. pre & post results, 2. redesign vs non-redesign units, 3. comparison to other hospitals.	Quality Management and Nursing	Pre: 30 current charts each from CCU and 7 West & Survey (FY 90). Post: Following integration of new roles.	Fewer staff members in contact with patients; improved patient satisfaction; improved physician satisfaction
Measure staff turnover in all affected departments. For qualitative measures, use staff satisfaction survey and focus groups and individual interviews, if deemed appropriate, for 1. pre & post results, 2. redesign vs. non-redesign units, 3. comparison to other hospitals.	Management Services, Human Resources & Marketing	Pre: FY 1990 & Survey (FY 90). Post: Monthly turnover; survey following integration of new roles.	Maintain turnover rates; improved staff satisfaction

must be defined. Each of these variables must be clearly understood and measurable in terms of quantifiable statistics or documented responses to questions.

Selection of methodology. A selection among available data sources for each variable must be made, as well as the determination of appropriate data collection methods.

Designation of timing and frequency. A base period must be selected for data collection and measurement of variables during a preimplementation period prior to work redesign. Postimplementation periods may be established on a periodic basis (monthly or quarterly) or a one-time study basis (six months after implementation).

Specification of expected outcomes. The expected outcome for each variable should be specified in order to develop various hypotheses that can be tested with the data collection results. It is important, however, to be careful not to bias the results based on these expectations.

Assignment of responsibilities. Responsibilities must be assigned for data collection planners, data collectors, data providers, data analyzers, and data interpreters.

Table 5.1 presents some of the components related to cost, service, quality, and satisfaction included in the evaluation model developed and implemented at Saint Joseph's Hospital of Atlanta.

Commitment of Resources

Data collection planners

The primary focus of data collection planners is to establish the framework for data collection and analysis. Technical skills are required for evaluating alternative data collection methodologies, determining the appropriate methodologies to use, and designing data collection tools (such as forms, questionnaires, procedures) and parameters for implementation (such as sample size, time periods, instructions). These technical skills include not only familiarity with data collection and analysis techniques, but also familiarity with departmental operations, existing hospital reporting systems, and criteria for evaluating among alternative methodologies.

Data collectors

The commitment of time required by data collectors can vary significantly, depending on the selected methodologies. Gathering data from existing hospital reports, for example, depends on the number of data elements to be collected, the time periods selected to sample, and the level of detail within the existing reports compared to the level of detail required for collection. Typically, collecting data from individuals (such as interviews, questionnaires) or from observation/measurement studies (time studies) requires a greater time commitment of resources. For example, consider the time required to conduct interviews with all department managers involved in work redesign, or the time required to observe how nursing staff spend their time (for example, skill levels, 24-hour coverage, weekdays, weekends). This time commitment can range from a few days to several hundred hours. Also, data collectors must be familiar with the operations under study, understand and adhere to the data collection process consistently, and demonstrate good documentation skills.

Data providers

Data can be provided from a variety of sources, such as routine reports collected within specific departments (quality management reports on medication errors) or reports maintained within a hospital data base (payroll data). Data may also be provided by hospital managers and staff through responses to questionnaires, interviews, focus groups, and other meetings or discussions. Data providers may also be directly or indirectly involved in observation/measurement studies. For example, data providers may be asked to log certain information as they perform their job function, or they may be observed as they perform their job function. In both situations, time must be taken to explain the observation study to the provider and to ensure that the study minimizes any disruption to the job function being observed.

Data analyzers

It is essential that the data analyzers understand the data collection process so that they can assess the completeness and reasonableness of the data collected. The data analyzers must be familiar with methods of tabulating and summarizing data, including the use of computer software programs to set up and manipulate data base information. The analyzers must also be familiar with statistical analysis techniques required to compute statistical measures and analyze trends and relationships among variables. In addition, it is essential for the data analyzers to be skilled in reporting results, explaining findings, and documenting outcomes.

Data interpreters

The focus of data interpreters is to review results, assess outcomes, and develop recommendations. Data analysis results (pre- and postimplementation) must be reviewed for completeness and reasonableness to ensure that the variables were measured as originally intended, and to question or confirm the results based upon expectations. The comparison of pre- and postimplementation results must be assessed in terms of the significance and implication of any changes. Such implications may demonstrate the success of the work redesign program or may indicate the need to investigate specific components of the program. It is important to keep in mind, however, that unexpected outcomes may be attributed either to unexpected operational circumstances or to inappropriately collected or analyzed data. It is the responsibility of the data interpreters to assess these situations and develop recommendations for continuing, expanding, or refining the work redesign model.

Hospital managers must commit resources, in terms of time and cost, to fulfill these roles. Who, however, should be assigned to these roles and time commitments? Before identifying and selecting among alternative considerations for these role assignments, it is important to establish general qualifications, or resource requirements. Consider the following qualifications:

- familiarity with departmental and hospital operations
- objective perspective
- knowledge of quantitative and qualitative data collection techniques
- knowledge of statistical analysis techniques
- available time commitment at a reasonable cost

Typical hospital resource alternatives that meet some or all of these qualifications include the following:

- management engineering staff
- other internal specialists
- individual hospital managers and staff
- committees of hospital managers and staff
- external consultants

Management engineering staff

Management engineering staff are well qualified, in terms of familiarity with hospital operations, data collection, and statistical analysis techniques. Because of their quantitative background, these individuals generally provide an objective perspective and are good candidates as data planners, data collectors, data analyzers, and data interpreters. Potential limitations among management engineers could be related to limited familiarity with alternative clinical roles and operations attributed to work redesign and limited exposure to qualitative data collection and analysis techniques.

Internal specialists

Other internal specialists within the hospital could include planning and marketing staff, systems and financial analysts, internal consultants and internal auditors, and administrative residents. These specialists represent individuals who are project oriented and often involved and familiar with various areas of hospital operations. Because of their project orientation, these individuals are familiar with data collection techniques and generally provide an objective perspective. These specialists are good candidates as data planners, data collectors, and data interpreters. Potential limitations among these specialists could be related to limited familiarity with clinical or technical operations and limited experience in statistical data analysis.

Hospital managers and staff

Because individual hospital managers and staff are most familiar with all operations affected by work redesign, these individuals are good candidates as data collectors and data providers. In addition, they can contribute valuable input to assist the data planners and data interpreters. Potential limitations among this group could be related to limited objectivity, due to their specialization, and limited knowledge of data collection techniques.

Committees

Committees of hospital managers and staff represent the assembly and organization of groups of individuals in order to take advantage of group dynamics, discussion, compromise, consensus, and decision making. Committees are familiar with hospital operations and provide a more objective perspective than individual managers and staff. The committees are good candidates as data providers and data interpreters, and they contribute valuable input to the data planners and data collectors. Potential limitations among committees could be related to limited knowledge of data collection and statistical analysis techniques.

External consultants

External consultants provide a valuable alternative resource for data planners, data collectors, data analyzers, and data interpreters. External consultants can also, at times, serve as data providers for comparative data based

Table 5.2 Comparison of General Qualifications of and Typical Assignment Roles for Hospital Resource Alternatives

Hospital Resource Alternatives	General Qualifications					Assignment Roles				
	Familiar with Operations	Objective Perspective	Knowledge in Data Collection	Knowledge in Data Analysis	Available Time and Cost	Data Planners	Data Collectors	Data Providers	Data Analyzers	Data Interpreters
Management engineering	Yes	Yes	Yes	Yes	Varies	Yes	Yes	No	Yes	Yes
Other internal specialists	Varies	Yes	Yes	Varies	Varies	Yes	Yes	No	Varies	Yes
Individual managers and staff	Yes	Limited	Limited	No	Varies	Limited	Yes	Yes	No	Limited
Committees	Yes	Yes	Limited	No	Varies	Limited	Limited	Yes	No	Yes
External consultants	Limited	Yes	Yes	Yes	Varies	Yes	Yes	Limited	Yes	Yes

upon their experience with other hospitals. Consultants are typically well qualified in all areas, with the potential limitation of their unfamiliarity with the specific operations of the hospital. Thus, additional time is often required for consultants to become familiar with the hospital's operations so that they may contribute effectively to the data collection and analysis process.

Table 5.2 provides a summary of the typical qualifications and role assignments of these hospital resource alternatives. The availability and cost of each of these resource alternatives vary depending on each hospital's environment, as well as the scope of the data collection and analysis requirements defined in the planning framework.

Based on the experience at SJHA, the most optimal commitment of resources to data collection and analysis appears to be a blend of the alternatives. Management engineering staff in conjunction with other internal specialists can provide a project team with significant technical strengths. Working in conjunction with a committee of hospital managers and staff provides enhanced familiarity with operations, additional objectivity, and expanded viewpoints for data interpretation. Working with individual managers and staff also enhances familiarity with operations and expands resources for data collection activities. External consultants are particularly useful in enhancing the data planning activities and can be used to alleviate the time commitments of hospital resources in all data collection and analysis activities.

Determination of Methodologies for Data Collection and Analysis

There are numerous methodologies for data collection and analysis from which to select for work redesign. How to determine the appropriate methodology to select for each variable identified within the framework of the work redesign evaluation is based upon several criteria. Before reviewing the criteria, however, it is important to first understand the basic approaches, requirements, and attributes of available methodologies.

There are three major categories of data collection and analysis methodologies: (1) data from existing reports; (2) professional information/expert opinion; and (3) measurement/observation.

Data from Existing Reports

Much data can be obtained from existing departmental and hospital reports. For example, departmental reports can provide information on the number of patients treated, the number of procedures provided, and the number of medication errors, while hospital reports can provide information on the patient length of stays, the staff hours worked, and the expenses of various departments. These reports can provide valuable historical information of patient profiles, departmental work load trends, quality-of-care indicators, and hospital costs. At SJHA, both departmental and hospital reports were used to obtain the information needed to evaluate a multiplicity of variables in our model. Some of these variables and reports were (1) skill mix and wage rate from payroll reports; (2) employee turnover from personnel reports; (3) mix of patients by DRGs and services rendered from service consumption reports; and (4) needlesticks, infection rate, medication errors, and falls from quality management reports.

Data may also be obtained from outside sources, such as published studies, articles, and comparative hospital data bases, such as those materials and publications available through the American Hospital Association (American Hospital Association 1992; Healthcare Information and Management Systems Society, 1991). In all cases, it is essential to obtain an understanding of the data source, how the data are collected, and how the data summaries are reported. This will help to ensure reliability—the data appropriately measure the required variables and provide the necessary level of detail.

The major advantages in using existing reports are that

1. the information is relatively easy to obtain;
2. the accuracy of the data is relatively good; and
3. the acceptability of the results is good, especially if the data are obtained from an ongoing reporting process.

The major limitations are that

1. the data may be limited in terms of the specific details needed;
2. existing reporting systems may be inflexible to change in order to meet new data requirements; and
3. outside source data may be limited in terms of understanding the data sources and specific data collection methods used.

Professional Information/Expert Opinion

Gathering professional information and expert opinions are methods typically used for obtaining qualitative information. The basic distinction among these methods is that data are gathered from individuals knowledgeable of the variable under study. In most cases, these individuals represent those hospital managers and staff being affected by work redesign. The key elements that determine the success of these methods are structured design and objectivity. Much thought and preparation must be devoted to developing structured questions that form the basis of these data collection methods. Moreover, these questions must be designed in an objective fashion to minimize any bias on the part of the data collector as well as the data provider. Six methodologies within this category are described as follows:

Individual interview

The data collection and analysis method of the individual interview is used to obtain information from a qualified individual through a one-on-one question-and-answer format. For example, individual interviews may be conducted with department managers affected by work redesign to assess their level of satisfaction with specific changes to their operations, as well as suggestions for improvements. Individual interviews generally require a structured format of questions to serve as a guideline for the interview process. The interviewer must be trained in terms of understanding the purpose of the study, how to select and approach respondents, how to establish rapport, how to ask questions, how to obtain responses, and how to document answers.

The major advantages of the individual interview are

1. the interview process is relatively easy to design and implement;
2. interviewees within the hospital provide readily available information; and
3. information can be obtained within a limited time commitment.

The major limitations are

1. interviewer bias may affect the results;
2. interviewees may try to provide expected answers rather than their true perspectives; and
3. interpretation and documentation of the responses may be unclear or misunderstood.

Focus group interview

The focus group interview is a modification to the individual interview process. In this method, information is gathered from a group of respondents through a question-and-discussion format. Focus group interviews generally require that the interviewer be prepared with a list of topics or general questions to serve as an interview guide. Respondents are given considerable freedom in responding to the topics and interacting with others in the group.

The major advantages of the focus group interview are

1. group interaction can provide valuable discussion and insight to the topic under study that may not arise through individual interviews; and

2. the group discussion may lead to follow-up questions and new issues that were not planned or expected.

The major limitations of this method are

1. more time is required to conduct these interviews, and often multiple sessions are required;

2. group interactions may lead toward a discussion or direction that strays from the desired topic; and

3. the interviewer must have skills related to group control, as well as the interview process.

Questionnaire

The questionnaire method is typically based on a written list of questions administered to a group of individuals. Numerous variations of the questionnaire method differ in the degree of structure (for example, a formal list of specific questions or a general list of open-ended topics), whether the objective is clearly specified or disguised, how the questionnaire is administered (for example, personal questioning, telephone, or mail), and the types of questions used (for example, open, multiple choice, or dichotomous). In all cases, however, the questionnaire method requires a significant design effort to determine what information is needed, the type of questions and questionnaire to use, the content and wording of individual questions, and the organizational format of the questionnaire. Two key elements that influence the success of the questionnaire are the clarity of the questions and the communication of instructions to the respondents.

The major advantages of the questionnaire method are

1. the versatility of the questionnaire provides a useful tool for many situations, objectives and variables;

2. experience with this method streamlines the design time and improves the validity of results; and

3. less overall time is required in comparison to measurement/observation techniques for data collection.

The major limitations are

1. respondents may be unwilling to provide information or may answer questions according to their perceived expectation of what answer is desired;

2. respondents may not have information available to answer specific questions; and

3. limited experience in questionnaire design may produce unclear questions and inaccurate responses (Boyd and Westfall 1964).

Individual interviews, focus group interviews, and questionnaires at SJHA

At SJHA, an analysis of the patient-focused model, including our redesigned roles, was conducted using three methodologies: individual interviews, focus group interviews, and questionnaires.

Individual interviews were conducted with the majority of professionals functioning in a redesigned role on the two pilot units. The interviews were semistructured and ranged in duration anywhere from 30 minutes to two hours. The primary purposes of these interviews were to determine the level of satisfaction with the newly redesigned role, to identify reasons for satisfaction/dissatisfaction with the role, and to obtain suggestions for improvement.

The hospital commissioned the Planning and Marketing Department to conduct focus group interviews to assess the following:

- Overall perception of work redesign

- Perceived benefits from work redesign

- Level of support for work redesign

- Employee satisfaction

- Training related to work redesign

- Work environment as a result of work redesign efforts

- Perceived effectiveness of work redesign

- Communication efforts related to work redesign

- Suggestions related to work redesign

Ten focus groups were conducted involving employees from throughout the hospital who had been or would be affected by our work redesign program. The groups were stratified as follows:

- Those employees functioning in a redesigned role on two pilot units (i.e., active participants)
- Those employees working on the two pilot units but not in a re-designed role (i.e., nonactive participants)
- RN staff hospitalwide (excluding the pilot units)
- Ancillary staff hospitalwide (respiratory therapists, radiology tech-nologists, medical technologists, physical therapists, and pharma-cists)
- Support staff hospitalwide (admissions, environmental services, food services, transportation, central supply, nursing, medical records, utilization review, business office, materials management, and phle-botomy)
- Clinical managers from both of the pilot units
- Department directors from ancillary, support, and nursing depart-ments that had been or would be affected by work redesign
- Clinical nurse specialists hospitalwide

The results of these focus group interviews were phenomenal! The depth and breadth of information obtained by using this methodology could not have been obtained by other means.

A very detailed questionnaire was administered to all employees func-tioning in a redesigned role. The purpose of the questionnaire was to validate findings revealed by the focus groups and to obtain a more comprehensive evaluation of work redesign, including the following:

- Satisfaction of participants with the redesigned roles
- Perceived adherence to the clinical imperatives—the guiding princi-ples or "rules" upon which the model was based
- Perceived effectiveness or worthiness of the redesigned roles

Exhibit 5.2 illustrates some of the questions contained in the questionnaire. Like the focus group interviews, this methodology, along with individual interviews, provided us with extremely valuable data upon which to make essential changes in the patient-focused model.

Flow diagram

A *flow diagram* is the schematic and graphic representation of the sequence of events or steps within some activity or process. For example, a flow diagram may be used to determine the specific number and sequence of steps involved in the patient admitting process before and after work redesign. The

Exhibit 5.2   SJHA Work Redesign Analysis

Please indicate your job title.

Clinical Associates	Service Associates	Administrative Associates
☐ Registered Nurse	☐ Service Associate I	☐ Administrative Associate I
☐ Pharmacist	☐ Service Associate II	☐ Administrative Associate II
☐ Respiratory Therapist	☐ Service Associate III	

Please indicate your unit.   ☐ 2 South   ☐ 3 South

Please answer the following based on *your* experience in redesign.

1. How satisfying is your role to you personally?
   - ☐ Very Satisfying
   - ☐ Somewhat Satisfying
   - ☐ Somewhat Dissatisfying
   - ☐ Not Satisfying at All

2. Has your role met your expectations?
   - ☐ Yes   ☐ Somewhat

3. In terms of costs, what percentage of the tasks you perform could be more efficiently performed by someone else?
   - ☐ None
   - ☐ Less than 25%
   - ☐ 100%
   - ☐ Greater than 25% but Less than 50%
   - ☐ Greater than 50% but Less than 75%
   - ☐ Greater than 75% but Less than 100%

4. How much of your time is spent on tasks that are recognized as unique to your professional discipline (RNs, RTs and Pharmacists only)?
   - ☐ None
   - ☐ Less than 25%
   - ☐ 100%
   - ☐ Greater than 25% but Less than 50%
   - ☐ Greater than 50% but Less than 75%
   - ☐ Greater than 75% but Less than 100%

5. For your unit, how much of your time would be required to perform all the services that are recognized as unique to your professional discipline (RNs, RTs and Pharmacists only)?
   - ☐ None
   - ☐ Less than 25%
   - ☐ 100%
   - ☐ Greater than 25% but Less than 50%
   - ☐ Greater than 50% but Less than 75%
   - ☐ Greater than 75% but Less than 100%

6. In what ways can your duties be changed to make your role more professionally rewarding?

7. In terms of costs, how could your skills be more appropriately utilized?

8. What needs to start happening on your unit for redesign to be effective?

Continued

Exhibit 5.2   Continued

9. What needs to stop happening on your unit for redesign to be effective?

10. Have you considered the training required to be successful in your new role? If not, what training would you consider necessary to ensure your success in this role?

11. Was there training provided that was not useful? If so, please give details.

12. Do you feel there will be sufficient change in the model within the next 6 months for most of your concerns to be addressed to your satisfaction? Why or why not?

13. Has enough time been provided for development of your role to adequately evaluate the effectiveness of it? Why or why not?

flow diagram requires the data collector to gather this information from the data provider through a series of questions, discussion, and documentation of diagrams. The data provider must be familiar with the operations of the activity under study, and the data collector must be skilled in documenting the appropriate level of detail, using appropriate flowcharting techniques to depict activity steps, sequences, decision points, and variations in the process. Figure 5.1 illustrates a flow diagram of the central transportation process at SJHA prior to and following the implementation of work redesign.

The major advantages of the flow diagram method are

1. a complex process may be represented in simplified terms, under-standable to both clinical and nonclinical professionals;

2. limited skills are required to learn the flow diagram method; and

3. less overall time is required in comparison to measurement/obser-vation methods for data collection.

The major limitations of this method are

1. the accuracy of the flow diagram results depends on the knowledge of the data provider, as well as the methodology skills of the data collector;

2. the method provides no basis for verification of results, unless multiple individuals are interviewed or observation methods are used to confirm the flowcharted activities; and

Figure 5.1   Saint Joseph's Hospital of Atlanta Central Transportation
Process

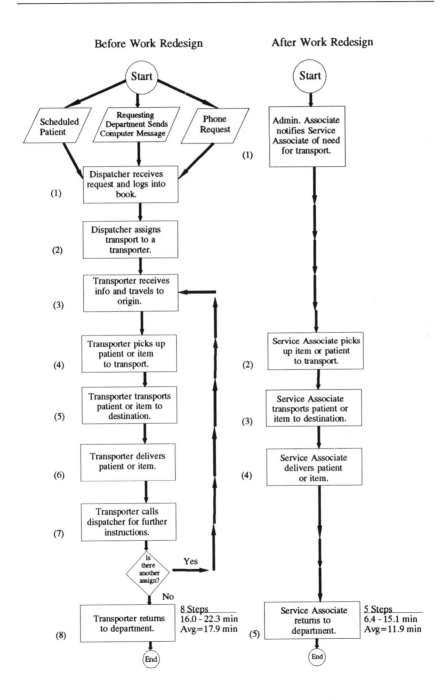

3. the more variations or complexities within the measured activity, the more complicated the flow diagram process becomes.

Structured estimation

Structured estimation is useful for obtaining quantitative information from individuals without a measurement or observation process. The structured estimation method structures an activity or process into basic steps, similar to the flow diagram method, and then questions the data provider to estimate quantitative information, such as the number of times performed or the amount of time required. For example, a structured estimation method can be used to estimate the time required to admit a patient, transport a patient, or perform an x-ray procedure. The method requires a thorough understanding of the process under study in order to structure and specify the detailed steps of the process. Table 5.3 delineates via this methodology the work flow steps and the actual time involved to perform a variety of tasks or functions at SJHA prior to the implementation of work redesign.

The major advantages of the structured estimation method are

1. routine and high-volume procedure steps and times can be estimated with high accuracy and confidence;
2. data can be obtained in a less threatening manner than observation methods; and
3. less overall time is required in comparison to measurement/observation methods for data collection.

The major limitations of the method are

1. the accuracy of the estimation results depends on the knowledge and estimating accuracy of the data provider;
2. reasonableness tests using multiple data providers or other observation methods should be used to ensure reliability of the results; and
3. variations and complexities within the process under study create more steps, more estimates, and more chance for estimation errors.

Attitude measurement/psychometric scaling

Attitude measurement/psychometric scaling is used to apply quantitative analysis to qualitative data in order to quantify variables such as attitudes and preferences. For example, this method can be used to assess patient perceptions toward specific quality-of-care indicators (for example, their level

Table 5.3 SJHA Process Purity and Complexity Work Redesign—
Preimplementation Study

Department	Activity	Work Flow Steps		Process Time (Min.)	
		Range	*Average*	*Range*	*Average*
Admitting	Elective admission	9–13	9.7	36–79	48.0
Admitting	Emergency admission	4–11	5.4	9.5–48.5	19.3
Laboratory	CBC test	16–24	18.0	9.4–17.4	10.9
Radiology	Chest x-ray	32–33	32.5	35.0–145.3	61.7
Respiratory Care	Aerosol treatment	6–14	8.4	26.8–61.3	35.4
EKG	EKG procedure	16–17	16.5	34.5–37.5	35.1
Transportation	Patient transport	8.0	8.0	16.0–22.3	17.9
Housekeeping	Room turnaround	11–12	11.5	20.0–47.0	32.2
Materials Management	Stocking unit	8.0	8.0	36.0	36.0
Dietary	Meal delivery	5.0	5.0	26.0	26.0

of satisfaction) or perceptions as to which quality-of-care issues are most important (for example, ranking quality-of-care indicators on a numbered scale reflecting level of importance). The attitude measurement/psychometric scaling method requires that questions related to qualitative information be structured in such a way as to establish levels of responses, such as levels of agreement, levels of preference, or levels of importance (for example, most unimportant, somewhat unimportant, neutral, somewhat important, most important). This structure provides a basis for quantifying the results, such as applying point levels 1 through 5 for the levels.

The major advantages of the attitude measurement/psychometric scaling method are

1. qualitative information becomes easier to summarize and present in quantitative terminologies;

2. the structured question format can be easier for data providers to answer than open-ended questions; and

3. there are various scaling methodologies available for the analysts.

The major limitations are

1. the results of scaling methodologies cannot be verified through the use of other data collection and analysis methods;

2. special skills are required to structure questions in the appropriate formats and to compute scaled results; and

3. although various scaling methods are available, their differences are often attributed to mathematical assumptions that are difficult to compare and contrast (Boyd and Westfall 1964; Guilford 1954).

Measurement/Observation

The primary uses of measurement and observation techniques focus on work processes and activities in order to specify work flows, quantify time requirements, measure variability, and assess relationships (for example, trends, correlations) among quantitative variables. The key elements that determine the success of these methods are the sample size and the degree of consistency or variability within the process being measured or observed. The larger the sample size of measurements and observations, the more reliable statistical results will be. The more variability, however, the larger the sample size required to enhance reliability. In some cases, significant variability in the data measurements may indicate the need to redefine the variable under study. Four methodologies within this category are described in the following.

Flow diagram with observation

The data collection and analysis method of a flow diagram with observation is a variation of the flow diagram method described earlier. With this approach, however, the data collector gathers information through observation of the events or steps of the activity or process being studied. Because of this, the data collector must be able to interpret and document the activity steps, sequences, decision points, and variations. Integrating both methods provides a basis for verification, through observation, of the flow diagram developed through professional information/expert opinion.

The major advantages of the flow diagram with observation method are

1. a complex process may be represented in simplified terms, understandable to both clinical and nonclinical professionals;

2. limited skills are required to learn the flow diagram method; and

3. the observation provides a basis for verification of the flow diagram results.

The major limitations are

1. the accuracy of the flow diagram depends not only on the methodology skills of the data collector, but also on how well interpretations of decision points can be made and how many variations within the process are actually observed;

2. more time is required to develop a flow diagram based upon observations, especially if the process has multiple decision points and variations within the process that require more and more observations to capture all possibilities; and

3. the more variations or complexities within a process, the more complicated the flow diagram process becomes.

Stopwatch time study

The stopwatch time study method is the most common approach to work measurement. This method typically involves the stopwatch timing of an operation and simultaneous "performance rating" (i.e., an assessment or judgment as to the working pace or performance of the data provider being measured). For example, a stopwatch time study may be used to measure the time required to perform a lab test, clean a patient's room, or transport a patient to radiology. It is necessary before conducting the time study to determine the "standard" method, specifying the sequence of events, the supplies/equipment needed, and variations within the operation, similar to the flow diagram method. Because of the complexity of many operations and the occurrence of delay factors (for example, patient not ready, elevator delay, procedure interruption), it is common practice to divide the operation into specific elements or steps for timing purposes. The data collector must understand the operation and must be skilled in determining the elemental structure of operations, observing and recording actual time requirements, and assessing performance ratings. It is also important, within this method, to determine the appropriate sample size of observations, which depends on the amount of variation within the timed activity, the number of elements identified within the operation, and the degree of accuracy and confidence desired (Buffa 1972).

The major advantages of stopwatch time studies are

1. the method provides a very accurate measurement of time;
2. the results are generally acceptable to managers and data interpreters; and
3. the method can be repeated over time to update standards or specific elements of the work activity.

The major limitations are

1. the stopwatch can interrupt the operation process and the behavior or performance of data providers, since people generally do not like being observed or timed;
2. the method is generally unsatisfactory for measuring complex operations with variations within the process, primarily due to the additional time required to obtain satisfactory sample results; and
3. the data collector and analyst must be skilled and experienced in order to produce reliable results.

Self-logging

The self-logging method is a participative work measurement technique in which activity information and time requirements are recorded by the data providers themselves as they perform the operation being studied. The activities to be measured must be adequately defined and described in advance. Appropriate forms are then developed to enable the data provider to maintain a log or a series of log-in and log-out entries, in order to record the activity performed and the time required. Mechanical time stamp machines, bar code technology, or computerized hand-held systems can also be used to streamline the logging efforts. For example, a self-logging method may be used to log and measure patient escort times, the time required by a phlebotomist to travel to the nursing unit, or the time required to code a patient's medical record.

The major advantages of the self-logging method are

1. the method is generally easy to set up and administer
2. the method is easy to understand and, therefore, generally acceptable to both the data provider and the data interpreter; and
3. moderate skills and training are required by the data collector, data provider, and data analyst.

The major limitations are

1. close monitoring is required of the data provider's recording techniques;

2. the method may be disruptive to the operation under study; and

3. data analysis may be time-consuming due to the volume of data collected, the need to interpret illegible or confusing data, and the need to eliminate incomplete or inaccurate data.

Work sampling

This method is based on making random observations of an operation or data provider and using the laws of probability and statistics to analyze activity times. The method operates on the premise that a random sample drawn from a large group will tend to resemble the group from which it is drawn. The larger the sample size, the more confidence there will be in the results. A primary use of work sampling is to measure work activities that span a long period of time by observing the activity at random intervals of time. For example, the work sampling method may be used to measure the amount of time during the day shift that a nurse spends providing direct patient care, or the amount of time spent waiting or idle due to delays, work fluctuations, or personal break times (Buffa 1972).

To use the work sampling method, it is essential that adequate sample sizes are taken, and that observation times and sequences are randomly determined. It is also necessary to fully understand the operation under study and to develop appropriate forms to capture data at random time intervals. Data collectors must be instructed and trained in the data collection method and must be familiar with the operation being observed since they must accurately record their observations into a format that can be statistically summarized.

The major advantages of work sampling are

1. statistically reliable results may be obtained in a relatively short time in comparison to other data collection methods;

2. work sampling data are easy to summarize and analyze; and

3. the method causes limited disruptions to the operation and staff being observed.

The major limitations are

1. the method is more useful for measuring major work activities that extend over long periods of time than detailed procedures or activities that require shorter times;

2. the data collection is typically limited to observing predetermined categories of activity and does not provide for detailed recording of specific activities or conditions that occur; and

Table 5.4 SJHA Comparison and Evaluation of Data Collection and Analysis Methods

Methods	Criteria	Availability of Information	Time Required	Training and Skill Required	Difficulty of Obtaining Data	Interruption of Work Operations	Accuracy of Results	Acceptability	Cost
Data from existing reports	Existing hospital reports	Moderate	Moderate	Low	Limited	Low	Moderate	Good	Limited
	Outside sources	Limited	Limited	Low	Low	Low	Limited	Limited	Limited
Professional information and expert opinion	Individual interview	Moderate	Limited	Limited	Limited	Limited	Moderate	Moderate	Limited
	Focus group interview	Good	Moderate	Moderate	Limited	Limited	Good	Good	Moderate
	Questionnaire	Good	Good	Good	Moderate	Limited	Moderate	Good	Moderate
	Flow diagram	Limited	Limited	Moderate	Limited	Limited	Moderate	Moderate	Limited
	Structured estimation	Good	Moderate	Moderate	Limited	Limited	Moderate	Moderate	Limited
	Attitude measurement/ psychometric scaling	Moderate	Good	Good	Moderate	Limited	Good	Good	Moderate
Measurement and observation	Flow diagram with observation	Limited	Moderate	Moderate	Moderate	Low	Good	Good	Limited
	Stopwatch time study	High	High	High	Moderate	Moderate	High	Good	Good
	Self-logging	Good	Good	Moderate	Good	Good	Good	Good	Moderate
	Work sampling	Good	Good	High	Good	Limited	Good	Good	Good

Key: (1) Low, (2) Limited, (3) Moderate, (4) Good, (5) High.

3. technical skills are required to set up and implement a work sampling study.

Selection of a Data Collection Methodology

Given these alternative methods for data collection, how do you determine which methodology to use? This determination should be based on an evaluation according to the following criteria:

1. *Availability of information.* Sources from which the data are most available (for example, existing reports, professionals/experts, measurement/observation).

2. *Time required.* The time needed to set up data collection methods, to collect information, to tabulate and compile results, to measure accuracy and reliability, and to establish desired measures of the variable under study.

3. *Training and skill required.* The amount of instruction and training needed by data collectors and data providers, and the knowledge, skills, and experience needed by data collectors and data analyzers.

4. *Difficulty of obtaining data.* The amount of effort and complexity required on the part of the data collector and data provider to gather information.

5. *Interruption of work operations.* Whether or not the data collection method is disruptive to the work operation process or the data provider being observed.

6. *Accuracy of results.* The potential to achieve valid and reliable data analysis results based on the selected methodology.

7. *Acceptability.* The level of confidence that data interpreters, such as hospital managers, have in the data analysis results.

8. *Cost.* The cost of the time and resources required to implement the data collection and analysis methodology.

A general comparison and evaluation of the data collection and analysis methods discussed in this chapter is provided in Table 5.4.

Design of Data Collection Tools and Parameters

The specific design of data collection tools and parameters depends upon the data collection and analysis method selected. *Data collection tools* are the forms, questionnaires, and other documentation required in gathering information from existing sources, professionals, or observations. *Data collection parameters* are the time periods, sample sizes, and other specifications required in order to implement the data collection process. Although the specific details of the data collection tools and parameters will vary from method to method (i.e., existing hospital reports, questionnaires, work sampling) and from variable to variable (i.e., quantitative and qualitative), there are general guidelines that apply to all data collection efforts.

Understand Operations, Variables, and Data Sources

Before designing the data collection tools and parameters, it is necessary to have a thorough understanding of the operations under study, the variables that have been defined to measure, and the availability of data sources. The operations under study can have a significant impact on the design of the data collection tools and parameters. For example, consider a work sampling study of laboratory technicians who work in one primary location and phlebotomists who travel to patients throughout the hospital. The data collection tools must reflect differences in their work activities as well as their work locations, and the data collection parameters must incorporate differences in the number of observers required.

The variables must also be well defined and understood in order to design the data collection forms and parameters appropriately. For example, measuring the turnaround time for stat laboratory procedures may be interpreted differently than a more refined variable definition of measuring the turnaround time, including both "order to completion" elapsed time and "order to results reported" elapsed time for stat laboratory procedures requested during the day shift from a specific nursing unit.

The availability of data sources must also be understood before designing the data collection tools and parameters. For example, the number of arterial blood sticks provided on a particular nursing unit may be captured through existing hospital reports or may require a self-logging data collection over a lengthy time period.

Understand the Skills Required for Each
Data Collection Method Selected

Gathering data from existing hospital reports requires different skills and training than designing a questionnaire data collection process, which, in turn, requires different skills and training than conducting a stopwatch time study. Individuals who are skilled in some data collection methods may not be skilled in others. For example, an individual not skilled in work sampling techniques may be able to conduct a data collection, but may not design the form to select random observation intervals or may not collect an adequate sample size of observations.

Obtain Resources

The resources required to design the data collection tools and parameters may include in-house specialists, committees, or outside consultants. In-house specialists who have the technical skills and experience with data collection methods generally also have a good understanding of departmental and hospital operations, as well as data sources. Committees are a valuable resource, in terms of establishing objectives, defining variables to be studied, specifying time frames, monitoring progress, and assuming responsibility to ensure that the data collection process is designed and implemented. Outside consultants can be a valuable, but sometimes costly, resource to supplement internal resources.

Specify Time Periods

Data collection tools must be designed to be used during pre- and postimplementation periods of work redesign efforts. As described earlier, some data collection methods require more time than others. Preimplementation data collection time periods must take into account the implementation plans for work redesign, as well as the time requirements of the selected data collection methods. Postimplementation data collection time periods may be established at specified points in time (such as six months after implementation) or at specified time intervals (such as monthly or quarterly). The selection of postimplementation time periods will depend on the requirements and complexities of the selected data collection methods, as well as the time frame of expected benefits from the work redesign efforts.

Develop Questions or Measures

Data collection methods within the professional information/expert opinion category require that appropriate questions be developed. Other methods, including collection of data from existing sources, measurements, and observations, require that specific measures be established. For example, a stopwatch time study of a portable chest x-ray procedure would require the specification of several work steps that would need to be measured, such as travel time, setup time, procedure time, and documentation time.

Develop Standardized Forms and Instructions

Each data collection method requires specific forms and instructions for gathering and documenting information. This step ensures that a standardized process is established for data collection and analysis. The standardized process provides three major benefits. First, standardized forms and instructions help to standardize the data being collected over different time periods, from different individuals, under different circumstances, for different patients, or in different samples, thus ensuring that all collected data are comparable and can be combined to develop aggregate results. Second, standardization helps to achieve speed and accuracy in recording data, thus ensuring that data are collected in a timely manner and are consistently documented in order to enhance data reliability. Third, standardized forms and instructions help to achieve speed and accuracy in handling, tabulating, and compiling data, thus ensuring timely analysis and accurate processing of quantitative and qualitative measures.

Pilot Test the Data Collection Forms and Instructions

In order to help ensure the appropriateness and clarity of the data collection forms and instructions, it is good practice to conduct a pilot test. In this way, the data collection forms and instructions can be tested to identify any needed improvements, to add, modify, or delete data elements, to alter form design, or to clarify instructions. This step is especially important if many data providers or data collectors are to be involved in the data collection study. For example, a questionnaire may be tested among a few respondents before widespread distribution, or work sampling observations may be conducted by a few trained observers for a few observations before all observers are trained and before full-scale data collection begins.

Specify Sampling Method and Sample Size

The precision of data analysis results depends on the sampling method and sample size of data. Four common sampling methods are (1) simple random sampling, (2) stratified random sampling, (3) cluster sampling, and (4) systematic sampling. *Simple random sampling* involves data collection based upon a pure random selection of data elements, individuals, or observations from a defined total group of all possibilities. For example, when selecting from a group of all department managers or all patients admitted, a simple random sample ensures that each member of the group has an equal chance or probability of being selected.

Stratified random sampling involves the subdivision of the group being studied into several subgroups, called *strata*, and then the selection of a simple random sample from each subgroup. For example, all department managers may be stratified according to those managers involved in the work redesign effort and those who are not involved, or all patients admitted may be stratified according to admission type, such as elective admission or emergency admission. Consider for a moment the previous discussion regarding focus groups conducted at SJHA. All employees who would eventually be affected in some way by work redesign were stratified into ten groups.

Cluster sampling involves the selection of a sample of defined subgroups, especially when the entire group cannot easily be identified nor stratified. For example, to sample patient satisfaction with a particular aspect of work redesign, such as the admission process, a cluster sample may be specified as the group of patients admitted during the upcoming week. Another example of a cluster sample that was used at SJHA was the respondents to the questionnaire that was administered to all participants of work redesign. Although "all participants of work redesign" were sought, the "respondents to the questionnaire" represented the cluster sample.

Systematic sampling involves establishing a scheme or system for selecting a sample. For example, selecting every tenth patient chronologically admitted to the hospital, or observing a nurse's activity every five minutes would represent systematic sampling.

Selecting among these sampling methods and following the guidelines for selecting samples is important to ensure that data analysis results are statistically reliable. Also, the larger the sample size, the more reliable the data analysis results. Statistics textbooks provide numerous formulas for determining appropriate sample sizes based upon the sampling method, the type of variable being measured (for example, a number, proportion, percentage, average), the degree of confidence desired (for example, 99 percent, 95 percent, 90 percent), the amount of sampling error tolerated (for example, 1 percent, 2 percent), and the amount of variation (i.e., standard deviation) in the data (Daniel and Terrell 1979).

Training and Informing Data Providers and Data Collectors

The design of data collection forms must be presented in generally understandable formats and language since many data providers and data collectors may need to become familiar with the forms. Data providers should be informed of the objectives of the data collection study and instructed in their specific requirements, whether responding to interview questions, completing a questionnaire, or being observed as they perform a work activity. Data collectors should similarly be informed and trained in asking questions, completing forms, and making observations. These efforts help to ensure that the design of data collection forms and parameters are generally understood before the data collection process is implemented.

Implementation of the Data Collection Process

Implementation of the data collection process entails data collection and analysis conducted prior to work redesign implementation and after work redesign efforts have been initiated. Preimplementation studies are required to establish baseline information on each of the quantitative and qualitative variables defined within the framework of the evaluation model. Postimplementation studies are required to either monitor progress on a periodic basis or assess progress at some designated point in time, in order to measure changes that may be attributed to the impact of work redesign.

As emphasized earlier, data collection implementation should be preceded by the assessment of data availability from various sources, the development of a plan for data collection, the commitment of resources, the determination of appropriate methodologies for data collection and analysis, and the design of standardized data collection tools and parameters. The primary steps for implementing the data collection process are described in the following.

Conduct Preimplementation Studies

Prior to initiating work redesign, data collection should be conducted for each quantitative and qualitative variable defined within the framework. This step provides for the establishment of baseline measures for each variable. The time required for conducting these preimplementation studies depends on the number of variables under study, the resources committed to the effort, and the data collection and analysis methodologies selected. Proper planning ensures that ample time is allowed to conduct the data collection prior to work redesign implementation.

Document, Summarize, and Develop Report Formats

Since many departments, managers, staff, patients, and physicians may be affected by work redesign, the data collection framework is likely to identify many variables to study. Consequently, the preimplementation studies can produce significant volumes of data and results. It is essential to provide adequate documentation of the data collection process, the data itself, and the results of data analyses. This documentation is important for answering detailed questions concerning the study or results, as well as for reviewing the process at some later point in time to ensure that postimplementation studies are conducted in a similar manner. The large volumes of data analysis results also need to be summarized to provide the most meaningful information related to each variable.

Conduct Postimplementation Studies

Subsequent data collection and analysis studies may be conducted on a periodic basis or at specified points in time. For example, periodic data collection can generally be used for those variables for which data are available from existing hospital reports. Limited additional efforts may be required to compile and summarize this information on a regular basis, such as monthly or quarterly. Periodic information can be used to monitor trends in variable measures over time throughout work redesign implementation. Data collection efforts that require a significant commitment of time or resources, such as work sampling or questionnaires, may be conducted at specified points in time, such as six months after the work redesign implementation, and annually thereafter.

Document, Summarize, and Develop Comparative Profiles

Postimplementation study results need to be documented, summarized, and compared to the preimplementation study results for each variable being analyzed. Postimplementation results should be presented in the same format as the preimplementation study results. This step will provide comparative profiles for each variable and will indicate any changes or trends in the various cost, service, quality, and satisfaction measures that have been studied.

Conduct Variance Analysis

It is important to determine if any changes in the evaluation measures have occurred and to determine if the changes are significant. Initially, these changes should be noted in simple terms, such as an absolute change in time required to admit a patient, or a percentage change in the number of patients satisfied with the admission process, providing an initial indication as to whether the measures show improvement, decline, or no change in performance. If there are positive or negative changes in performance, additional analysis should be conducted to determine if the changes are significant.

From a statistical perspective, formulas exist for measuring the statistical significance of any variable changes. Use of such formulas will determine if the change is likely to be attributed to chance or to the actual impact of work redesign. For example, if the initially measured time to perform a patient procedure ranged from 30 to 60 minutes and averaged 45 minutes, and the postimplementation study results ranged from 20 to 50 minutes and averaged 40 minutes, a statistical variance analysis can be used to test if the change is significant (i.e., attributed to an operational change, such as work redesign) or if, given the original data, it would have been just as likely to obtain an average of 40 minutes (Daniel and Terrell 1979).

Interpret the Results

The determination as to whether any measured changes in performance are attributed to work redesign is more complicated than performing a statistical variance analysis. In scientific experiments, outside influences caused by variables not being studied are controlled to minimize their impact. In hospital operations, it is impossible to control other changes that might occur between the preimplementation and postimplementation time periods. For example, the patients are different, the staff may be different, some technology may have changed, and other operational characteristics may have changed. Thus, the results must be interpreted to assess the possible influence of factors other than work redesign.

The data interpreters, as discussed earlier, must consider the impact of work redesign amidst other hospital changes in order to judge the performance impact of work redesign. Also, variable measures may change over time as a result of these other factors or the sampling process itself. There is also a general impression that performance improves over time as a result of being measured (i.e., if someone knows that something they control is being measured, then they will work to improve their performance). Thus, the performance measure may decline initially from the preimplementation results, and then improve as periodic postimplementation studies are conducted. It is beneficial, therefore, to conduct periodic postimplementation data collection studies whenever possible to ensure adequate evaluation of the work redesign model.

Appropriate Use of Evaluation Results

The data collection and analysis results of the work redesign evaluation process may be used to demonstrate the degree of success of work redesign, identify areas in which expected outcomes were not attained, and plan for the future development and implementation of the work redesign model. Results should be interpreted not only in terms of statistical trends and variances but also in terms of the reasonableness of the results. For example, are the measured variables providing the intended information? Are factors other than work redesign influencing the results? Are the results, whether positive or negative, within an acceptable range around the expected outcomes?

If the evaluation process has been properly executed, and if the results are statistically meaningful and reasonable, then the results may be used with confidence.

Demonstrate the Success of Work Redesign

Demonstrating the success of work redesign may include enhancements and improvements to cost measures (for example, increased productivity, streamlined work flow, reduced cost per patient day), service measures (for example, reduced patient waiting time, lower turnaround times, increased responsibilities of dedicated staff compared to centralized departments), quality measures (for example, decreased retake rates, decreased infection rates, decreased medication errors), and satisfaction measures (for example, improved patient, staff, and physician satisfaction). The successes should be communicated to staff, department managers, hospital administrators, and board members to demonstrate the benefits achieved through everyone's work redesign efforts. This step also serves to lay the groundwork for future expansion of the work redesign model.

Identify Areas in which Expected Outcomes Were Not Attained

If the data analysis results do not support expected outcomes, potential reasons for these variances should be evaluated. As discussed earlier in this chapter, nonattainment of expected outcomes may be attributed to statistical variations in the data results or the impact of operational changes or factors other than work redesign. Other potential reasons for these variances are that the implementation of work redesign job functions may have changed or may be functioning differently than expected, there may be errors in the data analysis, or there may be errors in the data collected.

Plan for the Future Development of the Work Redesign Model

This planning effort depends on whether the work redesign evaluation measures demonstrate a successful implementation or potential areas for improvement. It is likely that among all the quantitative and qualitative measures that are evaluated, some will demonstrate successful performance and others will identify shortcomings in terms of expected outcomes. Successful measures of work redesign provide support for future expansion of the model. For example, successful measures for a pilot test nursing unit may support the expansion of work redesign to other areas of the hospital, including other nursing units and other departments. On the other hand, identified shortcomings will indicate the need for corrective action.

Plans for the future development of work redesign may include additional training or retraining of work redesign staff; revision of the work redesign model, such as redefined roles, responsibilities, schedules, organization structure, or operating procedures; or revision of the evaluation framework, in terms of identifying new performance measures, revising data collection and analysis methods, or updating outcome expectations. The major changes that SJHA made after the results of the individual interviews, focus group interviews, and questionnaires were obtained were the following:

- The timetable for implementation was drastically revised. A commitment was made by the administration that further implementation would be postponed until necessary revisions were made to the model.
- A full-time work redesign coordinator was employed.
- The clinical associate role was eliminated.
- Each of the professional disciplines drafted proposals that outlined how each professional discipline would function in a more expanded role, which would represent job enrichment for these individuals. In addition, these professionals delineated how each of the disciplines would provide services in a more cost-effective and patient-focused manner, as well as how each of these professionals could function as a collaborative member of a multidisciplinary patient care team.
- The service associate role was revised.
- The administrative associate role was revised; one level of this job category was eliminated.
- The relationship between the pilot units and the central departments was more clearly delineated.
- Training for the service associate and administrative associate roles was curtailed until the problems identified were resolved.
- A comprehensive, formal, written communications plan was drafted for internal use.
- The project structure, including membership of all committees, for the work redesign program was revised.

As one can see, critical decisions were made based on this study.

The evaluation of work redesign or operational restructuring efforts is a unique challenge for hospitals. Evaluation endeavors will grow exponentially as the model is implemented in more and more areas of the hospital. It is imperative that administrative leaders of this project commit the appropriate resources, both financial and human, to the evaluation of this change, which, in reality, represents a metamorphosis of today's hospital.

References

American Hospital Association. 1992. *The Complete AHA Catalog—1992*. Chicago: AHA.

Boyd, H., and R. Westfall. 1964. *Marketing Research, Text and Cases* (revised ed.). Homewood, IL: Irwin.

Buffa, E. 1972. *Operations Management: Problems and Models* (3rd ed.). New York: Wiley.

Costis, H. 1972. *Statistics for Business*. Columbus, OH: Merrill.

Daniel, W., and J. Terrell. 1979. *Business Statistics, Basic Concepts and Methodology* (2nd ed.). Boston: Houghton Mifflin.

Guilford, J. P. 1954. *Psychometric Methods* (2nd ed.). New York: McGraw-Hill.

Healthcare Information and Management Systems Society of the American Hospital Association (AHA). 1991. *1991 Catalog—Healthcare Information and Management Systems Publications*. Chicago: AHA.

6

FINANCIAL IMPACTS OF WORK REDESIGN

Ann Scott Blouin and Richard Heim

Background Theory and Approaches to Work Redesign

The economics of health care has taken a financial toll on each provider of services in the industry. Every hospital has tried to come up with new and innovative ways to decrease their costs, while continuing to provide a high quality of care and a strong patient orientation—not an easy task to manage. As third party payers continue to reduce the payments for services, facilities are finding viable alternatives that not only save money, but enhance job satisfaction. Work redesign is one of these alternatives that is becoming a necessity in all health care facilities. This chapter will explore some of the financial indicators that can help to make work redesign easier to analyze and implement.

Work redesign began and has evolved for a variety of reasons:

- To decrease overall hospital costs
- To improve the patient care delivery system
- To decrease duplication of tasks
- To stimulate motivation
- To manage scarce professionals
- To retain employees
- To improve recruitment
- To increase job satisfaction
- To increase employee productivity

Each hospital can take these reasons and rank them differently based upon their individual situation. Each of these reasons has significant importance to the overall operations of a facility, as well as the financial position of a hospital. A key point to keep in mind is that in some hospitals, not all of these items can be reduced to a financial outcome. In work redesign, there may be quality and performance benefits that are difficult to quantify.

There has been a variety of approaches used to structure and implement the work redesign concept. Table 6.1 lists four different approaches and their basic concepts. Each approach has been variably used and modified to enhance the quality of work and increase the quantity of work.

Health care facilities have been experimenting with numerous types of work redesign. Some have been very successful and others have failed. There are important aspects of the approach that need to be analyzed before a program can be pursued. Here are some key questions that should be discussed:

- Does work redesign support the strategic goals of the organization?
- How can we continue to keep the focus on the patient and cut costs at the same time?
- Will the patient be hurt by these changes?
- How can we encourage the employees to work with us to get the job done more efficiently and cost-effectively?

All of these questions should be considered in the analysis of work redesign. They are the basics for exploring the financial aspects we will look at throughout the rest of this chapter.

Aspects Affecting a Cost-Benefit Analysis

Planning implementation

The key to a successful cost-benefit analysis is the degree of planning that will carry the project through to completion. The concept of work redesign must be fully supported by senior management. If senior management has a vision and a commitment to what the hospital would like accomplished, then a cost-benefit analysis will help support this program.

The changes that work redesign will bring about are not just at the staff level. You will be working on breaking down archaic departmental structures that are part of the overall hierarchy of the hospital. This is one key reason for having management support. To get started, you must establish a plan for this group to follow. These steps are graphically depicted in Figure 6.1.

Table 6.1 Approaches to Work Design

	Job Enrichment	*Job Characteristics Model*	*Japanese-Style Management*	*Quality-of-Worklife Approach*
Definition	Growth of the motivational factors (e.g., achievement, recognition, responsibility, and advancement) not the reduction in job dissatisfies	The idea that people will respond differently to the same job, and employers can get increased motivation, satisfaction, and performance by altering job characteristics	Treating employees according to a "family approach," which helps in the development of organizational cohesiveness	Improving the worklife by addressing the tasks, the physical work environment, and the social environment
Positives	Higher job satisfaction; diversification	Can structure work to make it more satisfying; match people with the jobs they wish to perform; workers will do better because work is rewarding and satisfying	Teamwork or group consciousness; creates a sense of harmony	Management must understand both technical and social systems; based upon the individual's ability to make judgments about what is or is not desirable in the workplace
Negatives	Management's reluctance to commit to long term; too many changes to old job classification system	Time-consuming; not always a correct match for every job	No individualization; lack of competition among employees	Must have and keep a very committed management team; social environment is sometimes very hard to analyze

Source: J. B. Cunningham and T. Eberle, "A Guide to Job Enrichment Redesign," *Personnel* 69, no. 2 (1990): 56–58.

Figure 6.1   Basic Steps of a Work Redesign Model

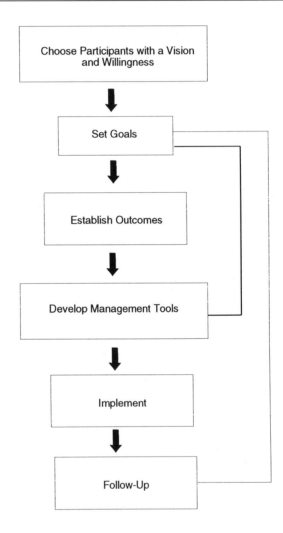

Members of the team exploring work redesign should be a cross-section of the people who will help make it a success. Along with senior management, key departments like human resources, support services, strategic planning, nursing, and finance should be represented.

Understanding cost concepts will help the entire group look for areas to improve the possible financial benefits from work redesign. Each of these cost areas may or may not have an impact depending upon a hospital's individual situation. Table 6.2 lists areas of cost that should be considered.

The costs associated with *managerial* and *operational control* are costs that department heads and directors typically work with on a day-to-day basis. Managers are directly responsible for these costs as part of the normal operations of their department.

Project costs are usually associated with an effort such as work redesign. Have you spent time and money on things that will be lost or sunk if the program is not implemented? Will the program of work redesign have some incremental costs associated with it? *Incremental costs* are the difference between the current operational costs and those that would be incurred as a result of implementing the work redesign program. What is the cost to the organization if they choose to turn down this opportunity? Knowing each of these types of costs will help you in the decision-making process.

Finally, *volume/statistical-based* costs are also considered. Work redesign may or may not have a significant impact on the statistical volume; you must distinguish between fixed costs and variable costs. Generally, the largest cost involved in work redesign is labor. There are some labor costs that do not fluctuate with volume and some that will rise and fall with the census or procedures performed.

Table 6.2 Cost Categories

Managerial/Operational Control
  Direct/indirect costs
  Controllable/uncontrollable costs
  Committed/noncommitted costs
  Budgeted/actual costs

Project
  Sunk costs
  Incremental costs
  Opportunity costs

Volume/Statistical
  Fixed costs
  Variable costs
  Semifixed costs
  Semivariable costs

Source: B. R. Neumann, J. D. Suver, and W. N. Zelman, *Financial Management: Concepts and Applications for Health Care Providers* (Baltimore: National Health Publishing, 1988).

Alterations in Work Content and Context

As work redesign is planned, the content of the job role and the environmental context affected by the newly designed functions must be considered. Each of these aspects, role content and environmental context, can provide important financial benefits for the institution.

In examining the actual job content, there are three areas that should be assessed. First, has routinization or the duplication of effort been reduced or eliminated? By what quantity? Second, has the flexibility of several types of employees to perform a task been increased (i.e., job enlargement)? Third, is the best value achieved for the complexity of work required? Are registered nurses reserved for professional duties? Have less complex responsibilities been rearranged and delegated to one or more nurse extenders?

Understanding and measuring the fixed and variable components of job content is a valuable cost-accounting approach. Henderson and Williams (1991, 48) estimate work redesign can reduce fixed staffing costs by as much as 25 percent. Through cross-training and cross-utilization of traditional fixed personnel, staff's flexibility and productivity can measurably improve. An example is broadening the role of the unit secretary/clerk to include patient hostess (for example, delivering dietary trays, mail and flowers) and supply acquisition/stocking duties.

In looking at the hospital environment or context of patient care, three factors can produce cost savings. First, have staff been granted more discretion or decision making in task performance? An example is the staff reducing the unit supplies to "just-in-time" inventory. If staff can be assured that supplies are available when and where needed, nursing will decrease routine overstocking and stockpiling in rooms and closets.

Second, have the number of job classes interacting with patients been streamlined? Increasing job content through job enlargement should result in fewer full-time equivalent (FTE) personnel in the hospital infrastructure. For example, registered nurses can perform basic respiratory treatments (eliminating or decreasing the number of respiratory technicians); Leann Strasen (1989, 34) confirmed the downsizing of a respiratory therapy department from 17 to 5.4 FTEs. In another example, registered nurses and house staff assumed responsibility for starting intravenous lines, rather than a separate IV therapy nurse.

Third, have coordination and effectiveness of hospital departmental functions been improved from the patient's point of view? If the amount of time spent scheduling, documenting, transporting, and coordinating different components of patient care can be decreased, financial savings can result from fewer FTEs and better and more appropriate utilization of remaining staff. The costs of these coordinating functions can be as much as 30–40 percent of total personnel costs (Hanrahan 1991, 33).

Thus, four future work redesign trends in work content and environmental context are the following:

1. Patient care functions and personnel will be decentralized to physically larger patient care units, decreasing the time coordinating care and increasing both direct patient contact and staff responsibilities.

2. Centralized departments like human resources, admitting, and information systems will be reorganized to better support patient care personnel and functions, improving both efficiency and effectiveness.

3. Automation will be increasingly important for rapid access to patient information, leading to improved utilization of resources and clinical decision making. Mowry and Korpman (1987, 11) estimate that 1.5 hours per nursing staff member per shift could be saved by using appropriate information technology.

4. Patient care will be "protocol driven" as in case management, eliminating unnecessary patient days and reducing length of stay.

Education and Training Costs

Work redesign efforts usually involve the cross-training of current employees to enlarge their jobs as well as educating other workers affected by the redefined responsibilities. The most common method is on-the-job training using current teaching resources or hiring consultants to perform this activity. A possible alternative is seeking preestablished training courses at an educational institution such as a community college.

Analysis of financial investment for training must include the full salary (direct and indirect) costs of those performing the education (in-house or consultants) and employees attending the meetings, in-services, and skills laboratory workshops. Work redesign benefits can then demonstrate that these costs may be easily offset by the savings. The cross-trained employee is viewed as a corporate asset, worthy of the organization's long-term investment.

Three reports of training resource hours provide different examples for the amount of investment required. In a differentiated practice work redesign, Koerner et al. (1989, 19) tallied training costs to be 6.4 hours of in-service specific to the project and 8.6 hours of associated documentation streamlining required per staff member.

Kirby and Garfink (1991, 27–28) report using a formal eight-week training program for the introduction of nurse extenders, including 100 hours of learning lab and 180 hours of clinical experience. The RNs who functioned as partners for the nurse extenders attended an eight-hour workshop to discuss role orientation.

Vanderbilt University Hospital estimated their work redesign cross-training costs to total about $70,000 (Urmy 1991). These costs were believed to be easily supported by an approximate 9 percent institutionwide reduction in staff.

So while work redesign education costs require planning consideration and tabulation, experiences gained from several models of work redesign justify the financial costs based on the excellent return on investment. Budgeting for training costs is important for financial planning; but it also legitimizes the organizational value of work redesign.

Ancillary Staff: Analysis of the Trend

The growing shortage of health care professionals such as registered nurses, physical therapists, occupational therapists, and pharmacists has led to an increase in the use of ancillary support staff. Many institutions have redistributed certain patient care and unit environment responsibilities to less skilled and less expensive nonprofessional employees.

Prescott et al. (1991, 27) note that reducing only 20 percent of the inefficiencies in information flow—charting routines and reassigning certain aspects of unit management to others—can save approximately 48 minutes per RN per shift. This time can be spent coordinating care properly so that length of stay is reduced through interdisciplinary collaboration, discharge planning, and patient education.

For example, in 1989 Mercy Hospital and Medical Center in Chicago developed the role of "clinical partner" to assist the registered nurse. These 75 partners in patient care, or nurse extenders, were formerly licensed practical nurses, nursing assistants or respiratory therapists or had held several other job titles before being cross-trained. Basic clinical functions such as phlebotomy, starting IVs and performing EKGs were added to the role of the nurse and her partner. In addition, therapies (physical, speech, occupational) were moved to the patient care unit, avoiding the cost and inconvenience of transporting the patient to a centralized location.

Significant financial benefits for Mercy have definitely accrued through the reduction of labor expenses and decreased patient length of stay. Mercy's receipt of a $1 million Pew Charitable Trust/Robert Wood Johnson Foundation grant reinforced the importance of work redesign to the board of directors and the community (Eubanks and Grayson 1991, 27).

Three other successful nurse extender programs have quantified cost benefits. Alta Bates Herrick Hospital in Berkeley, California, estimates personnel savings of $32,000 per year for each patient care assistant position. Total decrease in labor costs for 1990 were estimated at greater than $1.3 million. HCA-West Paces Ferry (Atlanta, Georgia) discovered that 44 percent of the activities formerly performed by an RN could be delegated to a general medical technician (Hanrahan 1991, 34).

As illustrated in Figure 6.2, the Illinois Hospital Association (1991) piloted the Patient Assistant Liaison (PAL) program in nine hospitals. Results indicated a significant benefit in increased nursing care hours per patient.

Although ancillary workers cannot replace professional staff, they can help increase the effectiveness and efficiency of patient care. Restrictions due to professional practice acts, state laws, recruitment market conditions, and

Figure 6.2   Nurses at Nine Illinois Hospitals Had More Time Available for Nursing Care after Nonnursing Helpers (PALs) Were Added

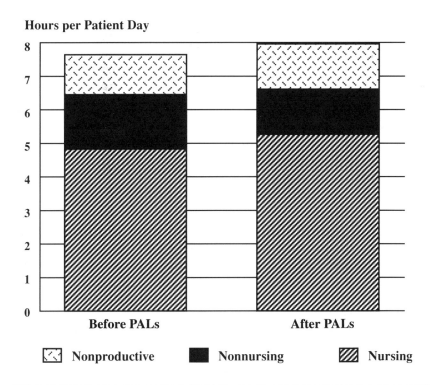

Source: Illinois Hospital Association.

educational/experience credentials should be considered when evaluating job duties that may be delegated to ancillary workers.

Improved Quality of Care: Financial Impact

"Scholars have suggested a possible relationship between the quality of nursing care and the work environment of nurses" (Farley and Nyberg 1990, 534). As the work content and environment or context for patient care is redesigned, improvements in the patient care quality can be documented and translated into economic benefits (Zander 1988, 24; Ethridge and Lamb 1989, 33–34).

How do the quality measurements equal positive financial results? In one experiment (Cohen 1991, 22–24), improved coordination and collaboration using nursing case management work redesign resulted in decreased length of stay (1.16 days per case), lower cost per case for 1,177 cases (total annual savings of more than $1 million), and opportunity for increased revenues due to more rapid patient turnover (potential additional revenues of greater than $1.3 million).

A similar revenue impact was derived using a different type of work redesign. ProACT® is a model that combines the benefits of case management and the expanded use of nurse extenders and RNs who function as a team. Brett and Tonges (1990, 42) estimated that 105 potential added admissions could generate more than $700,000 in additional revenues with the ProACT model of patient care delivery. What appear to be intangible or immeasurable results of work redesign can be quantified for financial analysis of net savings.

Impact on Nurse Retention

Over the past decade, it has become clear that nurses are unhappy with the myriad of nonprofessional clerical, housekeeping, transportation, and record-keeping duties that fell to them by default when hospitals downsized in the post-prospective-payment era. Hay Group research confirms that the current staff nurse job design emphasizes nonprofessional tasks; this leads to dissatisfaction and psychological burnout, promoting turnover (Henderson and Williams 1991, 47).

Basic financial indicators to evaluate professional nurse retention should be collected prior to beginning a work redesign effort. These measures can be compared during and after organizational changes are implemented. It is recommended that at least annual comparisons be collected for the following:

- RN turnover rate
- RN vacancy rate
- Recruitment advertising and marketing expenditures
- RN length of employment (job tenure) by job class
- Promotion from within hospital (percent)
- RN job satisfaction
- RN supplemental staffing utilization (FTEs and cost of agency, registry, and per diem staff)
- Management-to-staff ratio

The financial impact due to improved nurse retention can be examined through the administrative work redesign associated with implementing nursing shared governance. McDonagh (1990, 243–44) cites the experiences of three hospitals—Henry Ford in Detroit, MacNeal in metropolitan Chicago, and Saint Joseph's in Atlanta—in reducing RN turnover through the redesign process. In the years 1986–89, positive efforts decreased turnover from 30 to 14 percent; 50 to 14 percent; and 44 to 14 percent, respectively, for the three hospitals.

Recent estimates of the cost impact of RN turnover in the United States are as high as $20,000 per RN (Curran and Miller 1990, 538). This estimate included the costs of staff replacement, advertising, outplacement, and orientation. Evaluating the number of nurses who did not leave the organization is an important financial indicator of successful work redesign. If 25 nurses whose job dissatisfaction would have caused them to resign, remain with your hospital due to work redesign, the cost avoidance can equal $500,000.

Thus, the financial cost-benefit analysis for a work redesign effort should capture the indicators cited above regarding nurse retention. As Benner and Benner (1991, 74) note, "High turnover is extremely inefficient—the height of poor human resource and financial management."

Gains in Efficiency and Effectiveness

Health care delivery systems in the United States require serious revision for improved patient care. Indeed, the following statistics provide sobering substantiation that work redesign is desperately needed:

- Only 24 percent of nursing staff efforts are spent in patient care (McDonagh 1991).
- Greater than 50 percent of what RNs do has nothing to do with nursing (Hanrahan 1991, 37).

- No fewer than 105 hospital personnel (not including nurses, doctors, or housekeeping staff) are involved in a single patient's care during a 6-day stay (Weber 1991, 29).
- A typical 500-bed hospital has more than 500 job classes with an average of 6 employees per class (Hanrahan 1991, 33).

Let's further examine several instances where work redesign has resulted in improved efficiency and effectiveness of patient care delivery.

The ProACT work redesign model documented a 26 percent decrease in patient length of stay (Weber 1991, 30); a 4 percent increase in hours of direct care for patients; a 7 percent decrease in the actual costs per total hours of care; and a 3 percent decrease in actual labor costs per patient day (Brett and Tonges 1990, 41).

Saint Joseph Mercy Hospital (Pontiac, Michigan) found that while work redesign may or may not increase revenues, it can significantly decrease costs. Their chief financial officer estimated that a 1 percent drop in the cost per case could result in a $1.5 million savings per year. Their early work redesign results over the first 18 months included an investment of about $200,000 and an actual decrease of 5 percent hospitalwide in patient length of stay (Eubanks and Grayson 1991, 32).

A pilot unit at Lakeland Regional Medical Center (Lakeland, Florida) discovered that decentralizing laboratory services resulted in a decrease in results reporting turnaround time, from 157 minutes to 48 minutes. Simplifying the work process in diagnostic radiology, from 40 different steps consuming 140 minutes to 8 steps taking 28 minutes, significantly accelerated clinical decision making. Clinical nursing activities increased from 21 percent of the nursing staff's time to 53 percent, while direct care costs decreased 9.2 percent (Weber 1991, 25).

Another hospital's experience with a case management model of work redesign proves interesting. If length of stay can be reduced for patients whose reimbursement is prospective or limited, a reduction in patient charges can indicate improved profitability. From 1989–90, Southwest Community Health System and Hospital in Middleburg Heights, Ohio, was able to reduce total patient charges by $376,975 for its 15,079 discharges—an average reduction of $25 charge per case (Larter 1992).

To quantify how much savings or cost avoidance is involved, you can multiply the results of the actual minutes or hours of personnel time saved times their actual salary dollars. The administrator can then derive financial estimates gained with more effective use of personnel resources or possible staff FTE reductions.

Financial Indicators: Key in Evaluating Work Redesign

Basic Financial Management Concepts

There are entire books filled with financial equations and calculations that could be performed to help analyze the financial viability of any program. In analyzing work redesign, it should be approached from every angle that can make any kind of difference. Every idea should be looked at to determine its financial benefits or restrictions on the hospital.

To make the best management decisions, it is important to know the data that are available, and what they mean within your organization. Data come in a variety of different reports. Can the data you get support work redesign? Can the data be retrieved easily enough to make the analysis meaningful? Table 6.3 lists some key data that should be looked at first. All of these items are basic for a financial analysis. Not all of them will be valuable when you reach the end of your analysis; however, they should be considered for their appropriateness.

The important part of getting started is finding the data. Some items are easy to track down and find, while others may be harder or even nonexistent. This should not stop the process, however. Continue to explore other avenues of getting the necessary information. The goal may be achievable using other sources of data. One example is time studies. Many hospitals do not have formalized management engineering personnel who analyze the employees' tasks and how long it takes them to do those tasks. If not, you should begin by analyzing the basic elements of each position (if it is key to the redesign). List the major tasks the person performs, estimate the time it takes to do

Table 6.3 Key Data Elements for Work Redesign Analysis

Statistical	*Revenue*	*Expense*
Volume	Charge structure	Salary dollars
• admissions	• room rate	Employee benefits
• patient days	• additional charges	Supplies
• length of stay	• nursing time	Professional fees
• visits	• other operating	Bad debt
Time studies	Payer mix	Other expenses
• nursing	Revenue deductions	Salary comparisons
• nonnursing	Charity care	Procedural cost data
• ancillary professionals		
• support staff		

each, and then you can determine how much it costs to do those tasks by exploring the payroll records for this job.

After you have collected the data, you will need to begin analyzing work redesign for its financial viability. There are a number of financial management tools that can help. Probably the most effective and widely used analytical tool is a cost-benefit analysis. This analysis takes a look at all the financial implications of a program and groups them into either a benefit to the hospital or a cost. The data you have gathered can then be structured into a program profit and loss format. Exhibit 6.1 shows the basic format of a profit and loss statement.

This format is not designed to be final. Each hospital has its own form of profit and loss statement (sometimes called an "income statement").

Exhibit 6.1   Profit and Loss Format

Revenues		
Inpatient revenue	$100,000	
Outpatient revenue	1,000	
Total revenue		101,000
Contractual adjustments		
Contractual discounts	5,000	
Charity care	500	
Total adjustments		5,500
Net revenue		95,500
Other operating revenue	0	
Total revenue		95,500
Expenses		
Salaries and wages	50,000	
Employee benefits	9,000	
Supplies (office and medical)	2,000	
Professional fees	5,000	
Bad debt	500	
Insurance	1,000	
Utilities	500	
Other expenses	1,000	
Total expenses		69,000
Contribution margin		26,500

Items can be added or subtracted from this format to meet your hospital's needs.

Other financial indicators are the break-even analysis, net present value computation, payback analysis, and internal rate of return calculation. Each of these tools can be valid in helping a hospital make better management decisions. However, some of these concepts may not be applicable or necessary in all situations. We can now evaluate some more details regarding each of these indicators.

Standard Financial Indicators

Looking at financial data is really no different from sitting down and reading a story. This story, however, typically contains an extensive series of numbers and calculations. Don't look at the numbers as if they were a 4,000-page book. Instead, look at the numbers to determine the story they are trying to tell you. It is easy to pick up on key elements in a financial analysis. You will just need to know where to look.

We will concentrate the rest of this section largely on understanding how to come up with a cost-benefit analysis. The rest of the analyses and calculations become much easier to find if you understand how to properly assemble the data.

Cost-benefit analysis

The terms "cost" and "benefit" are used as generic terms in a cost-benefit analysis. "Costs" are considered additional expenses that the hospital would incur under work redesign. Costs may also be seen as a reduction of revenues. If, through work redesign, you determine that you should no longer charge patients for a particular service, this would be an example of a reduction of revenue or cost of the program. "Benefits" are increases in revenues or reduction in expenses. Obviously, altering the same number of FTEs from all registered nurses to a combination of registered nurses and nurse extenders should save the hospital salary dollars. This would be considered a benefit of this program. Finance personnel will be able to help you determine if something is a cost or benefit. The hardest part of this analysis is making sure that when you determine the changes that work redesign will have on the institution, you also determine if this change has a financial impact.

Financial impacts come in all shapes and sizes. The job is to find them. For example, work redesign may have an effect on outcomes for the patient. The patients should be receiving a different level of care that may decrease the time they spend in the hospital. This decrease in the length of stay (LOS) has financial ramifications throughout a cost-benefit analysis. There is an impact to revenues if patients are hospitalized fewer days. You will have lower gross revenues under this scenario. However, this does not necessarily mean that you will lose money with this decrease in revenue. Other aspects of revenues should also be considered. The payer mix of these patients is extremely important. If the patients leaving faster are commercial insurance patients, the hospital is genuinely losing money. However, if these patients are public aid or a variety of the fixed payers like Medicare, any HMOs or PPOs, then the hospital needs to do additional analysis to determine if they are in fact losing net revenues. Each of these fixed payers has an impact on the contractual adjustments calculated by the hospital. The difference between the charges to the patient for their stay and the amount of money the hospital receives from the third party is what is recorded in the contractual adjustments section of the income statement. If you can reduce the length of stay and charges, but you still get the same reimbursement from the payer, then decreasing LOS for these patients is a benefit to the hospital.

Work redesign will also affect your expenses. The most obvious change is a reduction in the labor costs. This change may not be as apparent if the staffing mix you propose has not changed much or you have hired three nurse extenders to take the place of one nurse. This proposed staffing mix is very important and should be analyzed completely, to make sure that patient care is still the highest priority and patients continue to get the highest possible quality of care. The expense classifications that automatically increase and decrease with labor costs are those associated with employee benefits. Typical employee benefits will consist of the taxes paid to federal and state agencies, health and dental insurance, contributions to retirement programs, and tuition reimbursement. It is estimated that employee benefits are approximately 15–20 percent of salaries, depending upon the package of benefits offered to the employees by the hospital. So, if work redesign reduces the level of salaries paid, then a reduction of employee benefits will take place as well.

Labor expense and employee benefits are the most obvious expenses to be affected. However, the analysis of work redesign should look much deeper than these two important changes. Some additional expense issues that are both costs and benefits to the program are explored in Exhibit 6.2.

You should evaluate all the aspects of the program that you wish to put together. The above are a few of the areas that hospitals may forget to think about when putting a program like work redesign in place. The potential that a system or environment change will have a financial impact on the hospital is high. If these areas are looked at and explored for that impact, you can

Exhibit 6.2   Additional Costs and Benefits to be Analyzed

Benefits

A change in the staffing mix could begin to have an impact on the professional fees of the hospital. Outside agencies are typically used when census is high and there are not enough nurses to cover the shifts. Outside agencies are very costly and any reduction in the usage of them is a benefit. This staffing mix change may allow you to call in the nurse extenders, thus reducing the outside agency coverage.

Reductions in the length of stay will create a benefit to the supply expenses. The total supply costs will decrease by the average supplies consumed by patients per day.

Increased job satisfaction will have a positive impact on reducing expenses. Recruitment and retention of registered nurses has already been cited as a potential savings of about $20,000 per nurse. These expenses consist of savings to areas like training, advertising, and especially outside agency coverage.

Costs

Initially, work redesign may also cost the hospital some money to recruit nurse extenders—not the recruitment of registered nurses, but of nurse extenders. Obviously, the expenses associated with the recruitment of nurse extenders should be lower than the saving recognized from nurse recruitment. However, the expenses associated with advertising and training for these new positions will be costly.

Another potential cost is the implementation of the program. We have talked extensively about the commitment and dedication from all levels of the organization. This time spent analyzing and implementing the program should be costed out and applied as an additional cost of the program.

The cost of implementation will also be increased in the initial start-up of a work redesign program. The potential for overlapping coverage and not fully understanding the positions of the others will take some time to work out. Take this into consideration as a cost of the program.

The hospital may also have the costs associated with attrition. Implementation of a work redesign program will change the staffing mix. A commitment to the staff that no layoffs will take place may cost or save money depending on attrition of registered nurses.

reduce the possibility of error when putting together the final profit and loss statement.

Once a cost-benefit analysis is completed, you could begin to use other financial indicators to help support the advantages of work redesign. All of these tools may be used in conjunction with the profit and loss statement that you have created through the cost-benefit analysis.

Break-even analysis

The first one we will look at is a break-even analysis. This methodology is typically used if the program you are analyzing has affected a volume statistic. Work redesign may not significantly improve revenues as much as reduce the overall expenses. In a break-even analysis, the task at hand is to target the overall impact to the hospital at zero. If you decrease the revenues, you will need to decrease the expenses to match. The contribution margin (profit or loss before applying indirect costs) of the profit and loss statement should be as close to zero as possible for a break-even analysis.

The standard break-even equation is

$$\text{Total Revenue} = \text{Total Cost}$$

or

$$\text{Revenue per Unit} \times \text{Quantity} =$$

$$\text{Fixed Costs} + (\text{Variable Cost per Unit} \times \text{Quantity})$$

When using this type of analysis, you should have an idea of which costs associated with changes in work redesign are fixed (for example, manager salary) and which are variable, or fluctuate with changes in patient census (for example, registered nurse labor dollars). The reason to use break-even analysis most likely will have to do with the staffing mix. If the proposal you put together asked for a change to 90 percent registered nurses and 10 percent nurse extenders and the cost-benefit analysis showed that the hospital would lose money, then you could look to a break-even analysis to help you consider a change to that mix. Based upon all the assumptions in the cost-benefit analysis, it may take a mix of 75 percent registered nurses and 25 percent nurse extenders to bring about a break-even situation. Two things to keep in mind are that (1) the staffing mix continues to maintain a high quality of care and (2) you have properly evaluated each assumption in the cost-benefit analysis. This would be the time and the place to check for any errors.

Net present value analysis

A net present value approach could also be adapted as a financial support item for work redesign. Typically, net present value is used to evaluate capital investment decisions. However, if your work redesign has a phased-in approach over a number of years or costs and benefits that will not occur for a while, then net present value is applicable. The point of using the net present value method is to calculate the current value of a future cash flow at a particular discount or opportunity rate.

The key to a net present value methodology is understanding the items needed to put one together and where they come from. Table 6.4 lists the necessary items and their sources.

The way you could take the information in Table 6.4 and transform it into a new present value analysis is shown in Table 6.5. This example shows that work redesign will increase the hospital contribution margin by $50,000 over three years. However, money three years from now will not

Table 6.4 Net Present Value Data Items

Data Item	Source	Example
Implementation costs	Valuation of time spent to develop the program.	$50,000
Revenue impact	Research of assumptions regarding LOS, payer mix, or any other revenue item.	$60,000 reduction
Cost impact	Research of assumptions regarding staffing mix, professional fees, and other expenses.	$160,000 reduction
Annual cash flows	Proposed profit and loss statement (contribution margin line item).	
Year 0		(50,000)
Year 1		(10,000)
Year 2		40,000
Year 3		70,000
Opportunity cost of capital	If you were to make a different investment, what rate of interest would you receive.	10%

Source: B. R. Neumann, J. D. Suver, and W. N. Zelman, *Financial Management: Concepts and Applications for Health Care Providers* (Baltimore: National Health Publishing, 1988).

be worth the same amount as it is today, so the contribution margin must be discounted to today's dollars. The discounting of these cash flows changes the contribution margin from $50,000 to $26,520. A contribution that is used in conjunction with net present value is the internal rate of return, or the discount rate at which the net present value is equal to zero (Neumann, Suver, and Zelman 1988, 439).

Payback analysis

Another method to consider is a payback analysis. Similar to the net present value method, payback is typically used to analyze a capital investment proposal. However, you can use this method with work redesign data as well. The payback analysis uses the same data as the net present value method to get the results. The goal of payback analysis is to determine the number of years it will take to pay back the original investment. Using the example in Tables 6.4 and 6.5, you should structure the payback calculation as follows:

Net Present Value

Year 0	(50,000)
Year 1	(9,090)
Year 2	33,040
Year 3	52,570
Total	76,520

To reach the $50,000 initial investment, you need to add the net present value amounts from each year until you reach $50,000. Thus, you will need all of Year 1 and all of Year 2 and still only have $23,950 of the original investment. You will still need to take $26,050 from the $52,570 in Year 3 to reach the $50,000 goal. By rounding this calculation (26,050/52,570), you get a 0.5 result. The results of the payback analysis are that it will take 2.5 years to achieve the goal of making enough to cover the original investment.

Table 6.5 Net Present Value Example

	Year 0	Year 1	Year 2	Year 3	Total
Contribution margin	(50,000)	(10,000)	40,000	70,000	50,000
Discount rate 10.0%*	1.0	0.909	0.826	0.751	
Net present value	(50,000)	(9,090)	33,040	52,570	26,520

*Values from a net present value table.

We have just taken a look at a number of financial management indicators that a hospital can use to analyze work redesign. Each of these can be used to help support the program when used in the proper way. The analysis should be as complete as possible, and should answer all the financial questions necessary to make the program of work redesign a success for everyone.

Summary

Interpretation of Measurements

Financial analysis of costs and benefits involved in work redesign is an important component of determining the program's success. This analysis is an excellent opportunity for collaboration among clinical, financial, information system, and human resource staff. Key financial estimates collected by the group include the following (McDonagh 1991):

- Retaining historical and continuing patient and personnel data bases
- Identifying and understanding costs (distinguish cost savings from cost avoidance)
- Interpreting meaning of revenue and expense variables measured
- Deciding what is the total initial investment involved (personnel training, capital acquisitions if needed)
- Quantifying long-term savings through measuring patient care standards, "ready for action" time, patient care liability costs, total salary expenses, improved utilization of professional staff, productivity, and staff retention

How does the administrator interpret the more elusive or intangible financial benefits possible from work redesign? Enhanced community reputation and the public's sense of a hospital's innovative status can result in increased patient market share and decreased staff recruitment and patient marketing costs.

Increased patient satisfaction can reduce liability problems. Lakeland reported a 4 percent increase in patient satisfaction, and fewer patient falls and medication errors in their redesigned areas (Weber 1991, 25). Improved patient care coordination no doubt increases patient satisfaction; other feasible savings accrue from diminished salary and supply costs, reduced patient length of stay and ancillary service utilization, and lower morbidity and mortality.

Higher physician satisfaction can mean more patient admissions and physician referrals. St. Vincent Hospital in Indianapolis, Indiana, reported a giant improvement in their medical staff's satisfaction with hospital services after work redesign. This improvement was no doubt due in part to the increase in nursing hours per patient day from 6.2 in the prepilot phase to 8.0 after work redesign (Weber 1991, 26).

Work redesign financial investment criteria include the following:

- Has patient length of stay decreased? Analyze the reimbursement impact based on hospital payer mix. Include the severity of illness/case mix adjustment.

- Have ancillary service charges decreased? Assess the impact on reimbursement.

- Has net loss/case decreased for any DRGs?

- Has net profit/case increased for any DRGs?

- Have physician practice patterns changed? Consider admissions, patient length of stay, use of ancillary tests.

- Have calculated costs for patients and departments changed? Include labor, supply, and capital expenses.

- Has new patient volume been accommodated without adding new expenses?

- Has market share increased in affected areas?

- Have positive impacts occurred in areas of greatest operational or financial problems?

Organizational Planning for Success

Work redesign offers substantial qualitative and quantitative benefits to the patient, the medical and hospital staff, and the organization's bottom line. Suggested steps in making certain your hospital's planning is complete include the following:

- Draft an outline for the overall work redesign program. This proposal should consider

  — description of program and objectives,

  — relationship to strategic and financial goals,

  — relevant baseline data,

  — process and procedure for implementation,

  — interdepartmental implications,

  — proposed benefits,

  — proposed costs, and

  — evaluation methodology.

- Develop a plan for financial goals to be included in the operating budget plans. Share financial savings goals with staff.
- Consider any needed compensation changes up front. Approach may include
  — pay for knowledge,
  — pay for performance,
  — skill-based pay, and
  — gain sharing or incentives for cost savings.
- Develop and revise as needed tracking mechanisms/data for interim and final points of evaluation.

It is important to recognize work redesign is a long-term investment in "doing things right" through improved efficiency and effectiveness in patient care personnel and systems.

References

Benner, R., and P. Benner. 1991. "Stories from the Front Lines." *Healthcare Forum Journal* 34 (4): 69–74.

Brett, J. L., and M. C. Tonges. 1990. "Restructured Patient Care Delivery: Evaluation of the ProACT Model." *Nursing Economics* 8 (1): 36–44.

Cohen, E. L. 1991. "Nursing Case Management: Does It Pay?" *Journal of Nursing Administration* 21 (4): 20–25.

Cunningham, J. B., and T. Eberle. 1990. "A Guide to Job Enrichment Redesign." *Personnel* 69 (2): 56–60.

Curran, C. R., and N. Miller. 1990. "The Impact of Corporate Culture on Nurse Retention." *Nursing Clinics of North America* 25 (3): 537–49.

Ethridge, P., and G. S. Lamb. 1989. "Professional Nursing Case Management Improves Quality, Access and Costs." *Nursing Management* 20 (3): 30–35.

Eubanks, P., and M. A. Grayson. 1991. "Restructuring Care: Patient Focus Is Key to Innovation." *Hospitals* 65 (15): 26–33.

Farley, M. J., and J. Nyberg. 1990. "Environment as a Major Element in Nursing Administration Practice Theory Development." *Nursing and Health Care* 11 (10): 532–35.

Hanrahan, T. F. 1991. "New Approaches to Caregiving." *Healthcare Forum Journal* 34 (4): 33–38.

Henderson, J. L., and J. B. Williams. 1991. "The People Side of Patient Redesign." *Healthcare Forum Journal* 34 (4): 44–49.

Illinois Hospital Association. 1991. "Report on Patient Assistant Liaison (PAL) Program." Warrenville, IL: Illinois Hospital Association.

Kirby, K. K., and C. M. Garfink. 1991. "The University Hospital Nurse Extender Model: Part I, An Overview and Conceptual Framework." *Journal of Nursing Administration* 21 (1): 25–30.

Koerner, J. G., L. B. Bunkers, B. Nelson, and K. Santema. 1989. "Implementing Differentiated Practice: The Sioux Valley Hospital Experience." *Journal of Nursing Administration* 19 (2): 13–20.

Larter, J. 1992. "Patient Charges 1989 and 1990." Unpublished data, personal communication. Southwest Community Health System and Hospital, Middleburg Heights, OH.

McDonagh, K. J. 1990. "The Financial Impact of Nursing Shared Governance." In *Nursing Shared Governance: Restructuring for the Future*, edited by K. J. McDonagh, 239–61. Atlanta, GA: K. J. McDonagh and Associates.

McDonagh, K. J. 1991. "Gold Medal Investment: The Financial Impact of Nursing Shared Governance." Paper presented at Saint Joseph's Hospital of Atlanta's conference, "The Olympic Challenge: Creating Models of Excellence through Organizational Design," Atlanta, GA, October.

Mowry, M., and R. Korpman. 1987. "Evaluating Automated Information Systems." *Nursing Economics* 5 (1): 7–12.

Neumann, B. R., J. D. Suver, and W. N. Zelman. 1988. *Financial Management: Concepts and Applications for Health Care Providers.* Baltimore, MD: National Health Publishing.

Prescott, P. A., C. Y. Phillips, J. W. Ryan, K. O. Thompson. 1991. "Changing How Nurses Spend Their Time." *IMAGE: The Journal of Nursing Scholarship* 23 (1): 23–28.

Strasen, L. 1989. "Redesigning Patient Care to Empower Nurses and Increase Productivity." *Nursing Economics* 7 (1): 32–35.

Urmy, N. B. 1991. "Sharing the Future of Healthcare: The Vanderbilt Experience." Paper presented at Saint Joseph's Hospital of Atlanta's conference, "The Olympic Challenge: Creating Models of Excellence through Organizational Design," Atlanta, GA, November.

Weber, D. O. 1991. "Six Models of Patient-Focused Care." *Healthcare Forum Journal* 34 (4): 23–31.

Zander, K. 1988. "Nursing Case Management: Strategic Management of Cost and Quality Outcomes." *Journal of Nursing Administration* 18 (5): 23–30.

7

WORK REDESIGN: GETTING READY
FOR AND DEALING WITH THE CHANGE

M. Gibby Kinsey, Vickie Mullins Moore,
and Marilyn Dubree

Changing things can be fun—and successful—sometimes! More often than not, however, change efforts fail because people really don't "sign up" or commit to the change. It's tough. There's no doubt about it! And, it's tough because people hang on to old habits and old behaviors long past their usefulness. For example, James A. Belasco (1990), author of *Teaching the Elephant to Dance*, asserts that "organizations are like elephants—they're slow to change." They both learn through conditioning. Trainers shackle young elephants with heavy chains to deeply embedded stakes. In that way the elephant learns to stay in its place. Older elephants never try to leave even though they have the strength to pull the stake and move beyond. Their conditioning limits their movements with only a small metal bracelet around their foot—attached to nothing. So, like powerful elephants, many companies, including hospitals, are bound by earlier conditioned constraints. "We've always done it this way" is as limiting to an organizations's progress as the unattached chain around the elephant's foot.

Project Management

Work redesign and the resultant changes that occur throughout the organization are so pervasive and all encompassing that it is important to manage a project of this magnitude with great care. If such a fundamental and radical change process is not well planned and implemented from the start, it can result in organizational chaos.

Belasco (1990) maintains that the single thread that runs through all of his "success" stories regarding change—and correspondingly is absent in most of his "failures" related to change—is the involvement of large numbers of individuals in drafting the vision. Multidisciplinary and multifunctional-level teams empower people to understand and to support the vision. It is important to design a project team for work redesign plans that include a variety of staff and incorporates the vast array of tasks that need to be completed in a collegial fashion.

The project structure for the redesign efforts at Saint Joseph's Hospital of Atlanta (SJHA) is displayed in Figure 7.1. The SJHA project was recently renamed from "operational restructuring," "work redesign," or "job redesign" to "patient-centered systems." The change was made because the term "operational restructuring" was never understood by the majority of staff; the terms "work redesign" and "job redesign" conjured up all kinds of thoughts in the minds of our employees, including loss of their jobs, that resulted in needless fear. So, the collective decision was made that the name of the project should more appropriately reflect the vision to create a patient-centered environment. The staff also wanted to convey the message that these efforts would reach beyond the patient unit level and would involve the entire hospital and beyond into the system's continuum of care efforts. And, finally, the staff wanted to convey that this project is really a journey rather than a destination and that a philosophy of continuous quality improvement or a systems approach is the underlying premise of this process. Each of the groups in the project organizational structure are described as follows.

Council for Patient-Centered Systems

The Council for Patient-Centered Systems is the final clearinghouse or decision-making body for the project. The functions of this group are broad and strategic in nature and include the following:

1. Develop the goals and objectives for the project including the time-table for implementation.
2. Evaluate the "success" of the project and communicate to appropriate others, such as the hospital board, administrative staff, department directors, staff, and others.
3. Address human resource issues and establish appropriate policies related to the project.
4. Ensure appropriate communications to all concerned; members function as "key communicators" regarding the project.
5. Receive information and recommendations from other groups; make decisions regarding certain patient-centered system issues.

Figure 7.1 Patient-Centered Systems Project Structure at Saint Joseph's Hospital of Atlanta

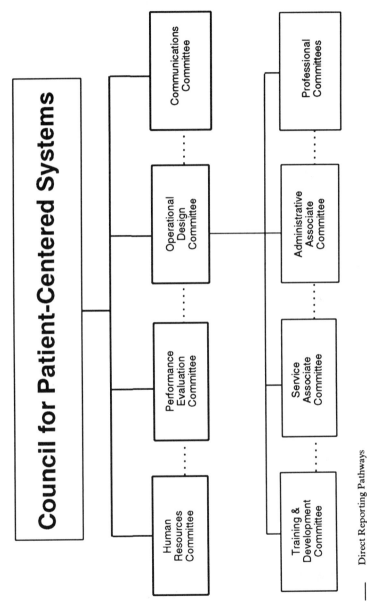

Membership on this committee is multidisciplinary, cross-functional, and multilevel and includes administrative and management staff as advisory members and various staff members from work redesign pilot units and other support departments.

Operational Design Committee

The Operational Design Committee reports to the council for patient-centered systems and is the working group for the project; its primary charge is to develop and operationalize the model. Because of this mission, this committee is also very large and is multidisciplinary, cross-functional, and, to a lesser extent, multilevel. This group consists only of staff personnel and department director level personnel. Administrative participation is in an ex officio or advisory capacity only.

Service Associate Committee, Administrative Associate Committee, and Professional Committees

The Service Associate Committee, Administrative Associate Committee, and Professional Committees are responsible for the development, implementation, ongoing evaluation, and revision of the various roles in the model. Each group reports to the Operational Design Team. Membership on each committee varies but is large in number and consists primarily of staff-level personnel.

Training and Development Committee

The Training and Development Committee is responsible for all aspects of training and development related to the project and also reports to the Operational Design Team.

Performance and Evaluation Committee

The Performance and Evaluation Committee is led by the director of Management Engineering; it has a reporting relationship to the Operational Design Team, but is directly responsible to the Council for Patient-Centered Systems. The charge of this group is to identify the variables related to cost, service, quality, and satisfaction that should be evaluated to determine the success of the model; to establish the methodology by which each variable will be measured; and to submit written evaluative documents on a monthly basis to the council.

Human Resources Committee

The charge of the Human Resources Committee is to identify potential human resource issues as a result of the changes in the organization and to address them proactively. In addition to the staff on this committee, the advisor to this group is an organizational development psychologist affiliated with the Employee Assistance Program. Like the Performance and Evaluation Committee, this group has a reporting relationship to the Operational Design Team but is directly accountable to the council.

Communications Committee

The primary function of the Communications Committee is to ensure that a formal, written internal and external communications plan is developed and implemented; that communication is timely and consistent; and that communication regarding the project reaches all of those concerned. This committee is led by the assistant vice president of Marketing Communications. Membership on this group is large and consists of staff, department head, and administrative level personnel. This group also has a reporting relationship to the Operational Design Team but is directly accountable to the council.

Steps toward Implementation

Four of the initial functions of the Council for Patient-Centered Systems will be to

1. develop the mission statement for the project;
2. develop the clinical imperatives for the project;
3. establish a model that is a fit strategically, culturally, financially, operationally, and legally; and
4. develop a formal, written internal and external communications plan.

Development of Mission Statement

Once the structure for the project including the key participants has been identified, the next step is to develop an institutional vision consistent with the mission and philosophy of the organization. If the organization has a clearly defined mission statement, it is essential that the leadership review that document and incorporate it into any mission statement for operational restructuring. Generally speaking, the mission statement will clearly define what the organization hopes to accomplish through restructuring. The mission statement should include the purpose and objectives that are expected to be followed in designing, implementing, and evaluating the restructuring effort.

If the primary reason for an organization to initiate a restructuring effort is financially driven, the objectives outlined in the mission statement will clearly reflect the objectives the leadership of the institution hopes to achieve. The criteria for evaluation of the success of the project will largely be financially based and the efforts of the team will be focused on achieving the financial impact outlined in the mission statement.

If the primary reason for restructuring is to improve staff, patient, and physician satisfaction and the organization is in a position where financial considerations are not all encompassing, the mission statement will look quite different in purpose and objectives, although the design and methods of implementation may look very similar.

Development of Clinical Imperatives

Clinical imperatives are the guiding principles upon which the patient-focused health care delivery model should be based (Exhibit 7.1). Of course, the clinical imperatives must be consistent with the mission statement and overall philosophy of the practice environment. The clinical imperatives should address quality, service, satisfaction, and cost to ensure that the overall objectives can be specifically defined.

Quality imperatives should reflect how excellence in patient care will be achieved or maintained. The specified or desired care delivery model should be stated in the clinical imperatives along with the composition of the care delivery team. This, of course, will be dependent upon the unique needs of the patients on each unit. Training requirements for members of the teams will be outlined to ensure staff are qualified for their expanded roles. Responsibilities for establishing standards of care and monitoring to ensure compliance should also be contained in the clinical imperatives.

The clinical imperatives should reflect service standards and a method for how they will be achieved and measured. Levels of service satisfaction for all constituents—patients, staff, and physicians—should also be included.

Any economic objectives should be stated in the clinical imperatives and should be considered as the model design and implementation schedule are created. As all of the imperatives for the project are stated, they become a cornerstone for development of the model to be implemented.

The mission statement, clinical imperatives, and model that is developed will evolve from the assessment of the organization and must fit the

Exhibit 7.1   Clinical Imperatives at SJHA

Clinical Imperatives

The following are the Clinical Imperatives or the guiding principles upon which the Patient-Focused Health Care Delivery Model should be implemented:

Quality of Care

We will preserve and maintain excellence in patient care.

Every patient will have a primary nurse.

Every effort will be made to ensure continuity of patient care.

Every effort will be made to minimize the number of health care workers with whom the patient comes in contact.

The individual composition of the teams will be dependent upon the unique needs of the patients on each unit and, therefore, could vary among units.

Each team member will be considered unique and of vital importance to the team and every effort should be made to convey this message to each member of the team.

Team members will be expected to perform those tasks for which they have been adequately trained.

Every effort will be made to utilize the knowledge and skills of the professional health care worker at the appropriate level in the most cost effective manner possible.

Those tasks deemed to be shareable will indeed be shared as appropriate among the members of the team, recognizing that each level of each job category has a primary function.

Members of the team will negotiate daily regarding the tasks to be completed on a given shift.

The functional department (i.e., nursing, radiology, respiratory therapy) will have responsibility for setting and monitoring quality goals.

Adequate training and ongoing education will be provided to ensure highly qualified staff.

Service

A collaborative approach between the unit and the central department will be employed to set service goals; the hospital-wide Quality Assurance Committee will approve final form.

Every effort will be made to achieve maximum efficiency.

Continued

Exhibit 7.1   Continued

The focus for the service provided to patients and physicians will be to continually improve the process by which the service is provided.

Satisfaction

SJHA will continue to measure, to the greatest extent possible, satisfaction of staff, physicians, and patients and will respond appropriately to findings.

Cost

The goal will be to control costs—rather than to decrease costs.

Overall

An ongoing evaluation of the patient-focused job redesign model will be implemented and maintained and will include a comprehensive assessment of variables related to service, quality, satisfaction, and cost.

organization. It cannot be said strongly enough, or too often, that one model will not fit every organization. A consultant who would attempt to "sell" a defined model to an organization, without taking into consideration the organization's strategic plan, culture, financial position, operational climate, and the legal and regulatory restrictions of the state, would be dooming the restructuring effort to failure. A patient-focused program that lacks fit in any one of these dimensions is weakened, but one that lacks fit on several of these dimensions is doomed (Leander 1992b).

Design of the Model

Strategic Fit

When developing a model, the strengths of the organization must be considered as well as the weaknesses. The competition must be defined and the model developed in such a way as to provide the organization any competitive advantage in the marketplace. A strategic fit must be accomplished as defined by case mix, specialty services, patient type, demand and competition for services, and medical staff composition.

Cultural fit

In order to ensure the model will fit with the organizational culture, the culture must first be determined and its strength assessed. According to Edgar

Schein (1990, 111), "Culture is defined as a pattern of basic assumptions, invented, discovered or developed by a given group, as it learns to cope with its problems of external adaptation and internal integration, and that has worked well enough to be considered valid and, therefore is taught to new members as the correct way to perceive, think, and feel in relation to those problems." The culture of an organization has everything to do with the people who make it up. The strength of the culture is a function of the stability of the group, the length of time the group has worked together, and the positive reinforcement or avoidance conditioning that has taken place as the group has dealt with problems or change in the past (Schein 1990). There may be cultural biases that need to be identified and overcome. Dysfunctional elements of the organization may also be present that will impede the acceptance of the changing environment. Regardless of the model designed or implemented, it will probably offer the most intense change the members of the organization will experience as a group. The reaction to this process will be a result of the culture of the organization, and its success will be largely dependent upon how effectively the leaders in the organization can ensure that the value system is maintained while the desired cultural changes are produced.

Financial fit

The financial position of the organization must be assessed, and model development and implementation must be consistent with the financial objectives and return on the investment that the organization must achieve with the restructuring effort. These economic objectives must be clearly outlined in the clinical imperatives to ensure that the evaluation of the project will include them as one of the measurements of success.

An organization looking to a restructuring effort as a short-term fix to a narrowing operating margin is not going to find a financial fit with any model, however. A critical mass of the patient units must be restructured in order to begin to see any significant operating efficiencies and reduction in the cost of providing care. The critical mass will vary in institutions, depending upon size, method of care delivery, extent of service deployment, staffing levels, and other factors. There is a significant financial commitment initially before any cost savings can be expected to be achieved. As a result, not only the design, but the implementation strategies and speed with which implementation occurs must fit with the financial position of the organization.

Operational fit

The design of a hospital's patient-focused model is based to a great extent upon the levels and mixes of patient demand for care and services, which vary across institutions (Leander 1992b). The way in which these services are currently being provided must be taken into account before a model can be developed to restructure the delivery in the future. The physical plant, current care delivery model, steps that have already been taken to stream-line departmental operations or improve services, and existing operational policies and practices should be evaluated as the model is designed.

Leaders in the organization must not lose sight of the operational effi-ciencies that exist already or be too quick to discount new ideas for changing traditional operational practices to achieve greater efficiencies. Opportunities to improve central departmental operations are often overlooked in the quest for designing the most efficient model for the patient care units. The entire organization should expect to look for opportunities within each department to streamline and improve operational efficiencies and customer satisfaction since not all services will be deployed to the patient unit.

Legal fit

Licensure laws, practice acts, and regulations vary from state to state. It is imperative that the licensure and regulatory restrictions of the state be thoroughly investigated and understood as the model is being designed. For example, it may be permissible for an unlicensed person to conduct radiographic procedures in one state, but another state may regulate that practice to a licensed radiology technologist. To develop a model that allows unlicensed personnel to take simple radiographs on the patient unit, spend time and money to train staff and build a radiology suite, only to learn that the state regulations governing that practice are prohibitive, would be very foolish indeed.

Communication Management

Internal communication

Although it may appear a monumental feat to ensure that the designed model has an organizational fit, the greater challenge by far is to gain the acceptance and ownership of the restructuring effort by the entire organization. The very essence of the program is contrary to the traditional way hospitals have operated and how people have worked and managed within them. Regardless of the model designed, initial resistance to the concept from all levels of the organization can be expected.

An understanding of the change process, resistance to change, and steps to gain acceptance to change is important to achieve since restructuring will probably generate the most radical change that staff in an organization will undergo in their professional careers in health care. Consequently, it is imperative that goals and strategies for communication management be developed, including who will communicate, to whom the communication will go, how information will be communicated, how often the communication will occur, and how consistency of the communication will be maintained.

Written goals and strategies for both internal and external communication should be developed. Due to the sensitivity of this type of project with various professional groups, the external plan should include a press release for the media as the project begins and guidelines on how often to release new information, who will communicate with external sources about the project, and what information will be included in any communication externally. Since questions may come from media about the project, it is important for the hospital communications department to have an understanding of the project so they can relate information accurately.

An important point related to restructuring is that there is a great deal of ambiguity in the initial stages of the project. As the project team sorts through design questions, not all the answers are apparent from the start. Because of the need to ensure that the model is congruent with the organization, the specific details that staff may request as to how jobs may be changed, what services may change in the way they are provided, and how that will occur may not be determined until later on in the design phase of the project. This ambiguity may understandably cause more than a little concern to staff accustomed to having plans presented to them with all of the details included. Depending upon the involvement of staff in decision making in the organization historically and the amount of time it takes to make decisions about these very important issues, the answers may not be forthcoming for some months into the project. This continued lack of answers to frequently asked questions can create anxiety when staff suspect that decisions have been made, but not communicated with all members of the organization. If there is one universal message for administrators of organizations undergoing operational restructuring, it is to communicate, communicate, communicate. Just when you think you have reached every person in the organization with the correct information, it is time to start communicating all over again. There can never be enough communication about the project at any level in the organization. Even when you don't feel like you have anything to say except "we don't have the answers to that question yet," it is communication that must occur over and over again.

Some recommendations for goals and strategies identified in the communication plan are as follows:

• Establish trust between staff and the leaders of the project by ensuring open communication of information at all levels in the organization.

- Ensure that timely, accurate information is distributed in a uniform and consistent manner.
- Establish and publish the mechanism by which decisions are made.
- Identify "key communicators" of information.
- Establish a mechanism by which the effectiveness of the communication strategies can be evaluated and make alterations in the strategies as indicated.

Once the plan is established, decisions as to the type and format of communication can be made, such as what collateral materials will be developed and made available to staff. An assessment should first take place of publications already in circulation to hospital staff that could be used to communicate information about operational restructuring. Whom does this publication reach and how widely is it read? Following that assessment, additional publications may be required to ensure that information about the project is widely circulated.

Verbal communication of information by consistent sources that are accurate and timely is a key element to ensuring that all people receive the same information at or about the same time. Forums for communicating information to staff may vary from hospital to hospital, but could include staff meetings, open employee meetings, in-service education programs, and telephone hotlines for staff to ask questions and receive answers.

Regardless of the forum used, information that should be made available to staff includes the reasons hospitals throughout the country need to consider restructuring and the specific objectives the institution will hope to achieve as a result of their specific program. The degree of involvement of the staff in designing the model will certainly affect how much information they will require and how quickly they will need to be informed. However, since this project can be fraught with many misconceptions and misinterpretations at all levels of the organization, it is prudent to ensure that sufficient information is available from the start to prevent as much anxiety and resistance as possible.

The nursing staff at Saint Joseph's Hospital of Atlanta are empowered to make decisions affecting their professional practice through a professional practice model of shared governance. In the initial stages of the restructuring effort, staff input was sought, and the established councils for professional practice, education, and quality assessment were kept informed of progress of the program at monthly council meetings.

A detailed assessment of the program showed clearly that the nursing council membership felt that more formal nursing input was desirable, and the leadership of the project was able to make the suggested changes in the design team membership to include more staff involvement. This change required that the new members of the group be educated to a level where they were able to be informed participants in the decision-making team. Educational programs were scheduled on a weekly basis to include topics such as changes in reimbursement for hospitals; increases in the cost of providing care; structural inefficiencies inherent in traditional hospital operations; shortages of health care professionals; trends in patient statistics, such as length of stay, age, and acuity; and consumer demands requiring changes in the delivery of care. Current literature was provided to the group for their reading and sharing with coworkers. Although the staff were very involved in professional practice issues within the hospital and were knowledgeable of current trends related to these issues, they found the information on broader health care trends surprising. Staff who do not have the opportunity to be as involved in decision making and who are not as empowered will no doubt be less informed; therefore, it is important that education begin at a very basic level to prepare them to understand and accept the concepts of restructuring.

It is helpful to communicate information about other hospitals across the country involved in operational restructuring, their program status, and their experiences of success and failure. A caveat to this suggestion is to remember that no two organizations are exactly alike, and that the experiences of others should not be taken as law, but as possible alternatives.

Early on, communication from the hospital president/CEO is important to send the message to staff that top administrative staff and members of the board of directors are committed to the project. Specific information about how the power to make decisions and implement change will be delegated, who will lead the project at all levels, how the project will be managed, and the expectation of participation and cooperation is important for staff to understand. The CEO at Vanderbilt chaired the project steering committee and was closely involved with the work of the pilot. His participation was important to the project team and to the unit staff as they began the pilot planning and implementation. His continued visibility and support of restructuring has been critical in communicating his commitment to innovation in patient care.

Although the level of staff involvement will vary, it is important for the staff to hear that they will be involved in making decisions that may change the way they do their jobs. Job security is a concern to staff at all levels of the organization. Staff are troubled by the objective to provide services with fewer people involved in the steps to accomplish the task. They are understandably concerned about exactly what that may mean to them and their future employment. The degree to which they will be affected will, of course, be in part driven by the objectives the organization hopes to achieve with the restructuring effort. This information should be communicated honestly, clearly, and repeated often so that staff know what to expect from the long-term impact of the project.

Restructuring provides an opportunity for human resource staff to become actively involved in planning for staff assessment, skills training requirements for jobs that may be changed or created, and the degree of success that the employee may expect to have in achieving a higher level of accomplishment. A human resources philosophy and policy statement may be drafted and communicated to allay the anxiety staff may have about losing their jobs. This statement may discuss how employees will be assisted to acquire the skills necessary to expand their roles, how they will be assisted to move into positions that require skills for which they are not able to be trained, and how the elimination of certain positions will be accomplished should that decision be made.

Finally, since communication must be two-way to be effective, it is important for staff to know how they can get accurate answers to their questions and how, and to whom, they can communicate their concerns. They need to be made to feel secure that it is safe to express a difference of opinion or to challenge a decision. Appropriate forums need to be created so that a free expression of ideas and opinions can occur.

External communication

Even though operational restructuring is becoming more widespread within health care, the importance of communication to other health care providers, professional organizations, regulatory bodies, and colleagues cannot be over-stated. As one nursing administrator stated when asked what she considered the most important thing to consider when beginning a restructuring effort, "Be prepared to read about your hospital in the local newspaper, professional journals, hear about what you are doing from peers at local health care meetings, from the hospital association in your state, and don't be surprised if the local television station shows up on your doorstep to ask you to explain several misconceptions about this new approach to health care delivery and why your organization would consider such a radical change." Her suggestion was to take the offensive approach and to contact the professional licensing boards of the state, the state nursing association, regulatory agencies, third party payers, including those employers with whom the hospital has managed care contracts, and peers in other hospitals in the immediate area and even to develop a press release to try to give factual information to the media rather than just respond to erroneous information they may have received. Employees who may have strong negative opinions about the project may contact those they think will be able to influence or change the direction of the hospital. It is important to communicate to those external to the organization that the intention is not to attempt practice changes that are in conflict with licensing laws, practice acts, or regulations, either nationally or on a state level. Equally important to communicate is that health care costs will not be inflated by requiring professional staff to perform tasks for which they are overqualified and that a less expensive staff member could perform.

At Vanderbilt University Hospital, a proactive approach was taken in regard to communication. Contacts were made with legislators, professional associations, regulatory boards, and key stakeholders. This strategy proved helpful both externally and internally, as staff within the hospital were interested in feedback from specific groups and individuals.

Although it is impractical to think that external communication could be as extensive as the communication within the hospital, it is critical that it not be neglected. Simply updating a group that is meeting for another purpose will often encourage others to ask questions or provide an opportunity to dispel rumors. Whenever there is a forum to talk about restructuring or to utilize the concepts when problem solving with those external to the organization, seize the moment to inform and educate others.

Role Redesign

Of the multitude of challenges related to restructuring the hospital of the future, by far the most challenging of these is redesigning roles or jobs.

First of all, exactly what is "job redesign"? According to Vaughn et al. (1991), job redesign refers to the process of determining what tasks and work processes will comprise a given job or given group of interrelated jobs, and it typically involves either job enlargement or job enrichment. Job enlargement involves increasing the number of operations that an individual performs in a given job cycle at roughly the same skill level. Job enrichment, on the other hand, concerns the amount of responsibility an individual is able to exercise in the work environment. When a job is enriched, the individual assumes higher-level functions and responsibilities not previously delegated to him or her.

Hackman and Oldham (1980) focus on the following five dimensions of a job that are most applicable to enriching jobs:

1. *Skill variety.* The degree to which a job requires a variety of different skills.
2. *Task identity.* The degree to which a job requires completion of a whole or identifiable piece of work.

3. *Task significance.* The degree to which a job has a substantial impact on the lives of other people.

4. *Autonomy.* The degree to which a job provides substantial freedom, independence, and discretion.

5. *Feedback.* The degree to which carrying out the activities required by the job results in the individual obtaining direct and clear information about the effectiveness of his or her performance.

There has been much evidence that job enlargement has increased employee productivity; some types of workers find the work less monotonous and more meaningful because they experience greater variety. Other studies show that increasing job variety results in job satisfaction and better attendance. One of the main criticisms of job enlargement, however, is that it leaves the basic nature of the job unchanged.

Job enrichment increases the employee's authority, responsibility, and autonomy. Consequently, job enrichment provides greater intrinsic rewards to employees. Early work on job enrichment at AT&T and in Great Britain indicates that it significantly increased productivity and job satisfaction while reducing turnover. However, a more recent review of 30 job enrichment experiments indicates that it has a more significant influence on quality of performance than quantity of performance. One consistent finding reported by several researchers is that job enrichment will be successful only if the individual possesses a high need for achievement. If individuals are low on this need, management may want to target other employees, recruit new employees, or provide training to increase such needs before enriching a job (Vaughan and Fottler 1991).

A summary of the job redesign literature indicates that cross-training of employees is likely to be more successful under the following conditions (Vaughan et al. 1991):

1. Job enrichment is given greater emphasis than job enlargement.

2. Organizational factors such as technology present few or no constraints.

3. Middle managers are provided with appropriate inducements to support job redesign.

4. Employee compensation is increased along with the employee skills and responsibilities.

5. Job redesign is a voluntary process targeted at individuals with a high need for growth and achievement.

At Saint Joseph's Hospital of Atlanta, our goal related to redesigning roles has been to develop a model that would be personally and professionally enriching to our employees. To do that, we agreed from the very beginning that employees have certain rights that should be considered essential rights:

- The right to be needed
- The right to be involved
- The right to a covenantal relationship
- The right to understand
- The right to affect one's own destiny
- The right to be accountable
- The right to appeal
- The right to make a commitment

This position supports our philosophy of shared governance and has driven much of our decision making related to redesigning roles. However, of paramount importance is to determine what actually makes sense operationally in the organization in terms of redesigning roles, "multiskilling," or cross-training employees in patient-focused care areas. At SJHA, a variety of models was considered. Exhibit 7.2 provides a general explanation of each of these models. At one extreme is the "multiskilling" model. In this model, all patient caregivers would be trained to autonomously deliver care to their patients. This approach to providing patient-focused care is appropriate for high-volume, routine patient services that are not constrained by licensure requirements—vital signs, activities of daily living, oxygen setup, and EKG. At the other extreme, care can be provided by a unit-based "specialist," who would be decentralized to the patient care unit rather than work out of the central department (i.e., respiratory therapy or pharmacy). This particular model works best if providing the service legally requires a license or the volume of demand for that service is too low to allow a large number of nonspecialists to maintain competency (Leander 1992a).

The Saint Joseph's Hospital of Atlanta Model

At Saint Joseph's, the multiskilling model was utilized to develop and implement three new support job categories: service associate, administrative associate, and clinical associate.

Exhibit 7.2   Various Organizational Models of Work Redesign

I. Multiskilling
Cross-train all direct caregivers of every team to deliver the service to their patients.

II. Integration
   A. Team-Based
       Cross-train one direct caregiver per team or include one "specialist" (who also performs other patient care activities) within each team to deliver the service to their care team's patients only.
   B. Shift-Based
       Cross-train one direct caregiver across all teams or include one "specialist" (who also performs other patient care activities) within one team to deliver the service to all patients.

III. Decentralization
   A. Dedicated
       Base a "specialist" within the operating unit's service area to deliver the service to all patients residing on that unit only.
   B. Focused
       Same as "dedicated" except the operating unit's "specialist" also delivers the service to patients of one or more other units.

IV. Centralization
The traditional approach—a "specialist" within the central department delivers the service to the patient of all operating units.

Source: Adapted, with the permission of the Patient Focused Care Association, from W. Leander, "Dimensions of Successful Service Redeployment: Why 'Service Redeployment' Succeeds when 'Department Decentralization' Fails," *PCFA Review* (Spring 1992): 2–7.

Service associate

The service associate is a unit-based individual reporting to the director of the patient care unit who assumes some tasks and functions from a variety of centralized departments, including environmental services, food services, transportation, central supply, materials management, nursing, and other professional departments. There are three levels of this job category. One level builds on the previous one; as one moves from Level 1 to Level 3, the amount of patient care responsibilities increase significantly. For example, the Service Associate 1 spends most of his or her time performing environmental services and transportation activities; the Service Associate 2 assumes more responsibility for central supply materials management activities and begins to assume nursing assistant functions. The Service Associate 3 is a patient care technician (PCT), with an expanded role: not only does the Service Associate perform nursing duties, but this individual also performs some tasks/functions typically performed in or by the laboratory, respiratory therapy, physical therapy, radiology, and so forth. So, this individual's role is very broad and expansive. As an example, Exhibit 7.3 delineates some of the responsibilities of the Service Associate 2.

Administrative associate

The administrative associate is the clerical/administrative individual in the model. This individual assumes some tasks and functions from a multitude of departments, including admissions, medical records, patient financial services, utilization review, and department secretary. This job category originally had three levels but has been revised so that it now has only two. The Administrative Associate 1 assumes the receptionist tasks and functions along with minor tasks and functions related to medical records, utilization review, and admissions; the Administrative Associate 2, however, performs order entry via the computer as well as the more complex activities related to medical records, admissions, and utilization review. Exhibit 7.4 reveals some tasks and functions performed by the Administrative Associate 1.

The implementation of these unit-based roles has been very successful, which is not to imply that there have not been difficulties. One of the greatest advantages has been the development of roles with a built-in career ladder that allows employees the opportunity to advance for the first time in their work career. Historically, career ladders in hospitals have been reserved for professional staff, such as registered nurses, pharmacists, and physical therapists. But, at SJHA, employees who want to be part of a team as we implement patient-focused care can apply for one of these positions if they are interested and meet the qualifications. During a recent evaluation of the work redesign model, employees commented very positively on what these role changes meant to them:

> "I've never been part of a real team before. It feels good!"
> Service Associate 2, formerly a Food Services Aide, SJHA

> "A chance to move up for the first time in my life."
> Service Associate 1, formerly a Food Services Aide, SJHA

> "I like patients. Now I get to do things for them. I like that. . . . Before this, the only thing I did was pass out trays and pick them up. Now I do a lot of different things."
> Service Associate 2, formerly a Food Services Aide, SJHA

Exhibit 7.3   Selected Responsibilities of Service Associate Level 2

Percent of Time Spent	Duties of Position
5–10%	Materials Management Related Responsibilities: a. Maintains par levels of all unit stock materials. b. Maintains reasonable levels of all nonstock materials.
10–20%	Central Services Related Responsibilities: a. Inventories area where chargeable and nonchargeable patient care items are maintained, entering count on hand-held computer. b. Sends inventory count by hand-held computer per telephone/modem to Central Services and Purchasing. c. Receives supplies ordered, verifies order is correct with pick tickets accompanying supplies. d. Identifies any discrepancy for patient chargeable supplies—"Lost Charge Report," and returns to Central Services for appropriate charging. e. When equipment alarms go off, can read messages—low battery, line obstruction, low/no fluids—so can relate to nurse. If alarm indicates low fluid/water level, those needing water to function would fill reserve tank. f. Checks P.M. date of equipment and if need to be scheduled for P.M. with Bio-Engineering, can make necessary arrangements.
Continuous	Guest Related Services: Answers phone, identifying location, their name, offers assistance, answers simple questions, whether patient is in their unit or not. Can identify which nurse is caring for patient caller is referring to, and connects caller with appropriate person.
60–70%	Nursing Assistant Related Responsibilities: a. Feeds patients. b. Makes occupied and unoccupied beds. c. Takes vital signs and records in TPR book and on graphic sheet in chart. d. Performs A.M. care (assists with baths, oral care, hair care, and skin care). e. Measures intake and output and records data on graphic and I&O sheets. f. Administers enemas as directed. g. Prepares patient for scheduled radiology procedures.
5–10%	Performs all Service Level 1 responsibilities as necessary according to staffing.

Source: Saint Joseph's Hospital of Atlanta (1992).

Exhibit 7.4   Selected Responsibilities of Administrative Associate
Level 1

Duties of Position

- Performs the admission process at the unit level:
  a. Verifies patient demographic information captured in the preadmission process.
  b. Obtains appropriate consents and places the correct ID band on patients.
  c. Assists in orienting the patient to the unit environment.

- Demonstrates proficiency in using the hospital information system (i.e., entering charges, utilization of correct pathway, etc.) and knowledge of other computer systems that exist in support departments.

- Introduces the concept of "business office patient service representatives" to individual patients and answers patient's initial questions regarding the business office.

- Reviews physicians' orders for STAT orders and alerts appropriate personnel.

- Works with physicians and their assistants on completing chart deficiencies.

- Assembles charts at discharge in appropriate order for medical records department and maintains dismissal chart logs.

- Functions as a monitor tech when appropriate.

"A great opportunity for corpsmen to really get to use their knowledge and skills and to contribute."

> Administrative Associate 2, formerly Nursing Department Secretary, SJHA

"People are more tolerant of others now because they're interested in one another's roles."

> Administrative Associate 2, formerly Nursing Department Secretary, SJHA

"I've never had a patient smile on the radiology table before."

> Clinical Associate, Radiology Technologist, Vanderbilt University Hospital

"The teamwork with nursing is something I've never experienced."

> Clinical Associate, Respiratory Therapy, Vanderbilt University Hospital

The patients love meeting someone on the unit that preadmitted them on the phone."
                Administrative Associate, Vanderbilt University Hospital

Clinical associate

The clinical associate is the professional role in the model. Like the service associate and the administrative associate roles, variations of this role are in place in a number of hospitals throughout the country. Typically, certain clinical and/or technical tasks and functions are performed by some combination—depending on the patient care unit—of professionals from six disciplines: nursing, respiratory therapy, pharmacy, physical therapy/occupational therapy, radiology, and laboratory. This role was evaluated on a pilot basis for six months on a medical-surgical unit and a coronary care unit utilizing RNs, respiratory therapists, and pharmacists. Table 7.1 delineates some of the functions that were shared among these disciplines in the coronary care unit.

Although the decision was made to eliminate the role of the multi-skilled clinical associate from the model after the trial period, numerous benefits were realized from having a combination of professional disciplines work together as a team on the pilot units. Undeniably, there is great added value in having nurses, respiratory therapists, pharmacists, and other professionals all consulting each other on behalf of patients and their care. We found when these discussions and consultations are face-to-face without today's numerous intermediaries—clerks, telephones, forms, and computers—they accomplish several things: They improve the quality and timeliness of clinical planning and care; they provide more cost-effective care; plus they nurture mutual respect and appreciation among these professionals. For perhaps the first time in their careers, these professionals concentrated on what they have in common rather than on their differences.

Despite these benefits, the role of the clinical associate was eliminated from the model because these individuals were spending the majority of their time performing tasks or functions that did not require their level of education, knowledge, and skills; in many cases they were spending as much as 75 percent of their time on tasks/functions outside of their discipline rather than on those unique to their discipline. In other words, unlike the roles we developed for our service and clerical personnel, we developed a role for our professionals that represented job enlargement rather than job enrichment. Because the hospital was committed to developing a model that would be personally and professionally enriching for employees, as well as one that would be cost-effective, the decision was made to revise the role of

Table 7.1 Shareable Tasks—Clinical Associates, CCU (RN, RT, Pharm)

Responsibilities	*RN*	*RRT*	*Pharm*	*All*
1. Set up hemodynamic monitoring equipment and lines.				*
2. Maintain and troubleshoot chest tubes.	*	*		
3. Initiate defibrillation/cardioversion.				*
4. Assist with set up of intra-aortic balloon pump equipment and lines.				*
5. Data management via HP bedside monitor.				*
6. Respond to ventilator alarms and perform basic troubleshooting.				*
7. Set up and maintain aerosol, humidity, and nonventilator metered dose inhaler.				*
8. Maintain an endotracheal/tracheostomy tube cuff. a. Assess cuff for leak. b. Inflate cuff to minimal occlusive pressure. c. Check cuff pressure using cuffolater.	* * *	* * *		*
9. Obtain blood sample for ABG analysis. a. Arterial line. b. Arterial puncture.	* *	* *		
10. Perform drug and drip calculations.	*		*	
11. Maintain IV therapy system. a. Bag, tubing, and filter.	*		*	
12. Set up and monitor IV infusion devices. a. Pumps. b. Dial-a-flow/Control-a-flow.	* * *		* * *	
13. Basic troubleshooting of IV infusion devices. a. Pumps/controllers.				* *
14. Obtain blood sample. a. Phlebotomy from peripheral site. b. Arterial line.	 *	 *		*

Source: Saint Joseph's Hospital of Atlanta (1992).

the professional staff in the model. Each professional discipline was charged with the responsibility to develop a role that would represent job enrichment for them and that would meet the following criteria:

- Each professional discipline will provide services unique to their discipline in a more patient-focused or customer-service oriented manner and will do so in a cost-effective manner.

- Professionals will function in an expanded role of some sort (i.e., perform additional tasks/functions or assume additional responsibilities).

- Professionals will be centrally based but will function as if they are unit based in that they will practice on a specific unit or service.

- Professionals will function more as a collaborative team member than ever before in the history of their career at Saint Joseph's.

The respiratory therapy, pharmacy, and radiology departments drafted a proposal and, in fact, entered into a "contract" that delineated how the professionals in their departments would meet the above criteria. This "contract" or "covenant" was mutually agreed upon and signed by the department directors of the support departments and the department directors for the patient unit. Exhibit 7.5 outlines some of the responsibilities of the "decentralized" pharmacist; Exhibit 7.6 portrays the performance standards for the radiology department that were mutually agreed upon by the radiology department and the coronary care unit. This professional model appears to be one that will both meet the objectives for our restructuring efforts and represent job enrichment for all participants.

Conclusions Related to Multiskilling of Personnel

The Healthcare Advisory Board's (1989) conclusions related to multiskilling of health care workers are as follows:

- Hospitals can reduce expenses by shifting tasks from high-skill, high-cost personnel (nurses, respiratory therapists, pharmacists) to lower-skill, lower-cost employees. For example, a service associate, LPN, or patient care technician can perform some tasks typically performed by an RN; a pharmacy technician can perform some of the tasks of a pharmacist; a laboratory technician can perform some of the tasks previously performed by a medical technologist. Some shifting of tasks are probably inevitable irrespective of the cost savings, given the current shortage of these and other health care professionals.

Exhibit 7.5   Pharmaceutical Care Services

1. Profile Review
    • Avoid duplicate therapy.
    • Effect cost saving (e.g., conversion from IV to PO therapy ASAP).
    • Effect dosage adjustment when indicated.

2. Chart Review
    • Review of past 7-day medication summary.
    • Screen charting compliance, especially for costly therapy.
    • Match disease states with drug therapy.

3. Patient Teaching; Admission/Discharge Counseling
    • Assessment of home medication therapy.
    • Instruction for dosage compliance after discharge.

4. Laboratory Results
    • Cultures and sensitivity done for appropriateness of antibiotic therapy.
    • Appropriateness of lab tests ordered.
    • Monitor for cyanide levels being done on high-dose/long-term Nipride therapy.

5. Nurse Teaching
    • In-services on new drugs.
    • Meet JCAHO requirements for appropriate sterile technique during IV drug/IV fluid preparation.
    • "Allergic drug reaction" definition and reporting.
    • Compatibility information.

6. Physician Rounds
    • Round with physicians before orders are written for most efficacious drug therapy.
    • Promote formulary control/compliance.
    • Provide on-site drug information.

7. IV Drug Monitoring
    • Screen for rate/dose match.
    • Monitor set changes.

8. Drug Usage Evaluation (DUE)
    • Identify needed DUEs.
    • Expand capacity for JCAHO expected DUEs done.
    • Promote practice drug evaluations, rather than less effective retroactive studies.

9. Pharmacist Intervention Documentation
    • Meets JCAHO requirements.
    • Documents cost savings.
    • Serves as a learning tool for others on the staff.
    • Documentation for continuous quality improvement.

Source: Saint Joseph's Hospital of Atlanta (1992).

Exhibit 7.6   Performance Standards for the Radiology Department's.
Involvement in Patient-Focused Care at SJHA

---

1. Order time to completion of procedure
"Stat" examinations: 15 minutes
"ASAP" examinations: 1 hour
"Today" examinations: 4 hours

2. Radiology response time (technologist response to floor via phone or
personal visit)
"Stats": <10 minutes
"ASAP" or "Today": <1 hour

3. Patient wait time in Radiology
Less than 5 minutes from arrival in Radiology to the start of the examination
Less than 5 minutes from the completion of the examination until the
patient leaves for return to his/her room

4. Turn around time of reports being available on the patient's chart
Within 24 hours of the examination completion

5. Technologist response to "code" situations
A technologist will respond with a portable machine to all "code" situations
within 5 minutes 100 percent of the time.

- Hospitals can maximize cost savings by cross-training nurses in high-
  skill, high-cost ancillary functions, such as respiratory therapy, as
  opposed to pharmacy assistant tasks, EKG, and phlebotomy. However, hospitals with low nurse vacancy rates and low nurse salaries
  may also benefit by cross-training RNs in the lower-cost ancillary
  function, eliminating the lower-paid ancillary personnel.
- The alternative for hospitals with high-salaried RNs is to cross-train
  nurse extenders in ancillary tasks.
- Hospitals should focus on cross-training employees within large departments, such as clinical laboratory, radiology, and food services.
  The similarity in skill requirements and the proximity of employees
  are key advantages. Table 7.2 identifies the most frequently cited
  skill combinations for multiskilled health care practitioners (Vaughan
  et al. 1991).
- There is currently too little evidence available to judge the magnitude
  of cost savings, if any, from shifting tasks to lower-paid employees;
  the success is clearly tied to salary differentials in each hospital's

market. Hospitals should experiment with this only if salary differentials are significant; it is not worth increasing organizational complexity—by adding different job categories—thereby exacerbating the problem of employee downtime.

Issues Related to Implementation

Sacred Cows

The "sacred cows" phenomenon can have a paralyzing effect on restructuring efforts, particularly redesigning roles. According to Kriegel and Patler (1991), authors of *If It Ain't Broke...Break It!*, "sacred cows" are those

Table 7.2 The Most Frequently Mentioned Skill Combinations for Multiskilled Health Practitioners (in ranked order) (n = 580 responses from 137 hospitals)

Combination	*Percent of Total Skill Combinations*
1. Respiratory therapist or technician and electro-cardiography (ECG)	9.0
2. Radiologic technologist and ultrasound	6.4
3. Laboratory technologist/technician and radiography	3.4
4. Radiologic technologist and special procedures (i.e., computed tomography, magnetic resonance imaging, and other medical imaging)	2.9
5. Radiologic technologist and mammography	2.6
6. Multiple business office functions (i.e., payroll, purchasing)	2.4
7. Laboratory technologist/technician and ECG	2.1
8. Registered nurse (RN) and respiratory therapy	2.1
9. RN and quality assurance/utilization reviewer	2.1
10. RN and discharge planning	1.7
11. Manager of multiple-support departments (i.e., housekeeping, laundry, and maintenance)	1.7
12. Radiologic technologist and laboratory	1.5
13. Other*	62.1
Total	100.0

Source: Reprinted, with permission, from D. G. Vaughan, M. R. Fottler, R. Bamberg, and K. D. Blayney, "Utilization and Management of Multiskilled Health Practitioners in U.S. Hospitals," *Hospital & Health Services Administration* 36 (3): 407.

* Each of the other mentioned skill combinations comprised less than 1.0 percent of the total.

systems and routines that have become standard operating procedure in many areas of our organizations. They are sacred because it is taken for granted that because something has been done a certain way forever and ever, it must be the best way to do it. The result is that we spend a lot of time, energy, and money feeding our sacred cows, supporting the system rather than having the system support us. It is very important to identify all of the sacred cows in your hospital, but it is just as important to decide what to do with them and when to do it. In other words, you have to decide which battles you are going fight. There are a variety of sacred cows. The most common ones are discussed below.

"Corporate Cows" are the most pervasive and most subtle—the values, the assumptions, the corporate culture, more or less the guiding principles of the hospital. If the culture of your hospital is bureaucratic, it is unlikely that operational restructuring will be considered in a positive way. If it is considered, only the CEO or the board or the executive staff will be involved in the decision making regarding this effort. Staff will have no input! On the other end of the spectrum is the hospital that is entrepreneurial in nature, fast moving, innovative, and risk taking. This hospital is lean and mean administratively—meaning it is not top heavy; it believes in and maintains shared governance and it empowers the staff. Such an organization will not be burdened by this particular cow.

"Company Cows" are archaic, complex policies and procedures. It is impossible to provide patient-focused care amidst a large number of company cows. How many times have you heard, "We can't do that because it's against policy?" Or, "You have to do this and that because it is company policy." When redesigning roles, it's absolutely essential that you charge your committee with the responsibility of rounding up all of the company cows—outdated policies, procedures, ways of doing things—and that you permit them to challenge the current way of doing things. Let them know that it's okay to ask questions such as "Why?," "Why not?," and "Who says?" Just think about your day in the hospital for a moment. If you're a nurse, do you consider it at least a tacit rule that you have to provide all of your A.M. care—including baths—before noon? And, isn't this the case even though your patient might just not want a bath until bedtime? And what about the housekeeping department? Isn't it a policy that all rooms be cleaned by 11:00 A.M.? Why is this? Pure and simple—it's a company cow!

"Departmental Cows"—or territorialism between and among departments—create the most harm in terms of efforts to redesign roles. Most of the time, departmental cows are based on the premise that other people's turf is sacrosanct. Consequently, turf wars are often fueled by fear on one side, and the desire to retain control and power on the other. Politics come into play and, typically, large numbers of employees are involved. Usually, one side will win and the other will lose. In most hospitals, one department stands out among the rest as the "biggest and best" or the most powerful—the one that has the most status. More often than not, this is the perception held of the nursing department. It is very important that restructuring efforts be perceived as a multidisciplinary, hospitalwide project rather than a nursing project. To achieve this end will require an enormous amount of interdepartmental team building over a long period of time.

Licensure/Regulatory Issues

Redesigning roles cannot be done without a meticulous review and analysis of all of the state practice acts pertaining to the various professionals in your organization, an assessment of the state regulations, and then, of course, knowledge of JCAHO regulations. You must have this information before you decide which tasks can be shared and which cannot.

In Georgia and Tennessee, for example, registered nurses, physical therapists, and occupational therapists have practice acts that govern their practice. These individuals, as well as pharmacists, must have a license to practice. Respiratory therapists (RT) are not licensed in Georgia. [They do have "title" protection, which means that even though other professionals can perform RT procedures, they cannot designate themselves a respiratory care professional (RCP). Medical technologists are highly regulated in Tennessee and Georgia, and JCAHO specifically requires that medical technologists perform all laboratory procedures (Department of Human Resources 1990). There are very few exceptions to this rule. One of these is that a phlebotomist—who does not have to be a medical technologist—can, in fact, perform some tests such as bleeding times, glucose tolerance, and accucheck.

On the opposite end of the spectrum is radiology. Radiology is not strictly regulated in Tennessee. Radiology is not regulated in Georgia and, in fact, diagnostic procedures can be performed by individuals with as little as six hours of training (Department of Human Resources 1989). Each state has a different licensure and regulatory situation. Moreover, this is further complicated by variations in union activity, professional associations activity, and the job market for specific disciplines. So, what does all of this mean?

By law, JCAHO regulations, practice acts, or some other means of regulation, there are certain things that only RNs, physical therapists, medical technologists, and so forth can do. For example, JCAHO (1992) requires that an RN assess the needs and coordinate the care of all patients; therefore, this is something that cannot be shared. A medical technologist could perhaps be cross-trained to perform some tasks and functions typically performed by other professional disciplines; however, no one else could be cross-trained to perform laboratory procedures. Anyone could be cross-trained to do radiologic procedures; radiologic technologists could perhaps be cross-trained to perform some tasks and functions from other disciplines. Certain respiratory therapy procedures could be taught to other individuals, and certainly respiratory care professionals could be cross-trained to perform a variety of tasks and functions from other disciplines.

According to Millman (1992), a health care policy analyst, the future regarding multiskilling or cross-training of professional personnel is uncertain. It appears that hospitals throughout the country are on somewhat of a collision course with lobbyists for the various professional associations. Millman cites the following from a report published in the *State Regulation of the Health Occupations and Professions*: "State legislatures seem to be increasingly willing to regulate technical professions, such as radiologic technicians and respiratory therapists, as well as subordinate professionals such as pharmacy assistants. The list of states which regulates these auxiliary professions grows every year."

One must question whether professional groups represent themselves or society's interests. There is no doubt that conservatives have an important function in professional associations. It should not be forgotten that the function of an interest group in a pluralistic society is to represent the group's shared interests. If it doesn't, it will not exist long. It is the legitimate purpose and obligation of such groups to raise quality questions. On the other hand, professional groups also contain practitioners who wear multiple hats as managers, employers, and educators. Among this group there inevitably will be those who see the advantages of change and the opportunity for moving the profession in new directions. The quality of leadership within the organization is the critical variable here (Millman 1992).

On the other side of this coin are the payers for health care. Certainly a significant driving force behind the restructuring of hospitals is the rapidly rising cost of health care and the resulting public and payer outcry for cost reductions. Undeniably, in this era of managed care and direct contracting, employers—as the payers for health care—require evidence that hospitals with whom they contract provide the highest quality care at the lowest possible cost. In addition, patients, as consumers, are more educated and informed than ever before, and they, too, are more demanding than in years gone by. To the extent that multiskilling or cross-training of personnel can be shown to be an essential component of cost-effective configurations, the greater will be the pressure on providing institutions to adopt these models of service.

The Leader Must Possess a New and Perhaps Different Set of Skills

The new patient care managers will not only be responsible for more personnel, they will be responsible for a very diverse group of people who are performing tasks and functions that have previously been performed in as many as 15 central departments. They will be responsible for professionals as well as nonprofessionals, perhaps clinical and technical personnel, and support personnel along with clerical personnel. The following is a list of the skills, characteristics, and traits that are crucial to the success of the manager in a restructured environment (Dupree 1989):

- Leads through serving
- Is vulnerable to the skills and talents of others
- Is intimate with the organization and its work
- Is able to see the broad picture—beyond his or her own area of focus
- Is a spokesperson and a diplomat
- Understands and speaks for the corporate value system
- Is an advocate for participative management
- Has consistent and dependable integrity
- Cherishes heterogeneity and diversity
- Searches out competence
- Is open to contrary opinion
- Communicates easily at all levels
- Understands the concept of equity and consistently advocates it

Prepare the Staff for Success

Operational restructuring and the redesigning of roles represents a whole new ball game. First of all, educate and train the staff well. It is preferable to select groups comprised of staff-level personnel affected by the process to identify training needs and to work in conjunction with others to provide the training. This process will assure them that what needs to be taught will indeed be taught. These individuals will also have to acquire a whole new set of skills:

- *Team building.* And this does not mean a one-time four-hour session, but instead refers to an arduous process that will take place over an undetermined, variable, but long period of time.

- *Delegation/directing.* Although this skill is essential, the extent of the need for this skill will vary depending on the patient care unit involved. For example, at SJHA the RNs in our coronary care unit are accustomed to an all-RN staff. So, many of them had never delegated patient care activities to anyone but a professional colleague, compared to our medical-surgical units, whose RNs were accustomed to working with nursing assistants and patient care technicians.

- *Communication.* This area cannot be emphasized enough!

- *Negotiation.* One of the clinical imperatives states that "members of the team will negotiate at the beginning of each shift and as necessary regarding the specific tasks/responsibilities to be performed/fulfilled during the upcoming shift." It would be a severe error in judgment to presume that staff are proficient in the area of negotiation.

- *Problem solving/conflict resolution.* Hospitals are creating a brand new, very different work environment for a diverse group of people. To expect them to just go at it and know how to solve their problems equitably and resolve conflict appropriately would certainly be naive.

Reward Participants . . . but How?

Hospitals have dealt with the issue of compensation in a variety of ways. Over 60 percent of hospitals pay cross-trained employees no more than other personnel (Vaughan et al. 1989). Figure 7.2 demonstrates that over half of the hospitals increasing pay of multiskilled employees keep the raise below $1.00 per hour (Healthcare Advisory Board 1989). Obviously, the most important thing to do is to determine that pay practices are relevant, up-to-date, and competitive with the market area. The following alternatives, however, should be explored:

- *Skill-based compensation.* Using this methodology, compensation may be based on the new skill or skill sets acquired. At SJHA, the minimum and maximum pay ranges were listed for each of the job categories that would be encompassed by each of the redesigned roles. With few exceptions, the minimum and maximum range for the redesigned role was established at the highest level of the job categories included in the new role. For example, Table 7.3 shows the salary ranges for each level of the administrative associate, which is the clerical/administrative role in our model.

- *Incentive bonuses.* Incentive bonuses can be in the form of monetary offerings or in the form of paid days off. For example, hospitals could offer a predetermined dollar amount (for example, $100 or

Figure 7.2 Over Half of Hospitals Increasing Pay of Cross-Trained
Employees Keep Raise below $1.00 per Hour

Salary Raise

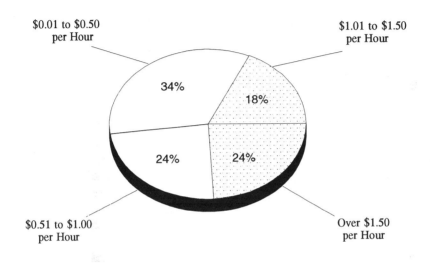

Source: Adapted, with permission, from Healthcare Advisory Board, *Million Dollar Cost Savings Ideas: Eighteen Tactics for Reducing Hospital Labor Costs,* The CEO Series, no. 1 (Washington, DC: Healthcare Advisory Board, 1989), 52.

$500) or a certain percentage (1 to 2 percent) of the employee's annual base salary to commit to and complete a certain amount of time, probably no less than six months, on a redesign pilot unit. At Vanderbilt, this percentage approach was used for staff working on the pilot unit. This methodology has been employed in a number of hospitals throughout the country.

- *Performance-outcome-based compensation.* This method of rewarding employees is probably going to become the wave of the future. Given the health care industry's focus on continuous quality improvement, and because the primary purpose of restructuring operations in hospitals is to improve processes and outcomes, it makes sense that compensation should perhaps be dependent upon successful attainment of certain predetermined outcomes related to the overall objectives for the project—cost, quality, service, and satisfaction.

Table 7.3 Salary Ranges for Administrative Associate Job Redesign Positions as of 1 February 1992

Administrative Associate 1 $7.80–11.70			Administrative Associate 2 $8.50–12.75			Administrative Associate 3 $10.55–15.82		
Positions	*Min.*	*Max.*	*Positions*	*Min.*	*Max.*	*Positions*	*Min.*	*Max.*
Data Entry Clerk	$7.80	$11.70	Department Secretary	$8.50	$12.75	Coder	$10.55	$15.82
Medical Records Clerk	$7.30	$11.40	Nursing Department Secretary	$7.53	$11.29	U. R. Assistant	$10.55	$15.82
Business Office Clerk	$6.97	$10.30				Q. C. Coordinator	$9.15	$13.72
						Financial Counselor	$8.95	$13.42
						Patient Services Rep.	$8.65	$12.97
						Monitor Technician	$7.78	$11.67

Source: Saint Joseph's Hospital of Atlanta (1992).

This method of compensating employees has been in place in other industries for many, many years and has been exceptionally successful. By using this methodology, employees are unquestionably empowered to make a difference—and they're appropriately rewarded depending upon the measurable difference they make.

Cost of the Project

Obviously, the cost of restructuring efforts is variable and dependent upon the type of changes as well as the magnitude of changes that the organization desires to achieve. The most significant factors related to cost are planning, space renovation, capital investment, consultation, and training and development.

Planning

The cost of planning is subtle, and therefore, extremely difficult to quantify. However, an attempt should be made to do so. Given the magnitude of change that will result from restructuring efforts, large numbers of individuals and groups should be involved in the planning process. It is likely that planning will take many months prior to the implementation of any changes in the organization. A myriad of councils, committees, task forces, and ad hoc committees will be assembled. An estimation of the cost involved for committee work and planning should be made using the following formula:

$$
\begin{array}{ccccc}
\text{Number of} & & \text{Average Salary} & & \text{Number of} \\
\text{Individuals on} & \times & \text{of Committee} & \times & \text{Committee Meetings} \\
\text{Committee} & & \text{Members} & & \text{per Month}
\end{array}
$$

$$
= \text{Average Cost of Committee per Month}
$$

Another consideration related to planning is the cost of replacing staff personnel at the unit level so that they can actually participate on the committees to which they have been assigned. For example, on a given committee, if there are six RNs, each of whom has to be replaced with another RN at time-and-a-half every time the committee meets, this cost should be factored into the cost of planning for the project.

Space renovation

Space renovation and its costs are obviously institution specific. Some hospitals have undergone major renovation as a part of their restructuring efforts;

others have undergone none. Types of renovations that might be desired, however, include

- decentralization of specific ancillary services, such as radiology, laboratory, and physical therapy;
- increased patient unit capability for storage and maintenance of equipment and supplies;
- reconfiguration of the "traditional" nurses' station to facilitate enhanced multidisciplinary work;
- patient server at or near each patient room;
- administrative space for expanded unit work related to medical records, admissions, patient financial services, and utilization review; and
- adequate space for multidisciplinary meetings and conferences required as part of the unit's new work.

A note of caution: renovations should be planned following the development of the model—not the other way around! Form follows function is appropriately applied in this particular situation!

Capital investments

Like space renovations, capital expenditures can range from minimal to extensive. The most common capital expenditures will result from

- equipment to provide decentralized ancillary and support services, such as radiology, laboratory, physical therapy, environmental services, admissions, and medical records; and
- computer upgrades or expansions.

The importance of providing the necessary equipment for the staff at the unit level cannot be stressed enough! Without the necessary equipment, the objectives for restructuring efforts—to improve service to patients and physicians as well as to maximize job satisfaction for employees—will not be met.

Consultation

It is likely that the use of an external consultant or consulting firm will benefit any hospital's restructuring efforts. Obviously, the number of different consultants—behavioral, organizational development, operational—and the extent to which they are used will determine the cost to the organization.

There is no doubt that the perspective and the momentum gained from the use of consultants can result in significant cost savings to the organization. On the other hand, consultants ineffectively or inefficiently utilized can lead to astronomical expenditures with minimal results. Factors that should be considered in making the decisions to retain the services of a consultant are

- scope of work to be performed,
- expertise/notoriety of the consultant/consulting firm,
- resources within the organization to work with the consultants, and
- outcomes or products desired along with the time line by which the outcomes should be produced.

Arrangements with consultants should always include agreements on at least

- fee structure;
- deliverables—the products of their work;
- expenses—covered and uncovered;
- use of internal human resources—for example, clerical, management engineering, and financial;
- use of internal material resources—for example, supplies and equipment.

Training

Training costs are not to be underestimated! In fact, over the life of the project, training costs might very well exceed those related to capital expenditures, the use of consultants, or even major renovations. Training costs should be considered with the following in mind:

- Amount of time required to train employees in the newly redesigned roles
- Staffing requirements to support the training
- Availability of trainers
- Time line for implementation

First of all, it should be emphasized that poorly implemented training plans will be far more costly than plans well developed and executed. Adult learners require and deserve learning opportunities that allow them undistracted learning and practice time. Because of this, plans must be made to provide structured learning experiences away from the employee's everyday work environment for however long is deemed appropriate to complete the training. Depending on the extent of training involved, this could be for a period of two weeks to three months. In addition, it is likely that employees participating in this training process will have to be replaced and, in many cases, with high-cost labor, such as agency personnel or overtime employees. These costs to the organization should be calculated as precisely as possible.

The availability of trainers is critical to the success of the training program. Depending on the time line for implementation, it is plausible that additional trainers will have to be hired; at the very least, the use of external resources will be needed. An enormous amount of time and effort will be required for the development of assessment tools, course outlines, lectures, training schedules, and evaluation methodologies.

Rewards for the Struggle

Organizational restructuring toward a more patient-focused approach to health care delivery was conceptualized in 1988. Benefits at that time were projected to be

1. increased direct care provided increased by 60 percent and total personnel related costs simultaneously lowered by as much as 40 percent;
2. long-term reduction in personnel of 15–20 percent;
3. the elimination of some positions;
4. downsizing or elimination of some centralized departments;
5. improvements in quality of care;
6. improved service delivery;
7. employee retention;
8. increased customer satisfaction; and as a result,
9. an increase in the market share (Weber 1991; Lathrop 1991).

Lakeland Regional Medical Center in Lakeland, Florida, was the first hospital to implement the patient-focused model in July 1989. Since that time, only a handful of hospitals nationwide have implemented a patient-focused approach to care delivery, yet those who have are reporting positive results. The results that have been reported to date have been able to substantiate and quantify most of the claimed benefits.

Improvements in Service Delivery

David Weber (1991) discusses the experiences of six hospitals and the results of their restructuring efforts to date. Considering that the majority of hospitals have entered the restructuring effort by piloting one unit and taking time for thorough implementation and evaluation of that unit before further implementation occurs, the results are indeed remarkable. Since the majority of services are provided at the bedside, turnaround times for test results are almost immediate. In fact, the routine turnaround times on patient-focused units are faster than STAT orders for tests on traditional units. A 70 percent improvement in laboratory turnaround times and an 80 percent improvement in radiology turnaround times were reported after only eight months at Lakeland Regional Medical Center.

Improvements have been documented in other hospitals in the service levels of pharmacy, EKG, respiratory therapy, medical records, utilization review, discharge planning, and nursing care. The time to clean and prepare a patient room following a discharge has been reduced to a phenomenally low 15 minutes at Vanderbilt University Hospital and Clinic in Nashville, Tennessee. The admitting process at Bishop Clarkson Memorial Hospital in Omaha, Nebraska, has been reduced from almost eight hours to 23 minutes! In the same hospital, the steps that must be taken for a patient to receive an antibiotic have been reduced from 12 to 5 (Weber 1991). At Vanderbilt, similar service changes were seen on the pilot unit. A chest x-ray previously took 50 minutes and 19 steps; on the pilot, the same process required 16 minutes and 9 steps.

Improved Quality of Care

Continuity of care is actualized on the patient-focused units for both the patient and the caregivers. Patients see fewer staff members throughout their hospitalization and become familiar with those people responsible for their care. From the caregivers' perspective, they see patients with similar diagnoses and care needs and are better able to predict the course of treatment, length of stay, and complications that may be anticipated and therefore provide higher-quality care to this aggregate group. This type of patient clustering has worked very successfully in the area of maternal-child health for several years with similar positive outcomes.

Quality indexes, such as errors in treatment, patient falls, medication errors, and satisfaction, have been compared to the same unit's experience prior to implementation of the patient-focused approach and also to other units in the hospital that provide care through traditional means. The improvements in all cases have been very impressive (Weber 1991). An improvement that was not anticipated, but that has been consistently demonstrated in the hospitals' quality data, is the reduction in nosocomial infection rates. This reduction is thought to result from a combination of several factors. Fewer staff come in contact with the patient; consistent caregivers have better knowledge of the patient type and complications that usually occur; and since they are consistently providing care to the patient, staff are able to detect subtle changes in the patient earlier and initiate treatment sooner. At Vanderbilt, the drop in missed medication dosages is felt to be directly related to the decrease in patient transports off of the unit, which previously led to missed medication administration times.

It is important to have historical quality data available for comparisons once a change in care delivery is implemented. During the assessment phase, it is suggested that a performance and evaluation team review the data available and if certain areas are lacking, that baseline data be collected before any changes are made. A multidisciplinary approach should be taken to determine the indexes that are going to be measured to evaluate performance and success in achieving the objectives. Specific indicators need to be established prior to implementation.

Empowerment of Staff

The shortage of health care professionals is one of the driving forces for hospitals to consider changing how care is delivered and who is best suited to perform the wide variety of associated tasks. Empowerment is closely tied to staff satisfaction and retention. Staff who feel empowered to make decisions about their practice and exert some control over the work environment are better satisfied than those who do not. It is important to remember that this does not only refer to nursing staff, but to all health care professionals providing care to the patient. There is stiff competition among health care professionals to provide care without being deferred from doing so because someone else got to the patient first. For example, the respiratory therapist and the dietician may arrive on the patient unit to provide services to a patient, only to find that the patient is off the unit for radiology services. This service was most likely scheduled for the convenience and productivity of the radiology department and to maximize utilization of the equipment. In the patient-focused approach to care, the primary caregiver would be responsible for assuring that the care was provided, and in many cases, would be the individual who was actually providing it. There is less time spent in scheduling and coordinating activities for the convenience of others, fewer people around whom care must be coordinated, and less time spent by all members of the team waiting for others to complete their duties.

Although staff initially express fear and skepticism about changes in their duties and reporting relationships, those who now work on a patient-focused unit express increased job satisfaction due to the empowerment inherent in the model. The expanded responsibilities gave them greater control over patient care, improved knowledge of the patient, and a sense of belonging to a team (Weber 1991).

According to Mary Ann Araujo, RN, executive vice president at Chicago's Mercy Hospital and Medical Center, "to be patient driven is to maintain a dynamic system of care delivery that fosters empowerment of all personnel to respond to the needs of the patient, rather than the routine of the system" (Eubanks 1991, 26).

Changes in care delivery should be evaluated in terms of whether they potentially enhance professional autonomy. Both case management and collaborative practice models are considered as enablers to the patient-focused models and are being implemented simultaneously with the models in some hospitals. These approaches also enhance professional autonomy and empower staff. The case management aspect of the ProACT® model implemented at Robert Wood Johnson University Hospital is expected to enhance collaboration and positively affect patient outcomes by reducing ICU length of stay and mortality rates (Ritter and Tonges 1991).

Increased Customer Satisfaction

Staff satisfaction

Empowerment was one reason staff satisfaction levels increased dramatically on the patient-focused units, but not the only one. Another equally important reason cited was the fact that staff were able to spend more time with the patients providing care, rather than in non-patient-care activities. Increases in the time caregivers are able to spend in direct care range from 20 percent to greater than 50 percent. The staff on the patient-focused orthopedic unit at Vanderbilt declared an astonishing 85 percent increase in the satisfaction with documentation requirements following implementation (Figure 7.3). Two percent of the nurse's time is now spent in documentation at Lakeland Hospital. The overall satisfaction with the patient-focused unit there translated into an RN turnover rate of 3 percent, the lowest in the hospital in 1989–90 (Weber 1991). The staff at Robert Wood Johnson report that they "enjoy the diversity and challenge of their new responsibilities, felt that their work is needed and appreciated, and like being a part of a team that interacts closely with patients to provide high-quality care" (Tonges 1991).

Physician satisfaction

When the idea of a patient-focused approach to care was introduced to the medical staff at Saint Joseph's Hospital of Atlanta, the response was very positive. Many felt that this represented a return to the "old way" of

Figure 7.3 Staff Satisfaction Measures: Work Redesign Study, Vanderbilt University

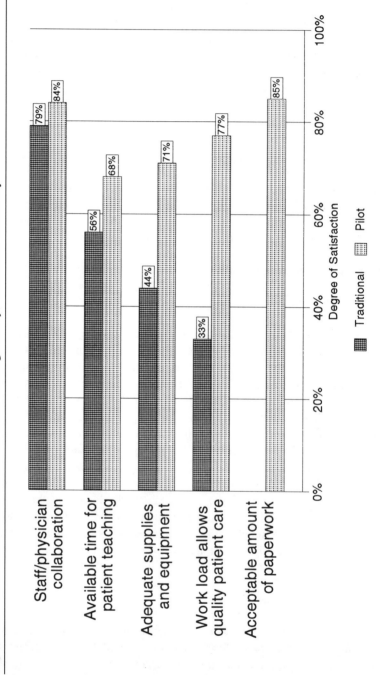

practicing—that is, where nurse generalists took care of all of the patient's needs without the aid of so many highly technical and narrowly focused practitioners. They also agreed that this would be a more cost-effective way to deliver care. This reaction is not the case in all hospitals embarking upon a restructuring program. Several physicians stated that they were openly opposed to this approach and felt that it would not enhance the delivery of care. The administration in those organizations pursued implementation despite the resistance, and both they and the medical staff are glad they did! Communication with the medical staff is essential from the beginning of the project, during design, implementation, and evaluation. Change of this dimension must be discussed thoroughly and often in order to give the physician the degree of comfort necessary as the project unfolds.

Physicians report that they are highly satisfied with the organization, care delivery, and efficiency of the patient-focused units (Figure 7.4). Because the service levels improved so dramatically, the physicians rank the patient-focused units as excellent in meeting the needs of the physician to provide care to the patient (Weber 1991). Benefits that physicians note include better preparation of patients for hospitalization through preadmission contact with nursing, increased nurse-physician collaboration, improved support services for patients and staff, improved problem solving by the nursing staff, and improved communication and coordination (Tonges 1991).

Patient satisfaction

The hospitals report marked increases in patient satisfaction on the patient-focused units (Figure 7.5). Patients judge that "hotel" services, such as cleanliness, food, and personal comfort needs, were greatly improved. More importantly, the response from caregivers, instructions and understanding of their care, obvious teamwork, and good morale of the team members were apparent. Patients expressed increased satisfaction regarding the obvious lack of transportation and wait time in central departments. As one patient expressed, "While being in a hospital can't really be described as a pleasant experience, it came close. . . . I felt like the staff were truly concerned about me and were arranging my care around my needs and comfort and not their own. I have been in a lot of hospitals, but this is the best way I have seen to take care of patients."

With demonstrated increases in the satisfaction surveys of all customers of the hospital, one can only surmise that an increase in the market share will follow. A competitive edge can be achieved in recruitment and retention of health care providers if the hospital provides an environment in which the employee is satisfied with the role expectation and amount of time devoted

Figure 7.4   Physician Satisfaction Measures: Work Redesign Study, Vanderbilt University

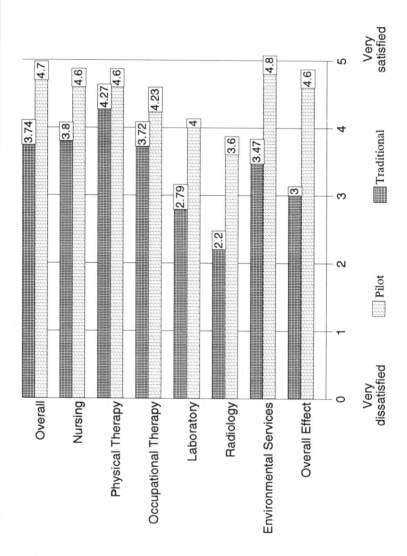

Figure 7.5 Patient Satisfaction Measures: Work Redesign Study, Vanderbilt University

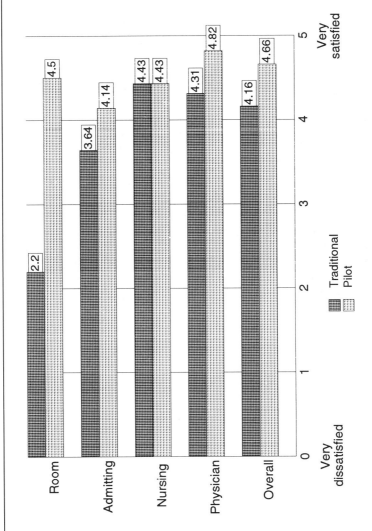

Figure 7.6 Hospital Labor Costs Today and in the Future (average costs in a 400-bed hospital)

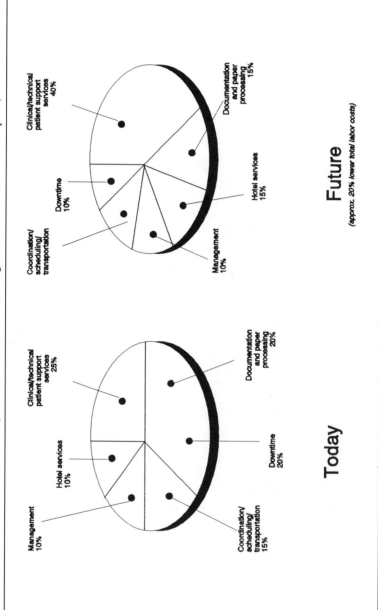

Source: Reprinted, with the permission of Hay Management Consultants, from J. L. Henderson and J. B. Williams, "The People Side of Patient Redesign," *Healthcare Forum* 34 (4): 44-49.

to providing care. Physicians will be more willing to admit patients into a facility that enables them to provide medical care efficiently and effectively and that is staffed adequately with professionals with whom they have a collaborative relationship. And finally, when patients have a choice as to where they receive medical care, will they not choose a hospital that has a reputation for being patient driven or where they have experienced a difference in the care provided?

Controlling Costs

The up-front cost of implementing a project of this magnitude is high, and since many of the hospitals reporting data are still in the pilot phase, it is difficult to quantify savings for the entire institution. However, the projections are that 15–25 percent reductions in fixed costs alone are possible from reductions that are achieved in scheduling and coordinating activities, documentation and processing times, and overall downtime of staff (Figure 7.6). For instance, Lakeland Regional Medical Center experienced a 9.2 percent reduction in direct bedside care costs as compared to a traditional unit (Weber 1991).

Hospitals have also experienced a decrease in the length of stay, which not only reduces the cost of providing care but denotes an increase in the ability of the institution to provide services more efficiently and of a higher quality. As patients are being moved through the system more efficiently, a capacity for increased admissions is created, which also has the potential to add to the revenue stream.

While the up-front costs are substantial and the financial returns significantly longer term, some organizations may question whether they can afford to restructure. Those who have come to believe in the service enhancements and improvements in customer satisfaction will no doubt question if any organization can afford *not* to restructure!

References

Belasco, J. A. 1990. *Teaching the Elephant to Dance: The Manager's Guide to Empowering Change.* New York: Crown Publishing.

Department of Human Resources. 1989. *X-Ray.* Chapter 290-5-22, pp. 553–584.46, 12 July.

Department of Human Resources. 1990. *Licensing of Clinical Laboratories.* Chapter 290-5-29, pp. 715–744.06, 5 September.

Dubree, M. 1989. *Leadership Is an Art.* New York: Dell Publishing.

Eubanks, P. 1991. "Restructuring Care: Patient Focus is Key to Innovation." *Hospitals* 67 (5 August): 26–27.

Hackman, J., and G. Oldham. 1980. *Work Redesign.* Menlo Park, CA: Addison-Wesley Publishing.

Healthcare Advisory Board. 1989. *Million Dollar Cost Savings Ideas: Eighteen Tactics for Reducing Hospital Labor Costs,* The CEO Series, no. 1. Washington, DC: Healthcare Advisory Board.

Henderson, J. L., and J. B. Williams. 1991. "The People Side of Patient Redesign." *Healthcare Forum Journal* 34 (4): 44–49.

Joint Commission on Accreditation of Healthcare Organizations. 1992. *Accreditation Manual for Hospitals,* pp. 79- 85.

Kriegel, R. J., and L. Patler. 1991. *If It Ain't Broke. . . Break It!* New York: Warner Books.

Lathrop, P. 1991. "The Patient Focused Hospital." *Healthcare Forum Journal* 34 (July/August): 17–21.

Leander, W. 1992a. "Dimensions of Successful Service Redeployment: Why 'Service Redeployment' Succeeds When 'Department Decentralization' Fails." *PFCA Review* 1 (Spring): 2–7.

Leander, W. 1992b. "Establishing a Rock-Solid Foundation." *PFCA Review* 1 (Spring): 8–13.

Millman, M. 1992. "Professionalism and Multiskilled Practitioners." *National Multiskilled Health Practitioner Clearinghouse* 5 (1): 8–9.

Ritter, J., and M. C. Tonges. 1991. "Work Redesign in High-Intensity Environments." *Journal of Nursing Administration* 21 (12), 26–35.

Saint Joseph's Hospital of Atlanta. 1992. *Communication Plan.* Atlanta, GA.

Schein, E. 1990. "Organizational Culture." *American Psychologist* (February): 109–119.

Tonges, M. C. 1991. "ProACT®: The Professionally Advanced Care Team Model." *Patient Care Delivery Models.* Rockville, MD: Aspen Publishing.

Vaughan, D. G., M. D. Fottler, R. Bamberg, and K. D. Blayney. 1991. "Utilization and Management of Multiskilled Health Practitioners in U.S. Hospitals." *Hospital & Health Services Administration* 36 (3): 397–419.

Vaughan, D., R. Bamberg, K. D. Blayney, and B. R. Wilson. 1989. *Hospital Utilization of Multiskilled Health Practitioners: A National Perspective.* Birmingham: University of Alabama.

Weber, D. O. 1991. "Six Models of Patient-Focused Care." *Healthcare Forum Journal* 34 (4): 23–31.

8

BREAKING MOLDS: HOSPITAL EDUCATION, WORK REDESIGN, AND THE AMERICAN WORK FORCE

Mary Claire Wilson and Stuart Gedal

Recently much of our attention as a nation has been focused on the unemployed and the difficult state of our economy. Are we losing some perspective on the massive shift in who is employed and who is becoming employed in our work force as a whole? This question deserves a great deal of attention because understanding the opportunities created by the answer to it is the key to our ability to remain a productive people.

We live in an era when only one of every six new entrants into the U.S. work force is a white male. African-Americans, Latinos, immigrants from all the nations of the earth, and women from every group now form the majority of new workers. Are we, as managers, supervisors, and coworkers, ready for all the implications this fact is having on the nature of work and what we are able to accomplish as a nation? Are those of us involved in work redesign projects ready to seize the many opportunities that work redesign offers us to be more responsive to the needs of this new multicultural work force?

Technology, Teamwork, and Multiculturalism

Even without the drastic demographic shift that is taking place today, major changes in the workplace are being created by the use of computer-based technology. We have lived with the less rapid changes created by machine-based technology for nearly two hundred years, and we have complained, as our parents have, often enough about that rapid pace of change! We are living, too, in an era of rediscovery of the social and productive value of teamwork. These are but two additional sources of change, and they, like the shift in demographics, are occurring at a pace and on a scale far more intense than the changes in past decades.

Hospitals are, in many ways, more sensitive to these trends of multiculturalism, technology, and teamwork than any other sector of the economy. The hospital work force, particularly in large urban areas, long ago became one of the most culturally diverse in our economy. Today, even small hospitals in the American heartland have their share of African-American and immigrant staff members. Indeed, other employers could well look toward hospitals to see in microcosm what is now happening in the work world at large.

The science of medicine is based squarely on biology, chemistry, and advanced research, and has perhaps, more than the computer industry itself, been influenced by sweeping advances in scientific knowledge. From diagnostic inventions such as MRI, CT scans, and ultrasound to treatments such as organ transplants, the hospital and the entire health care system is a technology-sensitive environment far beyond any yet imagined in industry, finance, or other sectors of the economy.

Redesign Trend

Work redesign represents a "high touch" response to these "high tech" trends (Naisbitt 1982). It is an attempt to ensure balance between people and machines, and create balance between those with specialized technical and professional skills and those with specialized roles. Work redesign happens when somewhere in your hospital's system, someone stops long enough or often enough to say, "We can do this another way!"

At Saint Joseph's Hospital of Atlanta (SJHA), work redesign was developed around the model of the multiskilled health care practitioner. Multiskilled health care practitioners have functioned in health care delivery settings for almost four decades. The multiskilling of nonnursing, non-allied-health staff, however, is a relatively new phenomenon. Multiskilling developed as a natural part of the broader work redesign process at Saint Joseph's Hospital of Atlanta. The process used to develop redesigned jobs reflected the combination of commitment, careful planning, and good fortune that are needed to make such a hospitalwide effort work.

A 1988 survey of 546 hospitals in the United States, conducted by Vaughan et al. (1989), found that 137 hospitals had multiskilled health care practitioner programs in place. These hospitals were spread out among 42 states and collectively had created some 580 types of multiskilled health care positions representing about 195 unique clusters of skills. In a 1989 study, the same researchers were able to identify some 75 training programs for multiskilled practitioners (Bamberg et al. 1989). These programs were based in both colleges and hospitals, and fell into two basic categories:

- Comprehensive training for a redefined, multiskilled job
- Discrete add-on training to expand the role of a clinical/technical provider into a new area

The range of hospitals and employees involved in the sites described by these two surveys strongly suggests that multiskilling of health care practitioners is more widespread than even its advocates have thought. When we examine the actual occupations to which the multiskilling concept has been applied, we also see that multiskilling has largely been restricted to professional, college-educated hospital staff such as nurses, respiratory therapists, technologists, and pharmacists.

As the patient care needs and human resource policies were explored at SJHA in order to plan the work redesign strategy, we came face to face with underlying issues of educational opportunity and social justice. We quite accidentally, but quite happily, found that work redesign had given us a tool to address these two issues in a positive way.

Developmental Approach

While a great deal of planning was undertaken as part of the work redesign process, chance opportunities played their role in the work redesign process by providing two tremendous opportunities:

- The opportunity to "experiment" with work redesign on a small scale before it was developed on a hospitalwide basis
- The opportunity to support work redesign with an extensive in-house education program focused on the needs of the educationally disadvantaged

The first opportunity was the chance to develop redesigned jobs on a small scale. Saint Joseph's was opening two new, physically separate units in newly constructed areas of the hospital—a medical-surgical unit and a critical care unit. This provided an open playing field of two small, closely managed units to develop the new team health care delivery concept and use it as a framework for work redesign. There were 23 beds in each of the two new units, and it was anticipated that nonmedical, nonnursing staff would number 34 in the medical-survey unit and 21 in the critical care unit. This provided the important opportunity to think of what has become a small, high-quality, closely monitored field test of various components of the work redesign process, and of the impact of its implementation.

The second opportunity was created by the Educational Services Department when it separately but simultaneously with the work redesign process instituted the People in Progress Program, a computer-based approach to basic skill enhancement and professional opportunities for all employees.

The work redesign teams created job descriptions for two types of support multiskilled health care practitioners, service associates and administrative associates. A career development ladder for each was then created as part of the staffing plan for our two new units. It was an explicit intention to carefully monitor and evaluate the implementation of the new jobs and the new training that would be required to create as well as to prepare and support employees and supervisors to implement and manage these new positions. It was important to ensure that the lessons learned from this process and its implementation would be applied in other areas of the hospital. If work redesign were successful on the two new units, this success would be used to promote the concept among managers, supervisors, and staff. Obtaining enthusiastic buy-in would be important to expand the process on a hospitalwide basis.

Service Associates and Administrative Associates

The small size of the two new units being opened encouraged us to experiment, to challenge each other, and to really figure out what was needed to make a team health care approach staffed by multiskilled practitioners work. The small scale of the initial effort was the key to its success and the eventual adoption of redesign on a larger scale. It took hours, days, and months of negotiations for administrators, managers, and supervisors to work together, first to build the trust necessary to negotiate, and then to hammer out the look of the new job structure. This process was further complicated by the fact that the new units with the new job and administrative structure had to be up and running when construction was completed. The process was open-ended and developmental, but it definitely had its bottom line.

The unique aspect of this design process is that the multiskilled health care practitioner model developed included multiskilled positions for support employees such as housekeeping, food service, transport, central supply, clerical, admitting, and nursing assisting staff. There was indeed success in implementing the targeted redesigned job clusters on the pilot units.

The new job structure creates two new categories of support employees as well as one category of professional employees (Figure 8.1). To date, the support categories have been the most successful and the best received by the

Figure 8.1   Patient-Focused Care

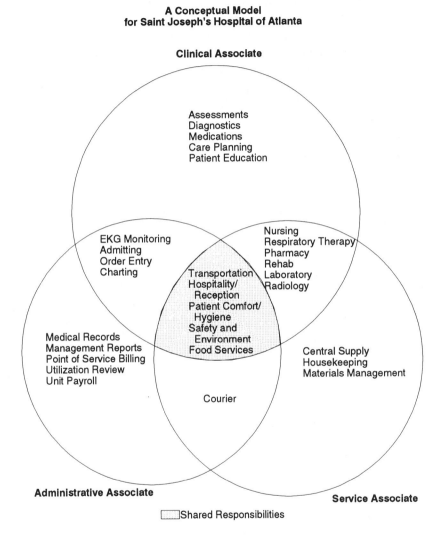

**A Conceptual Model
for Saint Joseph's Hospital of Atlanta**

Clinical Associate

Assessments
Diagnostics
Medications
Care Planning
Patient Education

EKG Monitoring
Admitting
Order Entry
Charting

Nursing
Respiratory Therapy
Pharmacy
Rehab
Laboratory
Radiology

Transportation
Hospitality/
Reception
Patient Comfort/
Hygiene
Safety and
Environment
Food Services

Medical Records
Management Reports
Point of Service Billing
Utilization Review
Unit Payroll

Central Supply
Housekeeping
Materials Management

Courier

Administrative Associate

Service Associate

☐ Shared Responsibilities

professional staff. Service associates carry out tasks traditionally associated with housekeeping, transport, food services, central supply, materials management, and varying degrees of patient care. Administrative associates carry out tasks traditionally associated with admitting, precertification, patient financial services, medical records, and utilization review. Two important aspects of the particular way this new structure was organized at the support, or nonprofessional, level are how these employees were supervised, and how enriched their career development prospects became.

The good fortune of having two new hospital units where we could try out the new work redesign model enabled us to develop a new administrative structure that parallels the service delivery structure. In the main hospital, housekeepers worked for a housekeeping department, transporters for a central transport department, and so on. In the new units, service associates worked for a supervisor who managed a team of administrative associates, nurses, and other members of the patient care team.

As the range of skills required by the new positions was examined, the skills were clustered for both service associates and administrative associates into three levels. There are clear differences in pay, required skills, responsibility, autonomy, and status for each level; the career ladders program gave us the vocabulary to describe each level as a rung on the service associate or administrative associate ladder.

Service Associate 1 is the entry level position for service associates and involves patient transport, food services, housekeeping, and other duties. The Service Associate 2 must demonstrate competency in all Service Associate 1 activities, as well as being certified or having two years of experience as a nursing assistant. The Service Associate 3 must master all the duties of Levels 1 and 2, must become certified as a patient care technician through a community college level course offered on-site at the hospital, and must assume some additional responsibilities, including phlebotomy, respiratory therapy, and radiology duties. All three levels require increasingly more sophisticated reading, writing, and math skills.

Administrative Associate 1 is the entry level for administrative associates. This position involves a variety of admitting and unit clerical duties. The Administrative Associate 2 employees interface with patients on the floor, interact more with nursing and medical staff, particularly around medical record keeping, and have some financial services responsibilities. The Administrative Associate 3 needs higher-level math, critical thinking, and reading skills to implement more complex record keeping, finance, and utilization review tasks.

Hospital staff members met in cross-departmental task forces to redesign support positions and identify training needs. Quality standards and monitors were developed for all the redesigned roles. The performance standards that created the job descriptions also laid the foundation for the training program. We began to look for ways to connect the potential for improved earnings, increased responsibility, and increased self-esteem to the newly redesigned service and administrative associate positions. We wanted to closely connect these new career tracks to the existence of an educational support program designed around adult education principles. If that connection could be defined, made explicit, and strengthened, we were confident that we would really have accomplished something.

What Is the Ladders Concept?

The People in Progress Learning Center was a response to staff needs for improved basic educational skills, including improved reading, writing, math, and listening skills for all employees, and English as a second language for the growing numbers of immigrant staff members. It was supported fiscally by Saint Joseph's leadership because it reflected the mission of the hospital to serve the disadvantaged, not just as patients, but as part of the hospital community, and because it represented a fiscally sound response to the labor shortage being experienced in allied health and patient care positions. This labor shortage is hardly unique to Atlanta or the state of Georgia. Perhaps one important lesson from our experiences with multiskilling is that work redesign should be considered as part of a broader strategy to address hospital labor shortages. A genuine effervescence seemed to take place between the work redesign project and the People In Progress Program. Work redesign created the very kind of career opportunities that motivated employees to take advantage of the People In Progress Learning Center to improve their basic skills and move up the career ladder.

It is only in retrospect that we can see how the redesign strategy that we developed for nonprofessional service and administrative staff fits into the broader picture of our human resources strategy. The fact that we had such a strategy in place enriched this part of the redesign experience and enabled us to achieve some very positive and satisfying outcomes for many employees from educationally disadvantaged backgrounds. We now see work redesign as a crucial piece of building a work force in our hospital that is able to respond to the challenges presented by technology, teamwork, and multiculturalism.

Developing the Training

In creating the three levels of service associate, we considered and grouped the skills required to perform the multiple tasks that were being reassigned, assigning them to the level that most closely possessed the necessary skills. For example, very few patient care responsibilities were assigned to the Service Associate 1 because these entry level employees did not yet possess the nursing assistant skills required for Level 2 or the patient care technician skills required for Level 3. Only those patient care tasks that could be taught in minimal time and could be easily monitored were assigned to Level 1. The challenge was to keep the smallest skills gap between the skills already possessed by the employee and the skills required for the new position. Training could then be focused on filling the gaps that remained.

Roger Kaufman (1991) proposes asking five questions when trying to decide what kind of training to do:

1. What organizational need are we addressing?
2. Where are the employees' current skills and knowledge relative to what is needed?
3. What skills and knowledge would be required to close the gap?
4. What interventions, such as training or hiring strategies, could be used to create those skills in employees?
5. What are the advantages and disadvantages of each potential intervention relative to cost and results?

According to Kaufman, it is essential that any chosen intervention be able to provide the desired results efficiently and cost effectively.

Initially, much of the training program was developed around a classroom/laboratory format with as many students in each class as possible in the interest of cost-effectiveness. Many of the more sophisticated skills had to be handled through cross-training in the appropriate departments. Clinical skills were validated as much as possible on mannequins, with the remainder handled on the unit under the supervision of a nurse. Periodic written and practical exams were administered, and remedial work was done with students who had not yet met the required minimal standards. Our costs were carefully tracked, along with other aspects of training, so that a cost-benefit analysis of the pilot unit training could be conducted and appropriate modifications could be made prior to hospitalwide implementation of the new roles.

At this point, the total training time has been shortened, the final exams and skills validations have been field tested, and improvements have been made in the instruments as well as the training methodology. An important component of the training process has been the "Train the Trainer" class for content experts, who are primarily clinicians or supervisors but are expected to deliver much of the on-the-job training. Fine-tuning of the entire training process has required extensive student assessments, data analysis, and feedback from the new managers on the pilot units. Plans to convert much of the training to a self-instructional format are under way because we believe we can maintain a high level of quality and consistency in the training while allowing the student to proceed at his or her own speed and determine the most convenient schedule. Furthermore, this approach contributes greatly to a cost-effective training process.

Service Associate Success Story

J.B., a middle-aged mother who is currently a candidate for a Service Associate 3 position, became involved less than a year ago in the work redesign project. Feeling a strong need for change in her position as a food services worker, J.B. elected to apply for a Service Associate 1 position. She performed well on the entry level skills assessments and was eager to enter the career ladder provided by job redesign and "go as far as she could go." After being accepted as a Service Associate 1, she was placed in a two-week training program to learn the responsibilities of the position. J.B. was a quick learner and decided not to wait for the nursing assistant course that would be provided on-site in about eight months. Instead, she enrolled in a local technical school nursing assistant evening course for which the hospital paid tuition reimbursement. After successfully completing that course, she was eligible to apply for a Service Associate 2 position, which she did within six months of entry as a Service Associate 1. She felt a need to work as a Service Associate 2 for several months in order to truly master all of the newly acquired patient care responsibilities, but she had not lost her determination to keep on growing.

Less than a year has passed since J.B. first heard about work redesign, and now she is enrolled in the patient care technician course provided on-site through a technical school, and she is well on her way to becoming a Service Associate 3. When asked what the benefits have been for her in this redesign project, her eyes sparkle and she says, "It has been such an ego builder!" Additionally, she reports that she has learned to work better with people, she has increased her education, and she has so much more job satisfaction. When asked about any concerns she has for the project, she mentions that you have to remain open-minded. You can't draw the line on what you will and won't do, you have to do it all. She adds that some of the Service Associates at Level 3 had problems with the housekeeping duties, which they thought were beneath them, and that sometimes the patients are surprised to realize that the same individual that just cleaned their room also is taking their temperature, giving them a bath, or delivering their meals. However, she quickly adds that patient satisfaction has been very high on her unit, with compliments such as, "You take such good care of me!" and "You pamper me!" She is very appreciative of the nursing staff on her unit saying, "They're so wonderful—they are always willing to help and answer our questions."

J.B. has plans to keep growing. She now wants to eventually become an RN. She points out that her enthusiasm for work redesign is not shared by everybody, particularly those required to add responsibilities they consider to be at a lower level. But for those like her, who have been locked into entry level positions for years with no growth opportunities, it is "total heaven" to have a mechanism provided for acquiring new skills and moving into higher, better paying positions.

Job Enlargement versus Job Enrichment

The main reason for the success of the service associate category has been the job enrichment inherent in each step up the service associate career ladder. Those who study work redesign measure it along two parameters: job enrichment and job enlargement.

Job enlargement entails extending the current job duties of an employee to include tasks that are new to the hospital or new to that employee's job description. For example, patient transport employees might be given the responsibility of transporting mobile equipment in need of repair to the maintenance area of the hospital. Job enlargement leaves the basic nature of the job unchanged.

Job enrichment, on the other hand, entails expanding the range of job tasks to include tasks demanding more skill, a larger variety of skills, more problem-solving, and more autonomy. Numerous benefits have been reported to be associated with job enrichment, such as greater job satisfaction, lower absenteeism, and reduced turnover.

The balance that is struck between enlargement and enrichment varies from hospital to hospital and the specific challenges presented by redesign in particular occupational areas of the hospital work force. It is important, from an education and training perspective, to go into the work redesign process with the awareness that different constituent or stakeholder groups within the hospital, even after they reach a consensus to move forward with a work redesign project, may approach the issue of what that balance should be with differing perceptions and interests.

What is clear is that top managers face the reality that there will be no teamwork where managers lack respect for the culture or backgrounds of the people who work for them. Frontline supervisors can already tell you that there can be little group effort where differences of language or lack of basic reading, writing, or math skills prevent communication or even preclude training for new types of more challenging, more productive, and economically rewarding jobs.

Link to World Education

The need for more highly developed basic skills among our support level work force is what gave rise to the People in Progress Program. This program is currently assisting employees to become "functionally literate," a term used to define the basic skills needed to function in today's complex, high-technology society.

As we moved into the work redesign project, we identified another need—the ability to identify the entry level basic skills that were essential for success in each of the new positions we were creating. Following a suggestion by the director of human resources for the American Hospital Association, we contacted a nonprofit company, World Education, in Boston, Massachusetts, to assist us in developing competency-based, job-related basic skill assessments for each of the newly created support level positions. Approximately 20 critical reading, math, listening, and writing competencies were identified for each position to create a "work sampler," or an entry level test to ensure that the candidate had the necessary skills to perform well in training and on the job.

Development of the work samplers required that World Education conduct actual site audits of the job functions and elicit input from all of the affected departments. Extensive field testing of the work samplers was performed and minor modifications were made.

At this point we feel confident that, from a testing standpoint, the work sampler is the best predictor of job success that we have. It is used in conjunction with prior job performance and manager recommendation in selecting all future service and administrative associates.

Conclusions

Potentially, work redesign represents the opportunity side of some converging social, economic, and technological forces that may otherwise prove extremely disruptive to our society and our productive capability as a nation. Not only in health care, but in manufacturing, finance, and other sectors, work redesign provides a friendly, receptive framework that gives shape and practicality to the teamwork and participative management theories being promoted by a growing number of programs in business and management.

The feasibility of work redesign and the growing experience with it across the country's hospitals challenge health care administrators to squarely face some fundamental work force issues and challenge the socially concerned—both within and outside of hospitals—to move beyond the role of critics and make our values come alive. By telling our work redesign story, we hope you will find pieces that fit your situation and begin to try them out.

References

Bamberg, R., K. D. Blaney, D. G. Vaughan, and B. R. Wilson. 1989. *Multiskilled Health Practitioner Education: A National Perspective.* Birmingham: University of Alabama.
Kaufman, R. 1991. "Toward Total Quality Plus." *Training* 51 (December): 50–54.
Naisbitt, J. 1982. *Megatrends: Ten Directions Transforming Our Lives.* New York: Warner Books.
Vaughan, D. G., R. Bamberg, K. D. Blaney, and B. R. Wilson. 1989. *Hospital Utilization of Multiskilled Health Practitioners: A National Perspective.* Birmingham: University of Alabama.

9

WORK REDESIGN: A JOURNEY, NOT A DESTINATION

JoEllen Goertz Koerner

Introduction

In the past 25 years many events, discoveries, and natural upheavals have changed the world—increased air travel, the moral revolution, launching of satellites, the women's movement, the sexual revolution, emergence of nuclear energy, the collapse of communism, and the continuing growth of technology and biomedical engineering. We are now living in an era marked by rapid change and transformation. Our current disequilibrium, both personal and professional, foreshadows an emerging new society. Roles, relationships, institutions, and old ideas are being reexamined, reformulated, and redesigned (Goertzen 1987). Health care is positioned by society to serve a unique and vital role in its survival. Thus, health care leaders must reassess the philosophy surrounding health and illness while designing a responsive and humane delivery system to serve society in the emerging new reality of the twenty-first century.

We are facing an era of "survival and thrival" within the volatile health care industry. The 1980s were coined the "whitewater era," with a focus on the self (Vaill 1989). The 1990s are being hailed the "era of chaos" by industry leaders (Kaiser 1990). An emerging focus on social consciousness notes movement from a model of domination to one of partnership. The role of leadership is shifting from a paradigm of direction and controlling to one of visioning and creating. Visionary and inspirational leadership, experienced in the context of democracy rather than bureaucracy, is essential to facilitate human and organizational potential and actualization through this crisis, leading to a transformed society.

Transformation and Consciousness Expanding Theories

A theory organizes observations, provides a vocabulary for communication, filters observations through a value system to provide understanding, and generates strategies for action. The prototype proposed for health care reform is founded on several theories that address evolution from a transformational and consciousness-raising perspective.

Transformational theory proposes that the keystone that unites the behavior of all things is the process of growth (Land 1973). Humanity manifests this universal drive toward growth on levels externally different from, but internally the same as, physical and biological forebears. Thinking, communication, socialization, technology, and ethics are examples of externalized and amplified acts of biological growth: the irreversible transformation of energy and matter into life and life-facilitating products.

In essence, the destiny of the simple cell, the individual human, and society at large is to reach out and affect the environment: "The drive of both the physiological and the psychological process of living is to assimilate external materials and to reformulate them into extensions of the self (Land 1973, 9).

The cell performs this process by ingesting its environment and transforming it into cells that match its own genetic pattern. The human mentally absorbs the cultural environment and affects it in ways that conform to culturally acquired mental patterns. These parallel acts of synthesis progress through five specific stages:

1. *Curiosity.* Searching for nourishment (food for the physiological cell and information for the spiritual, psychosocial human system).
2. *Learning and memory.* Digestion, assimilation, and internal growth (through a discriminating screening process).
3. *Creativity.* Assembling materials in new ways (mutation).
4. *Growth.* Affecting the environment through extension of internal patterns (self-extension).
5. *Responsibility.* Relating to environmental feedback (reaction to the environment from its response to the mutation).

The total act of growth is reacted to by the environment, and both the cell and the individual modify their subsequent behavior based on the feedback from the environment. If the conditions of nutrition and feedback permit new growth patterns, the result will be creative and responsible behavior. If not, the lack of alternatives results in a regression to more basic growth patterns.

Consciousness theory proposes that the total pattern of person-environment may be viewed as a network of consciousness, or awareness (Bentov 1978). Persons as individuals, and human beings as a species, are identified by their patterns of consciousness manifest in their behavior. An individual does not *possess* consciousness—the person *is* consciousness. Consciousness is the informational capacity of the system, the capacity of the system to interact with its environment (Newman 1986, 33).

Erich Jantsch (1980) notes that as the quantity of consciousness increases, the more numerous and varied are the responses to the environment. As the quality of consciousness increases, there is a higher frequency of response. The individual has a greater repertoire of responses in any given situation, and does so with increased agility or speed.

Transformation to a positive future calls for health care leaders to redefine our concept of health: health is the expansion of consciousness (Newman 1986). In this model, disease is viewed as one manifestation of health, rather than a negative state. Fused with its opposite, nondisease, it brings forth a holistic concept of health. Thus, the individual is viewed as an open system characterized by patterning that is constantly changing. Disease is viewed as a disruption in equilibrium, an invitation to reexamine one's lifeway, expanding self-consciousness, which may enrich life despite the outcome of the disease process. Disease may be experienced as a transformative rather than destructive event in an individual's life. This model has great implications for a society experiencing longevity and chronic illness. For some, the self-other awareness that emerges as a result of illness creates a quality in their life not experienced prior to the disordering event.

Transformation of the Health Care Delivery System

One cannot design the processes and structures necessary to transform our current health care system without acknowledging that it is influenced by, influences, and is nested within a larger social system. Further, one must acknowledge that any system is comprised of individuals possessing unique values and life patterns that influence the total system. Changing norms and behaviors are evident in most present-day societies along with changing patterns of needs among the work force. Thus, a transformational paradigm for health care must present a compelling vision that will inspire universal acceptance. It must also honor and enrich the society it serves through forms and structures that support personal and organizational transformation.

The Social Context Surrounding Transformation

Of all life-forms on this planet, only we can plant and harvest, compose art and music, seek truth and justice, laugh and cry. Because of our unique ability to imagine new realities, we are literally partners in our own evolution. Simultaneously, our planet is threatened with ecological catastrophe and nuclear annihilation. Today we stand at a decisive bifurcation—maintain our current cultural norms based on competition and dominance, which leads to destruction, or move toward a model of partnership and integration, which creates wholeness and health.

A reassessment of how systems are formed, maintained, and changed is rapidly spreading across many areas of natural science: chemistry, physics, mathematics, and biology. Raine Eisler (1987) notes that work completed by scientific leaders such as Ilya Prigogine, Isabel Stengers, Robert Shaw, Humberto Matruana, and Fritjof Capra presents an emerging body of theory and data referred to as "new physics" or "chaos theory." For the first time in the history of science, sudden and fundamental change that is irrational rather than linear and predictable, the kind of change our world is increasingly experiencing, has a scientific framework. New works investigating evolutionary change by biologists and paleontologists such as Vilmos Csayi, Niles Eldredge, and Stephen Gould, along with scholars such as Erich Jantsch and Ervin Laszlo, present data regarding cultural evolution in the social sciences. Important similarities regarding systems change and personal self-organization are emerging.

Another major contributor to an expanding social consciousness is the feminist study of cultural evolution, which encompasses the whole span of human history, focusing on the other half of humanity. Scholars such as Jean Baker Miller, Dale Spender, Florence Howe, Nancy Chodorow, and Carol Gilligan are providing data and insights that are opening new frontiers for women. They have uncovered a story that began thousands of years before recorded history (prehistory), demonstrating the presence of a matriarchal governance system that was peaceful and productive. History also reveals a bloody 5,000-year detour to patriarchal reign in a model of control and conquest. We currently face the potential consequences of this competitive cultural structure coupled with a very sophisticated level of technological development, putting our very existence into question.

Though one (chaos theory) emerges from the traditional male scientific paradigm and the other (feminist theory) from the female world view, Eisler combines them in her "cultural transformation theory." She notes that they share common ground: both acknowledge that the present system is breaking down, and both call for transformation to a different kind of future. She proposes movement from the current male system of domination to an integrated system of partnership (1987, 185–203), which will profoundly change reality at all levels (Table 9.1). Both men and women have the biological potential for many different kinds of behavior. The problem is not gender specific, but rather reflects the way both men and women have been socialized in our current cultural belief systems. In our male-dominated world not all women are peaceful and gentle, and many men are.

After living for 5,000 years in a dominator society, it is difficult to imagine another world. There have been other times of social disequilibrium when a fundamental systems transformation could have occurred. But each time when the thresholds signaled a shift from domination to partnership, it snapped back to its original shape (1987, 194). For the first time in recorded history we are at a threshold that shows signs of breaking, so that a cultural evolution could transcend the confines that have for millennia held us back. Lacking is a universal social guidance system, governing values, and a vision that could redirect the allocation of our resources and technology to enhance the well-being of humankind and move us into a new paradigm of partnership.

The Compelling Vision of a New Reality for Health Care

Prigogine and Stengers (1984) identify that bifurcations or evolutionary changes in chemical and biological systems involve a large element of

Table 9.1 A Comparison of Dominator and Partnership Systems

Dominator System	*Partnership System*
Male dominated	Male-female partnership
Warlike and suspicious	Peaceful and creative
Technological advancement	Spiritual/mental advance
Rigid hierarchy	Linking networks
Violence for social control	Love and duty
Conquest of nature	Harmony with nature
Domination	Caring and affiliation
Pursue own ends	Responsive to others
Food, sex, and shelter	Growth and actualization
Defensive habits of mind	Creative and interconnected
Nonproductive rigidity	Productive change
Conflict is destructive	Conflict is productive
Power over others: win/lose	Power with others: win/win

chance. Evolutionary theorist Ervin Laszlo (1985, 16) recognized that major shifts in human social systems also involve a large element of choice. "Humans," he observed, "have the ability to act consciously, and collectively, exercising foresight to choose their own evolutionary path. In our crucial epoch we cannot leave the selection of the next step in the evolution of human society and culture to chance. We must plan for it, consciously and purposefully."

Men and women are increasingly questioning the most basic assumption of contemporary society: that both male dominance and male violence or warfare are inevitable. A cross-cultural study by McConahay and McConahay (1977) found a significant correlation between rigid sexual stereotypes required to maintain male dominance and the incidence of warfare, wife beating, child beating, and rape. A growing number of such studies question and challenge the prevailing models of reality. By studying both halves of humanity, our knowledge about the possibilities for human society, as well as for the evolution of human consciousness, is expanding.

The emerging revolution in awareness is noted as the transformation from a dominator to a partnership consciousness (DuBois 1981). Men and women all over the world are challenging the male-dominator/female-dominated human relations model that is the foundation of our current world view (Simon and Kahn 1984). There is a growing awareness that the emerging higher consciousness of our global partnership is integrally related to a fundamental reexamination and transformation of the roles of both men and women (Eisler and Loye 1986).

The significance of this shift in awareness has profound implications for health care since 80 percent of the healers in the universe are women (Achterberg 1990). A new healing consciousness is emerging as the feminine perspective is influencing the curing and caring relationships that create and drive the health care system in Western society. Only when this shift is internalized can true collaboration and interdisciplinary teamwork emerge to integrate the health care needs and services for our society.

Leadership within the health care delivery system is called to create a vision based on shared values and beliefs, creating a collective dream for the future. A proposed vision for a new prototype in health care is the following:

> Disease is an invitation to higher being, thus health is the expansion of consciousness. An encounter with a health care agent or agency will offer a transformative life experience.

A metaphor is a basic way of thinking and a way of seeing that influences how we view and understand our world. It is typically used whenever we attempt to understand one element of experience in terms of another. A metaphor frames our understanding in a distinctive yet partial way. By highlighting certain features, it forces others into the background. To obtain a comprehensive reading of an organization, a clustering of different metaphors may coexist in complementary ways.

Garth Morgan (1986) has identified contemporary metaphors that describe organizations today as machines, organisms, brains, cultures, political systems, psychic prisons, instruments of domination, flux, and transformation. A review of these metaphors quickly discloses that many reflect the current cultural dominator bias.

Leland Kaiser (1991) proposes a new set of metaphors for health care agencies that support the movement toward interdisciplinary norms and the vision they create: hospital as cathedral, hospital as repair shop, hospital as theme park, and hospital as school. These metaphors, managed simultaneously, would create an environment and experience for the client that would be empowering and life transforming, or facilitating toward a peaceful and humane death. Further, the care providers in these metaphors would be working as partners and teams to create an array of comprehensive services for those clients served.

Life and death are the two most personal encounters of a spiritual nature. Thus, the hospital as a cathedral would honor and support a peaceful death in a manner consistent with programs developed for the birthing process. The focus of the patient caregiver would return to the sense of a calling in service of others. A reverential awe for life would be present in all activities within the organization.

The hospital has always been viewed as a repair shop. To strengthen this metaphor, advertising and posting of quality outcomes would facilitate consumer shopping and selection—and an occasional sale on elective procedures might enhance market share.

Just as Disneyland has created a theme park to address the diverse interests and needs of a varied public, so too the hospital of the future is called to create options that appeal to the publics they serve. The guiding principle would be to provide care to various target groups in a setting and manner consistent with the interests and values of the groups. Thus, the design of a pediatric unit would resemble a home, rather than an institution, for the child too ill to receive home care. Instruction and support of pregnant teenagers would occur in settings where they most frequently gather versus the sterile classroom setting in most inpatient hospital units. Taking the services to the public in a manner that honors their cultural values and state of consciousness would celebrate and strengthen the rich diversity present in our universe.

Health education and promotion are emerging trends that could unleash the potential for enriched physical and psychosocial welfare of the public.

A refocusing on primary and preventative care is replacing the traditional emphasis on treatment of disease. Currently 80 percent of all illness in the United States is related to lifestyle choices. Assisting individuals with pattern recognition regarding health behaviors and illness states can offer new alternatives for a healthy future, helping reach the objectives of Healthy People 2000 (Department of Health and Human Services 1990). Thus, the educative focus within health care is the primary vehicle for expansion of consciousness with its transformative impact on the client.

Replacing Hierarchy with Relationships

Structure

The organizational structure of the twenty-first century reflects the theme of our interconnectedness. Fritjof Capra (1982) identifies the movement away from a hierarchic, overcompartmentalized, and often mechanistic structural approach toward networks and relationships and change.

The preferred organizational shape is a spiral, a sphere moving through time and space. Spheres are circular organizational forms (Figure 9.1) that move from a reactive to a proactive stance, from the microcosm of the individual to the macrocosm of the organization, from the microcosm of the organization to the macrocosm of the universe (Kaiser 1991). A sphere moves from the notion of bureaucracy to a form of mutuality. In a sphere, one person's upside down is another person's right side up, and both perspectives are correct in seeing the whole. Empowerment comes from each one being receptive to the other's experience (Sun 1991).

Based on the model of DNA and genetic coding, spheres contain an intelligence mechanism (a working community or group) that navigates the system forward. Spheres within and between systems must become compatible and supportive, reflective of and reverberating with each other in harmony (Sheldrake 1988). The toxic patterns of competition are replaced with cooperative patterns of partnership within the community.

Corporate Consciousness

More important than the shape proposed is the awareness that accompanies such a structural model. An individual "ring of consciousness" reflects the totality of all learning and life experiences encompassed within an individual life. Anything outside the ring is within the "realm of nothingness," as it has not been experienced by the individual. A common phenomenon regarding consciousness is that individuals with a smaller ring attempt to pull people

Figure 9.1   Circular Organizational Chart

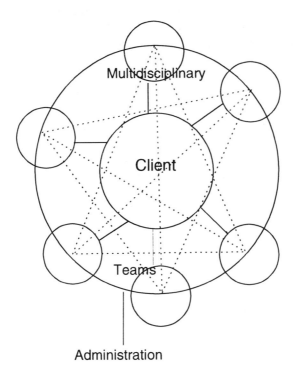

Administration

This chart reflects mutuality and integration focused on
the needs of the client. Administration plays a supportive,
facilitative role.

with a larger one into their own (Kaiser 1991). Expansion of consciousness
requires experiences beyond one's current reality, offered by a mentor who
lives in a larger ring. Further, mentoring someone with a smaller sense of
reality completes the circle of growth.

    Moving to a new prototype requires expanding the consciousness of
the total organization. The vision and energy of the group is then focused and
synthesized in a manner that gives birth to a new form. This activity must
be based on values and beliefs of the individual members (McCoy 1985).
The ability to integrate values into corporate vision, culture, and policies
produces excellence while contributing to the quality of life for the entire
organization as well as society. Thus, vision, values, and ethics comprise
the collective consciousness of the organization.

Community Building

Community reflects the capacity for relatedness within individuals—relatedness to other people, to events in history, to nature, to the world of ideas, and to things of the spirit (Henderson 1981). The feminist concept of community calls for a new way of being in the world, living in a connected sense with others and the universe. However, self-awareness must accompany other-awareness if true community is to exist. We must understand the impact of our presence and behaviors on the group as clearly as we articulate the impact of group behaviors upon ourselves and our work if a healthy, growth-producing community is to exist.

A true corporate community requires (1) a growth-producing culture that provides information and feedback to all members; (2) consensus-building relationships that utilize creative tension to move toward a collective vision on behalf of self and others; and (3) clearly differentiated roles that are mutually valued and well integrated to provide the full scope of services offered by the agency.

Land (1973) sees human behavior as a growth-directed activity. "Grow or die" is the imperative of life. Humankind extends the self within a cultural group and performs acts that facilitate growth of self and other. Subsequent behavior is maintained or modified, dependent upon the feedback response from the environment.

Just as organs determine the growth of cells, cultures determine the growth of the people living within them. The amount of growth expressed by individuals and groups is determined by the corporate culture. This culture determines the availability of information. Further, it determines the response of the environment to attempts at using the new growth that assimilated information produces. If the conditions of nutrition and feedback permit new growth, patterns of behavior become responsible and creative. If not, the lack of alternatives results in a regression to more basic growth patterns. Thus, growth cannot occur independently; it requires interaction and integration between the growing thing and its environment. Nothing grows totally from the inside. Something from the outside must be integrated if wholeness is to be achieved.

Consensus Building

Fear and competition lead to private combat for personal reward—all under the table. A supportive environment facilitates creative tension and healthy conflict. Peter Senge (1990) identifies creative tension as the integrating principle for moving a current reality toward a desired vision. The gap between where we want to be (our "vision") and where we are (our "current reality") generates a natural tension. It can be resolved by moving closer to either pole. Individuals and groups who learn how to work with, rather than against, creative tension, learn how to use the energy it generates to move reality more reliably toward their common vision. This growth cycle of creativity, which fosters intrinsic motivation, self-esteem, dignity, curiosity to learn, and joy in experiencing each other, follows the stages identified by Land (Figure 9.2).

As society moves from a posture of defense to one of self-actualization, the way we view conflict is being reexamined. The question is not how to eliminate conflict, but rather how to frame it as constructive rather than destructive. As individuals with different needs, desires and interests come into contact, conflict is inevitable. The feminine approach to nonviolent conflict calls each party to reexamine its own goals and actions as well as those of the other party. The result for both sides is productive change rather than nonproductive rigidity and maintenance of a dominant posture by one party. The aim is to transform conflict into creative energy rather than suppress it until it explodes in violence (Miller 1976, 86)

Communal conflict is a public encounter in which the entire group grows through the process of consensus building by exposing the question-able issue in an arena protected by the compassionate fabric of human caring. The theme of consensus is to value both the process and the product equally, living out the fact that we become whatever we do. In consensus building, the vision is released and a gestalt negotiated that creates a qualitatively different product than what each could create separately. The vision may be altered as it is lived out, thus the axiom "maintain the vision, but embrace the hybrid" must be honored. In working toward specific changes, each remembers that ultimately one can change only oneself.

Consensus building is based on the creative process, which is nonrational. A group norm for experimentation with various tools and processes allows all community members to connect with their intuitive knowledge. The process is nonlinear; at some level each member already knows what is essential to know. Supportive leadership and small groups best facilitate mutual trust and an ability to work together. Through clear and candid feedback in a supportive environment, all community members practice knowing when to wait and when to move ahead, when they are centered and when they are defensive and on guard. Time and space are essential to allow for experiencing alternative actions selected. Revisiting the issue and refining the process can be reenergizing for the group.

The key to successful consensus building is the ability to end or release a vision. Unless we are able to release or eliminate, we become constipated with old forms. To be able to release or end without knowing the next step

Figure 9.2   Components of Community

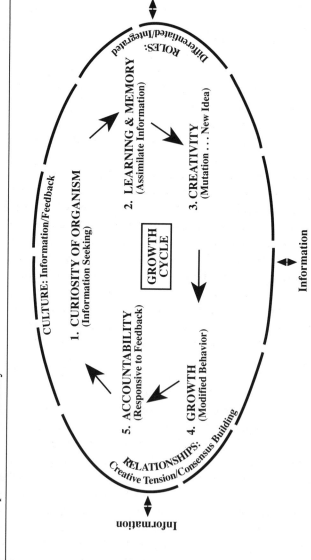

fully is the challenge in this process. We are only really free if we can risk everything on the next step. If we must know what will happen next, we are limited to what we can imagine. Thus, learning to trust the process is essential if a creative community is to evolve. Learning to end means taking our power seriously—our power to harm or heal, to love or to abuse, to create or destroy. Robert's Rules of Order give way to consensus building in an era of dynamic change. Thus, nonviolent change occurs as the spiritual and political dimensions of community life are integrated, creating a qualitatively different community. Metonoia, which combines adaptive learning with generative learning, provides the community with an opportunity to create, to become part of the generative process of life (Senge 1990, 14).

Transformation of Political and Economic Realities

Futurists such as Willis Harman at Stanford and researchers from the Club of Rome declare that to avoid major regional and ultimately global catastrophe, we must develop a new world system guided by a rational master plan for long-term organic growth rather than power and domination. This system must be held together by a spirit of truly global cooperation, shaped in free partnership (Harman 1977). This new global system will be governed by a global ethic based on greater consciousness of, and identification with, future as well as present generations and will require that power through cooperation, rather than power by confrontation, and harmony with, rather than conquest of, nature will become normative ideals (Sivard 1983).

These projections position human values and social arrangement as the main determinants of our future—not technology or economics. Our world will be determined by the way we humans conceive its possibilities, potentials, and implications rather than by power and dominance. James McHale (1969) states, "Our mental blueprints are its basic action programs."

Transcendent Leadership

At the organizational level, the power of management and leadership is being redefined as well. We have gone through various eras of management as humankind moved from an agrarian to a technological epoch. Today we are faced with the information era, with the knowledge worker the most prized asset within the organization. The role of management is moving toward transformational leadership where the leader is also a myth maker (Kaiser 1990).

The myth maker captures the spirit of the work force, which turns a dream into reality. John F. Kennedy was such a leader with his vision for a man on the moon. A transformational leader like Kennedy has skills on two separate domains: the horizontal dimension and the vertical dimension. The *horizontal dimension* reflects the skills a leader uses to mediate with the world. These "learned" skills include formal education, political acumen, interpersonal competence, and business sense. The *vertical dimension* is based on individual "knowing" and intuition. At this level the individual utilizes right and left brain, and integrates feelings and observations into decision making. This competence is demonstrated in a sense of timing, seeing the big picture, avoiding analysis paralysis, and creation of ideas that are novel and often outrageous (Agor 1989; Senge 1990).

Running an organization is more chaotic and less systematic than in previous decades. Executives are challenged to gain control of their own time and turn obligations into opportunities. The most difficult part of the job is finding time to contemplate and devise new ways to improve their system.

Jonas Salk (1983) identifies a new science of empathy, a science that will use the combined reason and intuition to draw conclusions from a totality rather than through isolated step-by-step "logical thinking." Intuitive leaders are establishing structures and policy that allow others in the organization to creatively intuit at their own level of function. Rules that inhibit individual judgment are being made flexible. A teaching-learning organizational format is emerging (Senge 1990) so that a trend toward "intrapreneuring" is noted in these progressive organizations. Within the contemporary health care organization such a shift in power must occur between organizations and the community, between administrators and physicians, between physicians and nurses, and between nurses and the client. This shift will require collaboration on decisions regarding what services are offered, and at what price. Further, there must be a sharing of the wealth between all parties that is equitable and not abusive.

Economics

Contemporary health care reflects a "scarcity mentality"—each sector competing for expanded funding to support escalating health care costs. A radical paradigm shift would reflect an "abundance mentality," which acknowledges that the industry already has billions of dollars allocated to its work. This shift would call for a sharing of power and resources across the continuum of care to provide affordable health care for all citizens, by a community of caregivers rather than a dominator medical model that focuses only on expensive, high-tech, acute care interventions.

If contemporary technology was not so singularly dedicated to the war effort, our cultural evolution would be vastly accelerated. The cost of developing one intercontinental ballistic missile could feed 50 million children, build 160,000 schools, and open 340,000 health care centers (Sivard 1983, 5). Even the cost of a single new nuclear submarine—equal to the annual education budget of 23 developing countries, in a world where 120 million children have no school they can go to and 11 million babies die before their first birthday—could open new opportunities for millions of people now doomed to live in poverty and ignorance (Sivard 1983, 26). What is lacking is the social guidance system, the governing values, that would redirect the allocation of resources, including advanced technological know-how, to higher ends. Post-communism trends offer us some hope for a new reality in this arena.

The same economic phenomenon is present within the health care industry. Currently, 13 percent of the U.S. gross national product goes to financing health care. This meteoric rise has been fueled by multiple factors including economic inflation, population growth, technology advances, and increased frequency and intensity of services. Since 1965 the percent of health care dollars going for hospital care has decreased slightly while the proportion for physicians' services has increased (PEW 1991).

Health care costs will not be influenced until payment is based on outcomes. It is essential to convene physicians, hospital administrators, nursing administrators, and payers around the same table to dialogue over the issues. No one discipline has the answer to problems as complex as those facing us today. However, comprehensive solutions would emerge through group effort couched in openness and vulnerability, because the power of sustained dialogue within a group is without measure.

Expenses must be viewed from a shared perspective. All health care providers could begin to examine ways to acquire capital equipment and supplies in a cost-effective, cooperative manner that does not exploit business partners or the public that utilizes the services offered.

Reimbursement systems must shift to reward outcome rather than ego. Interesting trends are emerging as a federal government is proposing a physician reimbursement package that will reward the primary care physician to a greater degree by reducing payment to certain subspecialty physicians such as cardiac surgeons. Another sign of change is the proposed cap on litigation activities, which would restrict the current malpractice activities in the legal arena. Rationing activities are emerging within some states as well as among payers such as Blue Cross and Blue Shield. Each of these innovations has potential to shift and reduce costs within the health care arena.

At the individual and corporate level, wastefulness and overconsumption must also be controlled. Western society demonstrates a pattern of overconsumption and waste; we are culturally obsessed with getting, buying, building, and wasting things as a substitute for satisfactory emotional relationships (Henderson 1981). Altruism and community service offered by health professionals would revitalize the spirit of both the provider and the recipient of such services.

A positive economic future will emerge when the roles of men and women are fundamentally rebalanced. Men and women will share in paid positions, household tasks, child rearing, and other social activities (Huber 1979). Traditional economic systems, whether capitalist or communist, are built upon the alienation of caring labor. This mindset devalues the contributions made to society by 2.1 million registered nurses, 3.4 million teachers, .5 million social workers, and 1.2 million child care workers. If the life-sustaining labor of nurturing, helping, teaching, and loving others is to be fully integrated into the economic mainstream, a fundamental economic and political transformation must occur.

A New Reality for Society

The universe is experiencing an era of turbulence and change that accompanies the end of an epoch and the emergence of a new world order. To those who look at isolated events it appears to be a time of chaos. New discoveries in the natural and social sciences demonstrate that it is the release of the enfolded potential of the universe. The universe is always in the process of becoming (unfolding) (Bohm 1980). The unfolding precipitates a crisis preceding transformation to a new order.

For millennia of recorded history, the human spirit has been imprisoned by the cultural bonds of dominance. Futurists are calling us to leave behind the hard, conquest-oriented values and traditions associated with the masculine and replace them with a movement toward partnership. Many today recognize that, in their present form, neither capitalism nor communism offers a way out of our growing economic and political dilemmas. To the extent that domination remains in place, a just political and economic system is impossible. Gradually, as the female half of humanity and its values and goals are integrated into the guidance mechanisms of society, a just political and economical health system will emerge.

The move to a new world of psychological and social rebirth will profoundly influence the health care delivery system. Hospitals will become arenas for personal transformation. Care will be delivered in ways and spaces that honor the diversity of clients served. Work will be facilitated by interdisciplinary groups and teams that include the client and/or community as a member. Reimbursement will be based on outcomes rather than status.

And, leadership will empower through myth and symbol, which will inspire all to new levels of consciousness—which is health.

In this new world, where the actualization of our higher evolutionary potentials—our greater freedom through wisdom and knowledge—will guide social policy, a primary focus of research will be on the prevention of personal and social illness, of both body and mind. Beyond this, our as yet untapped, but increasingly recognized, powers of the mind will be researched and cultivated, unleashing undreamed of mental and physical potentials (Loye 1983). Our thirst for knowledge and spiritual illumination, our longing for equality and freedom, our yearning for love and beauty will be realized, and we will discover what being human can mean.

> The reasonable man adapts himself to the world: the unreasonable one persists in trying to adapt the world to himself. Therefore, all progress depends on the unreasonable man.
>
> George Bernard Shaw

References

Achterberg, J. 1990. *Woman as Healer*. Boston, MA: Shamballa.

Agor, W. H. 1989. *Intuition in Organizations*. Newbury Park, CA: Sage Publishing.

Bentov, I. 1978. *Wholeness and the Implicate Order*. New York: Ark Paperbacks.

Bohm, D. 1980. *Wholeness and the Implicate Order*. London: Routledge and Kegan-Paul.

Capra, F. 1982. *The Turning Point: Science, Society and the Rising Culture*. New York: Simon and Schuster.

Department of Health and Human Services. 1990. *Healthy People 2000: National Health Promotion and Disease Prevention Objectives*. Washington, DC: U.S. Government Printing Office.

DuBois, E. C. 1981. *Elizabeth Cady Stanton, Susan B. Anthony: Correspondence, Writing, Speeches*. New York: Schocken.

Eisler, R. 1987. *The Chalice and the Blade: Our History, Our Future*. San Francisco, CA: Harper and Row.

Eisler, R., and S. Loye 1986. *Peace and Feminist Thought: New Directions*. World Encyclopedia of Peace, edited by E. Laszlo and S. Yoo. London: Peragomon Press.

Goertzen, I. 1987. "Making Nurses' Vision a Reality." *Nursing Outlook* 3 (May/June): 121–23.

Harman, W. 1977. "The Coming Transformation." *The Futurist* 2 (February): 5–11.

Henderson, H. 1981. *The Politics of the Solar Age*. New York: Anchor Books.

Huber, J. 1979. *Social Ecology and Dual Economy*. Frankfurt: Fischer-Verlag.

Jantsch, E. 1980. *The Self-Organizing Universe*. New York: Pergamon Press.

Kaiser, L. 1990. "Signs of Organizational Decline." *Hospital Forum* (March/April): 9–12.

Kaiser, L. 1991. *Building Consensual Vision.* Workshop presented at AONE Convention, San Diego, CA, 17 May.

Land, G. T. 1973. *Grow and Die.* New York: Dell Press.

Laszlo, E. 1985. "The Crucial Epoch." *Futures* 17: 2–23.

Loye, D. 1983. *The Sphinx and the Rainbow: Brain, Mind and Future Vision.* Boston, MA: New Science Library.

McConahay, S., and J. McConahay. 1977. "Sexual Permissiveness, Sexual Role Rigidity and Violence Across Cultures." *Journal of Social Issues* 33: 134–43.

McCoy, C. S. 1985. *Management of Values: The Ethical Difference in Corporate Policy and Performance.* Boston, MA: Pitman.

McHale, J. 1969. *The Future of the Future.* New York: Ballantine.

Miller, J. B. 1976. *Toward a New Psychology of Women.* Boston, MA: Beacon.

Morgan, G. 1986. *Images of Organizations.* Newbury Park, CA: Sage Publications.

Newman, M. 1986. *Health as Expanding Consciousness.* St. Louis, MO: Mosby Co.

PEW. 1991. *An Agenda for Action for U.S. Health Professional Schools.* Durham, NC: Duke University Medical Center.

Prigogine, U., and I. Stengers. 1984. *Order Out of Chaos.* New York: Bantam Books.

Salk, J. 1983. *Anatomy of Reality.* New York: Columbia University Press.

Senge, P. M. 1990. *The Fifth Discipline: The Art and Practice of the Learning Organization.* New York: Doubleday/Currency.

Sheldrake, R. 1988. *The Presence of the Past: Morphic Resonance and the Memory of Nature.* New York: Time Books.

Simon, J. L., and H. Kahn. 1984. *The Resourceful Earth: A Response to Global 2000.* New York: Basil Blackwell.

Sivard, R. 1983. *Work Military and Social Expenditures.* Washington, DC: World Priorities.

Sun, P. 1991. "New Thinking." In *At the Leading Edge: Visions of Science, Spirituality and Society,* edited by M. Toms. Burdett, NY: Larson Publications.

Vaill, P. B. 1989. *Managing as a Performing Art.* San Francisco, CA: Jossey-Bass Publishers.

INDEX

LIST OF CONTRIBUTORS

Ann Scott Blouin, M.S.N, R.N., is a health care consultant with expertise in organizational restructuring and shared governance, patient care delivery systems, operations improvement/ quality management, preparation for hospital accreditation, and professional staff salary compensation. Ms. Blouin is a frequent author in the *Journal of Nursing Administration* and is a clinical associate professor of nursing at Saint Xavier University and a lecturer at De Paul University, both located in Chicago. Ms. Blouin is currently completing Ph.D. and M.B.A. degrees at the University of Illinois, Chicago.

Kathleen A. Bower, D.N.Sc., M.S.N., B.S.N., R.N., is a principal in The Center for Case Management. Previously, Dr. Bower held a series of positions, including vice president of nursing, at New England Medical Center in Boston, Massachusetts. She was also the director of research and development for the Center for Nursing Case Management while it was based at New England Medical Center. Dr. Bower pioneered the development of nursing case management and has assisted nursing departments throughout the United States and Canada with implementing and refining Critical Path/CareMap™ and case management systems.

Marilyn Dubree, M.S.N., R.N., has held positions in clinical nursing, nursing education, and nursing administration and is currently the director of operational improvement at Vanderbilt University Hospital. In this role, she provides leadership and support to the task forces and design teams involved in work redesign and implementation of the housewide integrated patient care delivery model. Ms. Dubree was the project director for the Orthopaedic Work Redesign Project at Vanderbilt University Hospital and directed planning and implementation of this program. Previously, she was the associate director of surgical nursing at Vanderbilt University Hospital.

Stuart Gedal, Ed.M., is the director of Workplace Learning Programs for World Education, an internationally known nonprofit organization based in Boston, Massachusetts. Mr. Gedal has worked as an advisor and manager of workplace education programs in the hospital, printing, financial services, and precision manufacturing industries. He has coordinated and contributed to national and statewide curriculum design and training projects for adult and K–12 teaching and learning. His current projects include upgrade and enrichment programs for educationally disadvantaged employees in two states, project design for a collaboration of Georgia hospitals, and management of a field-based curriculum design project for a National Youth Apprenticeship demonstration project funded by the U.S. Department of Labor. Mr. Gedal received his master's degree at Harvard University.

Richard Heim, M.B.A., is a division director for MacNeal Hospital in Berwyn, Illinois. As the manager of finance, he worked on a number of initiatives related to work redesign and incentive compensation and the financial benefits of each. As a division director, he is watching these programs develop throughout the hospital.

M. Gibby Kinsey, M.B.A., M.S., R.N., C.N.A., has administrative responsibility for ancillary and support departments at Saint Joseph's Hospital of Atlanta. In addition, she functions as an internal consultant to the organization and is the administrator for hospitalwide projects related to operations, such as operational restructuring and case management. Ms. Kinsey has over 20 years of diverse experience in the health care industry; her area of expertise is operations analysis and management. Prior to her employment with SJHA, Ms. Kinsey was a senior consultant with one of the leading health care consulting firms in the country. Ms. Kinsey is a published author and has spoken throughout the United States on topics related to change management, empowerment, challenges for women in leadership positions, and operational restructuring.

JoEllen Goertz Koerner, M.S., R.N., is the vice president for patient services as Sioux Valley Hospital, a 548-bed tertiary care center in Sioux Falls, South Dakota. Ms. Koerner has served on statewide and national task forces on differentiated practice. A frequent lecturer and consultant on large-scale organizational change, Ms. Koerner has completed the Wharton Fellows Program for Nurse Executives at the University of Pennsylvania and is a Fellow in the American Academy of Nursing. She is a doctoral candidate at the Fielding Institute in Santa Barbara, California.

Vickie Mullins Moore, M.S.N., R.N., C.N.A.A., is an assistant vice president with administrative responsibility for the critical care division at Saint

Joseph's Hospital of Atlanta. SJHA is unique in that the coronary care unit and emergency department have restructured to provide a patient-focused approach to care delivery. As the administrator for these areas, she focuses primarily on the evaluation of cost-effectiveness, customers, and staff of the care delivery system. Ms. Moore is a frequent author and consultant regarding such topics as shared governance, quality assessment/improvement, cardiovascular program development, and chemical dependency among professional nurses.

Richard J. Stephen, M.S.I.E., is the director of management services for Saint Joseph's Health System, which includes Saint Joseph's Hospital of Atlanta, Saint Joseph's Hospital of Dahlonega, and other Mercy Care entities. The department is an integral part of the financial planning division and has primary responsibility for improving productivity management within the organization. With 18 years of experience in management engineering, operations research, and health care consulting, Mr. Stephen provides technical assistance to all hospital managers in the areas of operations review, productivity standards development, assessment of staffing needs, budgeting, quality improvement, performance monitoring, and decision support.

Mary Crabtree Tonges, R.N., M.S.N., is a consultant with the Center for Case Management, in South Natick, Massachusetts, and a doctoral student in organization and policy studies at Baruch College of the City University of New York. She is an author, lecturer, and consultant in nursing administration with particular expertise in work redesign and alternative nursing practice and care delivery models. Ms. Tonges was previously the vice president of nursing at Robert Wood Johnson University Hospital, New Brunswick, New Jersey, where she led the team that created the Professionally Advanced Care Team (ProACT) model. The work that she and her colleagues have done has been published in a series of articles in *The Journal of Nursing Administration, Nursing Management, Healthcare Forum, Nursing Economics, Modern Healthcare, Hospitals, Orthopaedic Nursing,* and as a chapter in *Patient Care Delivery Models.* Ms. Tonges received a B.S.N. from the University of Iowa and an M.S.N. from the University of Illinois, and she is a Commonwealth Fund Executive Nurse Fellow.

Mary Claire Wilson, M.S., CT(ASCP)(IAC), has served as the director of Saint Joseph's Hospital of Atlanta's education department for 11 years. She is responsible for general orientation, nursing orientation, and coordination of clinical courses, and has spearheaded the development of the Values Integration Program, the People in Progress Learning Center, and the Professional Development Series. Ms. Wilson's work in systems theory, educational media, instructional design, and self-instructional program development is even more beneficial in today's era of quality, cost-containment, and the growing workforce skills gap than it was 10 years ago. Ms. Wilson has published a number of clinical papers in national journals and has received an award from a national physicians organization for the best scientific paper presented by a nonphysician. She conducts numerous workshops, both on clinical topics and on health care education and training, and has been selected as an outstanding young leader in allied health by the American Society for Allied Health Professions.

ABOUT THE EDITOR

Kathryn J. McDonagh, M.S.N., R.N., C.N.A.A., is the president of Saint Joseph's Hospital of Atlanta and the senior vice president of Saint Joseph's Health System. Ms. McDonagh began her tenure at Saint Joseph's in 1983, serving first as the assistant nursing administrator and then as vice president for nursing and vice president for patient services. During these years, Ms. McDonagh was instrumental in the pioneering of shared governance, an organizational model in which nurses at all levels are empowered to participate in decision making regarding the practice of nursing. Saint Joseph's was among a handful of hospitals in the country to develop this model.

Along with several nursing administrators and managers, Ms. McDonagh routinely consults with other hospitals and nursing organizations seeking to implement shared governance. Under her leadership, Saint Joseph's is pioneering another administrative model. This time, the focus is on creating a patient-centered health care system through the redesigning of work within the medical facility.

Ms. McDonagh also served as the first president and chief executive officer of Saint Joseph's Mercy Care Services, another subsidiary of Saint Joseph's Health System. Mercy Care started as a volunteer effort of SJHA employees, primarily nurses and physicians, who were dedicated to the needs of the more than 20,000 homeless people in Atlanta. From its early volunteer efforts in the mid-1980s, this program blossomed into a multimillion-dollar network of community outreach efforts in the Atlanta area.

Ms. McDonagh attended Providence Hospital School of Nursing in Southfield, Michigan, and the University of Detroit. She received her graduate degree at the University of Michigan in Ann Arbor. She has conducted numerous speaking engagements on such topics as nursing shared governance, community outreach programs, emerging health care trends and work redesign in hospitals. Ms. McDonagh has published extensively on the topics of nursing administration, ethics, and shared governance. She is the volume editor of *Nursing Shared Governance: Restructuring for the Future*.